SHOULD I
STAY OR
SHOULD I
GO?

SHOULD I STAY OR SHOULD I GO?

SURVIVING A RELATIONSHIP WITH A NARCISSIST

RAMANI DURVASULA, Ph.D.

POST HILL PRESS

A POST HILL PRESS BOOK
ISBN: 978-1-61868-878-1
ISBN (eBook): 978-1-61868-877-4

SHOULD I STAY OR SHOULD I GO?
Surviving a Relationship with a Narcissist
© 2015 by Ramani Durvasula
All Rights Reserved

Cover design by Spiro Designs
Jacket photograph by Jill Davenport CPT
Interior design by Neuwirth & Associates

The information in this book is meant to provide a clinical opinion and advice, but is not meant to be a substitute for clinical care. Every case is different, and while this book provides a framework and guidance, it may not be applicable in every specific situation.

Post Hill
PRESS

Post Hill Press
275 Madison Avenue, 14th Floor
New York, NY 10016
http://posthillpress.com

To the "Muse-Ladies" in my life:
My daughters Maya and Shanti Hinkin
My sister Padma Salisbury
My mother Sai Durvasula
And in memory of my grandmother
Ratnamala Gunupudi (1924–2014)

Love is a striking example of how little reality means to us.

—PROUST

Whoever loves becomes humble. Those who love have, so to speak, pawned a part of their narcissism.

—FREUD

CONTENTS

CHAPTER 9

PROLOGUE

A scorpion sat on the shores of a river one day, needing to get to the other side, but the river was too wide, and there were not enough stones to jump across. He begged the various water birds—mallards and geese and herons—if he could catch a ride, but they pragmatically turned him down, knowing too well his cunning and his sting. He caught sight of the lovely swan making her way down the river and charmingly pleaded to her attributes.

"Please, beautiful Swan, take me across the river. I couldn't imagine harming something as beautiful as you, and it is not in my interest to do so. I simply want to get to the other side of the river."

The swan hesitated, but the scorpion was so charming and convincing. He was close enough to sting her right now, and yet he did not do it. What could go wrong? The trip across the river would take only a few minutes. She agreed to help him. As they traversed the river, the scorpion expressed his gratitude and continued to offer his compliments about her loveliness and kindness compared to all of the other negligent river birds. As they arrived at the other riverbank, he prepared to jump off. And right before he jumped off of her back, he lifted his tail and stung her.

Crying and injured, the swan couldn't understand why he'd done this, after all the promises, all the flattery, the logical explanations.

"Why did you sting me?" she asked.

He looked at her from the river bank and said, "I'm a scorpion. It's who I am."

In my clinical work with clients who find themselves in the devilish and toxic web of a relationship with a pathologically narcissistic or exploitative person, this fable is a painful and powerful teaching tool. They get stung over and over again, and even when they *know* harm is coming, they still believe this time will be different. Invariably, the outcome is always the same: more bad behavior and negligence from their partner, more self-blame for the problems in their relationship, no change in behavior by the "scorpion."

In this haunting parable about the scorpion, he has more insight than the average narcissist, at least owning up to the fact that he is what he is. Those who become involved with human narcissists should be so lucky as to have self-aware narcissistic partners who know that their bad behavior is simply who they are. Unfortunately, narcissists, unlike the scorpion, are masterful at blaming other people for their discontent. In essence, the scorpion would blame the swan for agreeing to take him across the river. After all, she could always have said no . . .

IS THIS YOU?

They met in the years after graduate and medical school through mutual friends. With their freshly minted degrees and careers, happy hours, holidays with friends, and long weekends, the world was full of possibility. Rachel was tall and willowy, successful in a marketing job, enjoying all of the attention coming her way. John was a physician, just starting out, smart, attractive, young, and sexy with his scrubs and his sharp wit. He started courting her and pulled out all the stops. He had a nice car (check), a great job and lots of professional possibilities (check, check), he pursued her arduously (check), they went to great restaurants or they cooked for each other (check), took long weekends when he could get away (check), and he was inordinately charming (check).

John was very sure of himself and, within months, neglectful. He wouldn't show up on time, if he showed up at all (he was a busy physician), rarely listened when Rachel spoke about her work (doctor's hours are long), showed little interest in her friends or family after a while, despite charming them initially (he loves me and he's busy, so when we have a moment, he just wants to be with me), and yawned and looked at his phone frequently when she needed a sounding board about some workplace transitions (he may be getting important calls; he is a busy surgeon). But they still went out to the right places, had fun, the sex was good, and before long he suggested that she come live with him in his comfortable home. Her lease was up, and at 29, it was time.

John made it clear that he didn't want her making big changes to the house—he was used to things the way they were—but he would love a woman's touch (which she soon saw meant cleaning up in between the days the housekeeper came). She rushed about to ensure that the house was the way he wanted it. Before she met him, and in the early days of their relationship, Rachel was cool and relaxed, coming home from work and tossing off her shoes in the middle of the living room, or not caring about the occasional sweater she left on the floor at the end of a long day. Now she was keyed up, wound tight, making sure everything was just so. But they fell into a rhythm, she slowly warmed up the home, she cooked him wonderful dinners, and they enjoyed the additional time living together afforded them. His occasional coldness, distraction, need for "alone time," and demands that their life look a certain way seemed excusable, since he was a busy doctor giving them a lovely lifestyle. So she focused on the good parts of their relationship. Rachel enjoyed her work, and John never minded her long hours because his were longer. Between their two salaries, they lived very comfortably, and she could purchase what she wanted and have nights out with friends without thinking twice. When their schedules allowed, they entertained—and showed off their gracious home and life.

Rachel's mother and friends praised her and even resented her. Her home with John was comfortable and their lifestyle enviable. Her mother told her repeatedly, "hold on to this one—he will give you a good life, he has a steady job, he's fun, he's handsome. . . ." Her friends were slowly getting married, and commitment was in the air. Every so often she would see one of her friends fly into panic mode at losing a fiancé or boyfriend, terrified that time was ticking away and having to "go back out there." That only reinforced her drive to overlook the red flags and focus on what was good.

That summer, about one year after meeting, John whisked Rachel off to Cape Town, South Africa, where he had a business meeting, and then asked her to marry him. The ring was like something out of a movie, and he then took her on a glamorous safari. The trip was a grand adventure, with good meals, great wine, great sex, and the feeling that she was living in a fairy tale (although one with an angry prince). She would look the other way at his entitled behavior at hotels, during safari tours, and in the airport. When he became neglectful, dismissive, or nasty, she looked at the two carats on her left hand and convinced herself that he wouldn't make that kind of commitment if he didn't really love her. You can't expect someone to be Mr. Sunshine every day, right? They called their families, they told their friends, and the two of them—and her ring—made the post-engagement rounds. They slid back into their rhythms at home and began to discuss wedding dates. Her friends and her mother reminded her that she was a lucky girl who had everything—the romance, the Romeo, the ring.

John started coming home later (doctor's hours), though it was sometimes clear he had been drinking. One night in the bathroom Rachel noticed that there were marks on his back, as though he had been scratched. He became possessive and secretive about his devices (iPad, phone)—even taking them into the bathroom and rarely leaving them unattended—and often shut the computer when she walked into a room, smiling widely and saying "hi, love, thanks for coming in and distracting me from my work."

One Saturday while she was running errands, Rachel had taken one of John's coats to be cleaned and found a receipt for a night when he claimed to be on call. It was from a local bar, with the time stamp revealing that at the time she texted him and he said he was checking in on a patient, he was actually paying his tab.

She confronted him, and he became rageful. "How dare you accuse me of this? Do you know how fucking hard I work? For fuck's sake, I was grabbing a pile of papers near Joe Morgan's stuff when he swung by the hospital, and I grabbed his receipt and some other things by mistake. Look (opens his calendar)—here is the call schedule. What the hell is wrong with you? Are you going to screw up everything we have because you are so insecure?"

She fell to her knees and began to cry, begging him for forgiveness, not wanting to lose all they had together, hearing her mother's voice that she wouldn't find another guy like this again, feeling she had no right to accuse him, and even if he was out for a drink with friends and didn't tell her about it, he deserved down time to decompress. Doubt kept creeping in about everything. Once confident, she now began second-guessing herself; her instincts were bothering her, but John would always make her feel crazy when she raised any questions about his behavior. Sometimes he even accused her of cheating.

Rachel began to notice that he wasn't always nice to other people when they were out and about. Demanding the best service, to be at the head of the line, complaining about the table at a busy restaurant—John was impatient and demanding with service people. It was embarrassing and yet, at those times, he would simultaneously draw her close and tell her how beautiful she was. It felt confusing and unsettling.

Over time, the late nights continued, and Rachel felt more and more isolated. When he did come home on time, John wanted her to be ready to go out, or have something made to eat. But when he would give her an estimated time of arrival, it was 50/50 whether he would show, and she ate a lot of home-cooked meals alone. About once a month she would call him out on his behavior and he would rage at her with a tirade about her selfishness, that "she had it easy and he worked so hard, did she just want to put a tracking system on him?" He would also turn it on her and ask her "why are you asking me so many questions? Are you trying to hide something?"

She had other things going on in her life: A reorganization at work was making her work life challenging, and her sister had developed breast cancer. The stress was taking a toll on her, and he rarely asked about it. When she talked about it, he would barely listen or sometimes even blame her for her difficulties at work, and he would minimize her sister's experience, citing medical statistics about prognosis, rather than simply comforting her in her time of fear and concern for her sister.

During these months, Rachel was planning the wedding, and it was going to be a show: a posh resort hotel in Santa Barbara with no expense spared, Vera Wang dress, high-end gourmet food from a friend who had a catering business in Montecito, wine they hand-picked from local wineries, a band they had heard performing one night in a local bar, and friends flying in from all over the country for a weekend to "celebrate their love." There were numerous decisions to be made, and John would be engaged and participating in them half the time, and not give a damn the other half—it felt completely unpredictable. She would make a series of decisions when he failed to show up to a meeting and then undo them all when he finally did, with him often berating her for her choices (which he told her to make in the first place, or didn't show up to assist with). Doubt. Second-guessing.

But she was engaged and had the ring, the home, the dress, the upcoming wedding, the rewarding job, and the successful fiancé—living the dream. One night Rachel opened up to John more about some of her dreams in the arts and a program that summer in Tuscany. Six weeks, and they could rent a home, she could paint and write, and he could take a break and join her for part of it. He laughed at her and mocked her ambitions, calling her lazy for wanting to take a leave from her job, telling her he thought it was a joke that she fancied herself an artist, and that his work was too important for him to be jumping off to some ridiculous artist's enclave in the middle of nowhere. While she appreciated that perhaps it wasn't practical, John talked at her like she was foolish and ridiculous. It felt like an audible click to her—her dreams being clipped right in front of her. And Rachel started to believe him and doubted herself more.

About three months before their wedding, a co-worker who had met her fiancé at a work event saw her husband at a "gentleman's club" type of establishment. Her fiancé was clearly a regular, was escorted discreetly with one of the women into a back room of the establishment, and later was seen kissing her while he was standing at his car. Rachel's co-worker decided to let sleeping dogs lie and not stick his nose in it.

In the weeks to come, Rachel and John were at a holiday event at her workplace, and the co-worker who knew about the strip club shenanigans was there as well. John was rude that evening, dismissive of her, and at times behaving in a manner that felt inappropriate to many observers (flirtatious with a young, attractive intern). At that point, the co-worker took Rachel aside and shared with her his concerns about her fiancé. He suggested they talk again during the week. On Tuesday after work that week, they stepped out for a cup of coffee, and he spoke to her about what he saw and his concerns about John, especially after his conduct at the party.

Rachel went to her usual drill; she defended him. *It couldn't have been him; I bet he was home with me that night; he is a doctor; he wouldn't do that.* She then became angry at her co-worker, who had been a longtime friend and whose wife was also a friend, wondering why he felt the need to do this. But she left their coffee meeting unsettled, and John wasn't home yet. He finally arrived after she had already gone to bed. The next day she made a few inquiries at the hospital, and her detective work revealed that John was not there that night. The co-worker's story stuck with her. She asked her co-worker what club it was, and the next time John claimed to be on call and he didn't come home, she went by the club, and his car—a shiny new Tesla—was in the lot.

Rachel went home and waited for his return. She called him out the minute he walked in at 2:30 a.m. He clearly smelled like someone else, and she was enraged. Initially, he was infuriated at the accusation, and when she told him she had seen his car, he accused her of being a "stalker bitch." But John didn't have much wiggle room, so the next day he sat with her and said that perhaps they just needed a vacation. He was gentle and loving. He apologized, said he was there with a buddy from work who liked those kinds of places, and that he understood how it would have felt weird to her to see that. He suggested a long weekend away, an island, first class all the way, just the two of them. A last break before the wedding.

The tropical breezes, the view from the bed, the long sexy mornings—before she knew it, the strip club and his inattentiveness slowly became a distant memory. During the trip she made him promise—please, never again—no more strip clubs or any of that.

He agreed. The wedding was less than two months away, the late nights had abated, and she just chalked up his behavior to some last bachelor jitters. They were back on track.

The wedding was a success—an unforgettable weekend, beautiful weather, everyone and everything was fabulous, and the photographs a testament to that perfect day. The honeymoon was joyful, the sex rapturous, a perfect start to a perfect life. The doubt faded.

They came back to regular life. John and Rachel went back to work, they put away the wedding gifts, and life returned to its usual rhythms. But she was married now, and that had to mean something, right? They played the role of successful young married couple quite well and then two years later she was pregnant.

It was joyous news, as she had looked forward to a family. But the more pregnant she became, the more he detached. Rachel was a bit anxious during the pregnancy, often asking John for reassurance, and he stuck to his story of late hours, not listening, and telling her that it would be over soon and they would be a family. She had fantasies of him massaging her feet, picking out names, putting together furniture. But his behavior was the usual: little empathy for her discomfort, little interest in the process, lots of concerns about how she would balance a baby and him.

The baby arrived—a beautiful boy. And their rhythms changed. John insisted that Rachel leave her job; his practice was growing and money was good. They moved to a bigger house, in the best neighborhood, and then they had a daughter. Pregnancy and children became a rhythm, and before long Rachel was drawn into the cadence of motherhood, house, life. John's late returns home often made less of an impact because she fell asleep exhausted as soon her children went to sleep. He worked and made money; she raised the kids. Rachel hated having to "ask" him for money (something she never had to do as an adult), and he would frequently question her and call her out for her "life of ease" at home with the children while he worked hard, but after seven years out of the job market, she believed that she was not of much use to anyone with her outmoded skills.

In the nine years since they were married, the patterns were the same as before: late nights, lots of secrecy, not listening, and little support. But they were really good at putting on a show for other people. A review of their holiday cards revealed big smiles, great vacations, suntans—a perfect façade. Rachel felt like she couldn't complain despite her concerns, her loneliness, and the million subtle ways she felt unheard and disconnected. The kids were ensconced in the finest of schools, their home was beautiful, and to the world, they had it all.

As the kids grew older and had more of a routine, she was awake at night, and John still didn't come home. Sex was infrequent, and she sometimes reiterated her request that he not ever go to the strip clubs again. He would always laugh at that suggestion. He remained secretive about his phone and computer but got it right often enough that the fights would come and go. And she would hold on. Self-doubt was a normal place for her. She felt like she had transformed from once being a confident and self-assured executive to being a quivering nerve, obsessing over small details at home, and tense with their children. She was as beautiful as always, and when other men paid attention to her, it would feel like a foreign experience because her husband had stopped noticing her a long time ago.

At a routine doctor's visit, the doctor informed Rachel that she had an abnormal pap smear, and she subsequently found out that she had HPV. Since she had never had sex with anyone but her husband, she then knew that she had a much bigger problem than his strip club visits. She sent the kids to her mother's and confronted him when he got home. A huge argument ensued, with screaming and accusations, and the enormity of what he had been doing became known to her, as she finally asked to see phone bills and other records. He had had numerous affairs over the years, typically adult dancers, cocktail waitresses, and reality stars in training. He had even acquired an apartment for his girlfriend du jour. Receipts revealed that he had spent nearly $100,000 on gentlemen's clubs, airline tickets, vacations, rent, and gifts for these women. She asked him to leave, and in the subsequent months he begged to be allowed back. Her mother asked if she knew what she was doing, kicking him out. Men make mistakes, his apologies felt so sincere, was she really ready to strike out on her own as a single mother with two kids? More self-doubt. It felt like everyone was in on it. She eventually let her mother know about the HPV and the rest of it, and her mother finally understood.

There were months of back and forth and apologies, and even while he was apologizing, John was going home to the apartment he shared with a 24-year-old girlfriend he met at a bar. The divorce was long and arduous, as he would frequently hide assets, and untold tens of thousands in legal fees later, they were divorced. In the years after the divorce, his lifestyle (which he endlessly posted on Facebook) consisted of young and younger girlfriends, new haircuts, faster cars, weekends in Vegas, and an unwillingness to pay his children's tuitions and other expenses. His clever attorneys left Rachel in a position of financial uncertainty. His family believed the many terrible things he had shared with them about her and offered her little support. However, Rachel says she is now at peace, but having to manage his inconsistency with the children, his not showing up for weeks at a time, breaks her heart, as the kids still love him.

In the aftermath, the one question was "did you see this coming?" Post-mortems are always so clear—hindsight is 20/20—we are all fortune tellers after the fact.

The cheating, the lying, the meanness, it was there from the beginning. What once could be packaged as him being confident, self-assured, hardworking, and successful revealed itself for what it was: The voices of others telling her she was lucky to have such a successful guy. Her mother transferring her own scripts onto her daughter. Ultimately, she thought her love would transform him. She believed the rescue fantasy.

In order to make the marriage last for the 10 years it did, Rachel silenced her instincts, was overtaken with doubt, isolated herself from the world because she was so ashamed, and gave up on herself. When asked if she thought she could have stuck it out, she reflected on asking for only one thing: that he not go to adult clubs. And he was unable to honor that one request. Strangely, it was the strip club attendance that ultimately broke her—beyond the decade of disrespect, rudeness, meanness, neglect and simply not being heard. She was still surprised about how easy it was to get snowed by lifestyle and the expectations of others.

This is one story. Of one who stayed and then ultimately left. For reasons of anonymity, it is in fact the amalgamation of many stories, woven into a fairy tale and cautionary tale.

This book is a guide. On how to stay. Or how to go.

Rachel said that "if I listened to those early red flags, I may never have gotten in, or if I knew that he would have never changed, I would have gotten out and jumped into a new life sooner. For as long as I stayed, I wished I had better strategies, because I am still dealing with the legacy of self-doubt and the sense that 'I am not good enough.'"

Our experiences make us who we are, but figuring out a way to cut our losses can allow us to accumulate better and more respectful experiences and spend our time in truer places.

What is your story?

Should you stay?

Should you go?

Keep reading. . . .

CHAPTER 1

A SURVIVAL GUIDE

Obsessed by a fairy tale, we spend our lives searching for a magic door and a lost kingdom of peace.

—EUGENE O'NEILL

You can only witness something so many times before you want to do something about it. To say something about it. And to share what you have learned. As a psychologist, a teacher, and a witness.

Directly observing so many people's lives wrecked, sense of well-being shattered, and psychological health ruined by being in relationships with narcissists, I felt that there had to be an honest survival manual. One that is not predicated on hopeful advice, or the idea that everyone can change, or prattle about forgiveness, or that the beast can become a prince. Rather, one that is grounded in the real terrain of this diagnosis; one that provides a realistic roadmap of expectations and management.

I have been a professor of psychology at California State University, Los Angeles for 16 years, and, while there, I have been the recipient of a decade of research funding from the National Institutes of Health to examine personality disorders in a very specific way, as they relate to health and disease. This work has forced me to closely examine the nuanced nature of personality disorders, including narcissistic personality. In our work studying hundreds of patients, I have witnessed the chaos created by these personality patterns not only for the clients but also for those around them. Simply put, personality disorders are bad for your health. I have been licensed to practice psychology for 18 years, and in those years I have carefully observed the stubbornness of these disorders. The people who have them simply do not change. One factor I have consistently noted is that sometimes we can change *behaviors* in people with narcissistic personality disorders, but the changes often do not stick around for the long term. Most important, I noticed that the subtle changes in behavior that we may create do little to improve how they behave in *relationships*. It is in relationships that people with narcissistic personalities inflict the greatest damage. You may be able to teach a narcissistic person to show up on time to meetings, but you cannot "teach" genuine empathy.

Finally, my career evolved at what may have been the most fascinating time of human psychological history. When I started out as a professor, laptops were non-existent, the concept of a smartphone felt futuristic, the Internet was in its infancy, and television shows involved actors and scripts. I watched a culture shift from "pride goeth before a fall" to "if you got it, flaunt it" in the blink of a decade. The human race decentralized, and it is increasingly every man (woman) for himself. Depth has been traded for superficiality, and it has been a costly psychological transaction. In doing therapy, teaching about personality disorders, and conducting research on personality disorders for a very long time, it all comes together. Not only knowing the diagnoses and the patterns but also learning some hard-and-fast facts. Those facts and observations are contained herewith.

Fitzgerald may have captured it best when he classified narcissists such as Tom and Daisy Buchanan as *careless:* "They were careless people, Tom and Daisy—they smashed up things and creatures and then retreated back into their money or their vast carelessness or whatever it was that kept them together, and let other people clean up the mess they had made." Narcissists are precisely that: careless.

They barrel through life, using relationships and people as objects, tools, and folly. While they often seem as if they are cruel or harsh, that is in fact giving them too much credit. They are simply careless. And they do expect other people to clean up their messes.

But carelessness is cruel. Frankly, the motivation for their behavior does not matter; what matters is the outcome. And that outcome is damage to other people's well-being, hopes, aspirations, and lives. Carelessness captures it, but it is not an excuse. Or as Anais Nin so beautifully notes, "Love never dies a natural death. It dies because we don't know how to replenish its source. It dies of blindness and errors and betrayals. It dies of illness and wounds; it dies of weariness, of witherings, of tarnishings. Every lover could be brought to trial as the murderer of his own love. When something hurts you, saddens you, I rush to avoid it, to alter it, to feel as you do, but you turn away with a gesture of impatience and say: 'I don't understand.'"

This is a book about hopelessness that is meant to bring hope. To offer real solutions based on reality and not simply wishful theorizing. This book is meant to be a primer and introduction to narcissism, to help you figure out if you are in a relationship with a narcissist and what that entails. But it will also place narcissism into a context. Reading through a checklist and picking out symptoms may be the first step, but it also helps to understand that these folks, harmful and challenging as they appear, are also not all bad. We fall in love with them, we build lives with them, we have children with them, and sometimes we can't let go of them. Even as they destroy us. Understanding these subtle dynamics may help you to be kinder to yourself and, perhaps, help you feel sane.

The Secret to Survival

This book is predicated on one simple secret: *Narcissists are not going to change.* That simple premise, I hope, will be a life-changer, because for many readers, it may pull their attention off of blaming themselves, feeling anxious, doubting themselves, frustrating themselves by working on communication and reading piles of relationship advice (that presumes that the other person is actually listening), or waiting for a bus that is never going to appear. Relationships with narcissists are held in place by hope of a "someday better," with little evidence to support it will ever arrive. I hold to my conviction on this—99 percent of people with narcissistic personality disorder *will not change*. What you see is what you get, so either get used to it or get out. Relying on your partner to change is not an option. The only changes you can make are in yourself: understanding the moving parts, managing your expectations, and making decisions accordingly. That is what this book is about.

This book provides an in-depth description of narcissism, as well as of the ominous Dark Triad (more on this in Chapter 3). It is meant to help you identify the red flags and common patterns, connect with how they make you feel, decide the right path, and then execute it. But most of all, it will serve as a reminder of the grim truth that narcissists will not change, and that you may not want to spend your life like Sisyphus, rolling the rock up the hill day after day, only to start again the next morning. It will show you how to break a cycle that you may not even realize you are stuck in.

Narcissistic personality disorder and other personality disorders are different than psychiatric patterns considered more "syndromal," like major depression. Personality disorders are patterned ways of responding to the world and of responding to one's inner world. Under times of stress these patterns become even stronger. Because they are patterns, they are also predictable. These patterns reside in the narcissist, not you, but their patterns cause a great deal of disruption in their relationships with everyone around them.

A Provocative Prescription

This book will no doubt be controversial in my field of practice and to many readers. I am, after all, a psychologist, and we are in the business of treatment and change. But I have seen little good evidence of consistent interventions that work with folks with narcissism. Maybe a few inches of progress, a polite acknowledgment that they were not always as graceful as they could have been, but like our friend the scorpion, "getting it" doesn't mean changing it. To quote William James, "A difference which makes no difference is no difference at all."

I'm also not going to tell you that you should leave. It would have been easy to write a book like this from a singular premise: You are being treated badly, so get out. But life is complicated and it is never that simple. Some people are unwilling to abandon these relationships, and a singular prescription (just walk away!) is likely to leave many people in these situations feeling even more alone and without any options. This book addresses that fork in the road using an honest framework. It was meant to address both options—and perhaps the same reader may opt to stay for a while, but then down the road he or she may choose to depart. There is no judgment being offered for either option—you are the only authority on what is right for you. Being given the tools to stay, but in an informed manner, makes this an essential survival guide that recognizes that romantic relationships are complex and nuanced territory. While narcissists may seem like one-trick ponies that behave in patterned ways, the rest of us are not. Even narcissists do not come in one size only. There are many different variants, which can leave us feeling many different ways. This book provides realistic advice on how to deal with their patterns, and it may permit people to stay more comfortably, transition out slowly, or leave in as composed and safe a manner as possible.

Writers are sometimes imprisoned by words and grammar, and in order to retain consistency throughout the book I use the pronoun "he" when referring to the narcissist (rather than "they"). Most extant research on personality disorders suggests that narcissistic personality disorder is more prevalent in men (e.g. DSM-5), and this may in part be due to the fact that boys and men are reinforced for the traits that comprise the disorder (just as girls and women are often socialized for traits such as dependency). Keep in mind that there are many narcissistic women out there, and many readers may have been impacted by female narcissistic partners (if you can make the "pronoun leap" as you read the book, it is my hope that this book is useful for all readers, regardless of the gender of their partners). This is not meant to be a book that unfairly targets men, but this usage may raise an issue for some readers and I wanted to ensure that the rationale was clarified, even if it is not optimal.

Violent Relationships

One of my major concerns as I laid out the framework for this book was that many of these patterns are observed in relationships characterized by domestic violence or intimate partner violence (IPV). The patterns and dynamics, such as the control, the coldness, the inconsistency, the charm, and the manipulation are all very much a part of narcissism. Frankly, in the myriad interviews I conducted as well as clinical cases I draw upon for this book, physical violence and emotional abuse (yelling, bullying, insulting) were endemic. Many times, and repeatedly, couples would come to the precipice of violence or abuse, and while blows were rarely exchanged, objects were thrown, doors were slammed.

One in three women and one in four men has been the victim of domestic violence, and domestic violence represents 21 percent of violent crime in the U.S. It remains a public health crisis in our country and world. Domestic violence requires an approach that is different and more acute than what is laid forth in these pages; it requires immediate attention to safety, the possible involvement of law enforcement, and the safeguarding of children. This is not meant to serve as a primer or guidebook to managing a violent relationship, even though many of the themes of the book will be relevant to women and men who are in physically violent relationships. The Appendix of this book features resources for people who are victims of domestic violence/IPV. So while this book may serve as another resource for you if you are in an abusive relationship, you are urged to seek out immediate assistance for your safety.

Co-Dependency

My other main concern in writing this book relates to the phenomenon of "co-dependency." According to the *Oxford Dictionary of Psychology,* co-dependency is defined as "a relationship or partnership in which two or more people support or encourage each other's unhealthy habits, especially substance dependencies." While the term has largely been focused on the dynamics of substance abuse in relationships, it has expanded to be more inclusive of any relationships in which people stick around and foster the other's bad behavior. In that way, simply staying in the types of relationships I will be describing in this book can be viewed as co-dependent, because by not leaving you are saying "it is okay for you to treat me this way."

Alan Rappoport, a psychologist who writes on narcissism, describes the relationship with a narcissist as "co-narcissistic," and we will delve into more about what he says later in the book. According to Rappoport, the co-narcissist is an audience to the narcissist's need to chronically be on stage and receive attention. Rarely does the performer respond to the audience, rather he just receives their adulation as gratitude for a performance well executed and then exits the stage. In our current psychology and self-help parlance, terms like co-dependency cast suspicion and criticism on someone for remaining in a relationship with a narcissistic partner. That can be an unkind stance, which often results in people becoming frustrated with someone who sticks around with a narcissistic partner. Many people stay in relationships with narcissists because they do not understand the dynamics of narcissism. Most people are *convinced* that their partners will change. Once you understand the disorder, and the tools for how to manage it, you may be less likely to endure the same treatment.

You *Can* End the Cycle

A relationship with a narcissist is in essence being in a relationship with someone who will never listen to you or hear you. As a result, you can be as precise in your communication as a robot, and it will not be heard nor will it matter. Admittedly, as I listened to the many stories shared with me for this book, even I would furrow my brow and think *why the hell did you stay?* It is easy to write off someone who stays in one of these abusive, narcissistic relationships as a fool, as a "co-dependent," or somehow complicit. Relationships are a two-way street, but that does not mean anyone should have to endure chronically bad treatment. I hope this book will not only help you understand how you got in and why you hang in there, but also give you enough information so you can make better choices and preserve yourself, so you can end the cycle of doubt, discomfort, and anxiety.

I have journeyed through this territory professionally, empirically, educationally, and experientially. The information contained herewith may well make some people angry, professionals in the field and narcissists alike. It is my hope that it may help even more people. I am firm in my conviction that this message must get out there: You *can* take your life back, even when you are in a relationship with a pathological narcissist. And, hopefully, in some cases, even avoid being here in the first place or going back to it again.

CHAPTER 2

NARCISSISM IS THE NEW BLACK

This Narcissus of ours
Can't see his face in the mirror
Because he has become the mirror.

— ANTONIO MACHADO

hese days the new "N" word is narcissism.

Most people know it's not a nice word, but few people know what it really means. But just like Supreme Court Justice Potter Stewart said all those years ago about pornography ("I know it when I see it"), it's the same way with narcissism.

The selfie. Reality TV. Social media. What's your brand? Am I fabulous? Will you follow me back? Narcissism is, indeed, the new world order. It is the reality TV star who can talk for 15 minutes about her new hair extensions or handbag. It is the professional athlete, such as Lance Armstrong, who says to the cynics and the skeptics: "I'm sorry for you. I'm sorry you can't dream big and I'm sorry you don't believe in miracles." It is musicians, such as Kanye West, who was quoted in *W Magazine* saying, "I made that song because I am a god . . . I don't think there's much more ex-planation." It's people like Bernie Madoff, who bilked investors of billions while living a life of extraordinary luxury and maintaining a grandiose illusion that people wanted to believe. A *Vanity Fair* article on the financier captured his narcissistic behavior perfectly:

"'Bernie is not what you would call Mr. Nice Guy, not someone you would want to have a beer with,' one insider volunteered. 'He was imperial, above it all. If he didn't like the conversation, he would just get up and walk away. It was 'I'm Bernie Madoff and you're not.'" If we were to post a rogue's gallery of prominent narcissists, it would go on for thousands of pages and be populated by celebrities, businessmen, prime ministers and presidents, athletes, musicians, artists, producers, and perhaps even your next door neighbor, your boss, or the guy sleeping next to you right now.

What *Is* Narcissism?

The Diagnostic and Statistical Manual of Mental Disorders, Fifth Edition (DSM-5) defines narcissistic personality disorder as a "pervasive pattern of grandiosity, need for admiration, and lack of empathy." It is further characterized as "variable and vulnerable self-esteem, with attempts at regulation through attention and approval seeking, and either overt or covert grandiosity." The person with narcissistic personality disorder is typified by symptoms including fantasies of unlimited success, beauty, or ideal love, the belief that he is special and unique, entitlement, interpersonal exploitation, envy, arrogance, superficial "close" relationships, and low levels of insight.

Pathological narcissism takes in more territory than just the DSM criteria. Narcissism is ultimately a disorder of self-esteem. Narcissists' grandiosity, quest for greatness, and braggadocio can result in most people viewing them as confident, smart, and successful (which they may ostensibly be), however you only need to scrape away with your fingernail to reveal that under the shiny top coat are people who cannot regulate their feelings and exist to obtain the approval of others. On days they receive praise, they have a great day. On days they are criticized, it is all doom and gloom. It is easy to feel as though you are on a roller coaster. There are also days when they are deeply vulnerable and prone to shame, so this isn't a simple picture. While the central pillars of narcissism are the self-esteem deficits that manifest as grandiosity, entitlement, lack of empathy, and admiration seeking, the "tells" of narcissism are a bit more far reaching, and we'll explore them in detail in the next chapter. Narcissism also meanders into other diagnostic spaces, specifically its affinity with psychopathy.

Narcissism is very much a "disorder of superficiality." Given that the entire world is trending towards greater superficiality in all endeavors—work, school, parenting, and love—the narcissists' propensity toward superficiality no longer seems that unusual. Narcissists fall in love (and quite often), however it is often a rather superficial experience, focused on variables such as excitement, validation, appearance, and success. Even so, love is very real for them, and it is unfair and inaccurate to say that a narcissist is "incapable" of love. It is often "love-lite"—a surface-level experience that is usually quite seductive and sweeping and then devolves into something uncomfortable and empty when day-to-day life sets in. When it comes to love, narcissists are sprinters and not marathoners. It is often a rather grandiose experience, with numerous references to "falling in love at first sight," and a "once-in-a-lifetime" love story. Trust me, before long you will hope it is once in a lifetime, and that it never happens again.

The Dark Triad

The Dark Triad is a term developed and presented by Delroy Paulhus and Kevin Williams from the Department of Psychology at the University of British Columbia. In a 2002 paper in the *Journal of Research in Personality*, they beautifully delineate the Dark Triad as composed of three overlapping but distinct traits: Machiavellianism, psychopathy, and narcissism. Machiavellianism is manifested through exploitation and manipulation of other people, cynicism (especially in matters of morality and ethics), and deception (especially in relationships). In simple terms, people who are Machiavellian know how to work every situation to their advantage and do so coolly and smoothly. Psychopathy is pathological selfishness; consistent violation of laws, rules, and norms; lack of remorse; and cold and callous attitudes and behavior. Psychopathy can feel especially dangerous because of the lack of remorse and guilt, as well as a chronic unwillingness or inability to take responsibility for anything. The Dark Triad traits are highly related to and overlap with narcissism, and, as you will see, rarely are we dealing with "clean" narcissism, but rather various traits of the triad combining to make one extremely challenging person.

It Starts Early

The theories on the origin of narcissism are thick and deep. There are two primary influences: early environment and our larger culture. Early environmental explanations usually focus on relationships with parents. The two key theorists on narcissism, Heinz Kohut and Otto Kernberg, both agree it has an origin in the parent-child relationship but have slightly different takes on it. Kohut focuses on something called "mirroring," or the experience of getting approval from parents in a consistent and realistic way. A parent or parents who are off their game (for example, one or both are absent or are narcissistic themselves, so they lack empathy for their child or are distracted by other influences, such as substance use or other mental illness) cannot provide this consistent mirror. When this occurs, the child cannot develop a realistic sense of self and gets stuck in an undeveloped world view. Children are grandiose by nature, and those magical thoughts and superhero assumptions get compassionately shaped into a realistic sense of self in the presence of consistent mirroring. Without that, the immature childhood worldview can persist. Charming in a six-year-old, not so much in a forty-six-year-old.

In addition, this experience of mirroring also results in the child developing mechanisms for what is called "self-soothing," basically the ability to manage emotions appropriately and on his own. Like a child, narcissists hold on to the grandiose view of themselves and keep looking to the world for a mirror, so they remain dependent on the world for validation and approval to bolster their self-esteem. In addition, narcissists never quite learn how to regulate their moods, so they are inconsistent, can have strong sudden shifts and rages, tend to project their emotions onto other people, behave badly, and find external ways to numb their emotions (drugs, alcohol, and sex are among the most classic ways).

Kernberg argues it a little differently but in a similar vein; he focuses on the idea that the children who have unempathic parents (narcissistic parents) will remain emotionally hungry throughout their lives and then develop their outer world instead of their inner world. Subsequently, they will overdevelop a skill set that the parents value (for example, appearance, academic achievement, athletic prowess, playing the violin). Because they never developed skills such as emotional regulation, and become masterful at compartmentalizing themselves, separating their world of achievement from everything else, they become grandiose around their talents. If they experience any sense of weakness or vulnerability, they cut off that part of themselves (a process called splitting).

Thus, for the rest of their lives, they oscillate back and forth between grandiosity and emptiness. More recently, psychiatrist Alexander Lowen, in his book on narcissism, posits that narcissism has often been linked to the experience of shame and humiliation in childhood—usually at the hands of parents who were controlling. A classic example of using power and control in childhood is spankings that are far out of proportion to the offense the child committed. Children who are also chronically exposed to criticism or mockery, or those who come from settings in which feelings are invalidated ("stop crying, it wasn't that bad"), learn that power is the way in human relationships and feelings are not okay (in other words, they learn to exert power over their feelings as well).

Ultimately, it leaves the child learning one thing: how to use power to influence his or her own relationships. Narcissists often have a history of rebellion, especially in their teen years, and Lowen believes that this may be due to a power pushback. The rebellion can shift the balance of power in the family, and the child then learns to use manipulations like rebellion or acting out or even submissiveness to get his or her needs met (rather than having been taught to appropriately express those needs).

Healthy Narcissism

Now that we've discussed the possible origins of narcissism, it is also important to distinguish between what is termed "healthy" narcissism and pathological narcissism. There is some disagreement on the term "healthy narcissism," which includes the ability to advocate for yourself, sometimes putting your needs ahead of others but remaining mindful of the impact of your choices on others, the ability to exert an opinion respectfully and ask that others recognize it, maintaining self-confidence, and pursuing ambition but not at the deliberate cost to other people. These are the general traits that fall under the umbrella of "healthy narcissism." When people stand their ground, but do so in a way that reflects an awareness of how their conduct and behavior are impacting other people, that is healthy self-advocacy, and it is sometimes termed healthy narcissism. (I prefer calling it healthy self-advocacy given the connotations of the term "narcissism.")

Many times, the bravado of a narcissist is misunderstood as "self-confidence." There is a difference—and it is a critical distinction. Self-confidence is trust in your abilities, your personal characteristics, and your insight and judgment. Self-confidence is bred through consistent presence in loving and supportive environments, validating experiences, and successes. A self-confident person is often a good problem solver and stress manager, self-reflective and able to clearly observe, articulate, and take ownership of his faults and vulnerabilities. Because self-confident people have a well-formed sense of identity and values, they do not feel the need to disrespect other people, because they know who they are and do not feel threatened by other people or their views.

The truly self-confident person is not empty and is in command of his emotions and sense of self, and this is manifested through empathy and genuineness. This is the opposite of the narcissist. Unfortunately, at first blush, because narcissists are able to clearly voice their opinions, speak highly of themselves, and are often ostensibly successful (wealthy, powerful, or leaders of some kind), it is easy to think they are high in self-confidence. But the key characteristics of narcissism—lack of empathy, arrogance, disrespect for other points of view, entitlement, and grandiosity—are not typically in the self-confident person's playbook.

The pages of this book will help you understand the difference between someone who is self-confident versus narcissistic. The confusion in these terms, however, frequently allows narcissists to get pretty far down the path (and into your life) before you realize that this is not self-confidence, but rather showmanship and bluster.

As you read through the pages of this book, you will also recognize that on some days or at some times in your life, you also have some of the more "unhealthy" traits of narcissism (you become grandiose about a new opportunity, you become a bit demanding about good service in a restaurant, you take lots of selfies and await those "Likes"). Keep in mind that we all engage in some of the "bad narcissism" patterns from time to time, but when it hits critical mass and characterizes your behavior in a predictable manner, that is when it jumps the rails into "pathological narcissism."

A key element of what makes narcissism pathological is that the pathological narcissist rarely, if ever, considers the impact of his or her actions or words on others (unless those others are useful to the narcissist). In addition, the unstable self-esteem of the pathological narcissist is the core conflict (whereas in healthy narcissism a well-integrated sense of self and identity are retained). As we cut to the core of what narcissism is really about, the differences between healthy self-advocacy and confidence versus pathological narcissism will become clear. Yes, sometimes we do put our needs and wants before others, but typically (and ideally) we do so after considering the impact of our actions on others.

What Is a Personality Disorder?

Our personality is basically our unique "pattern of response." It sets the course for how we as individuals typically respond to situations, stressors, and day-to-day life. It represents a framework for how our inner worlds are organized, and it is specific to each of us. In that way, personalities are like fingerprints – different for everyone. Our personalities in some way make us predictable—to ourselves and to the world—even when we are being "unpredictable." Personality is both innate and developed through our interactions with our environments. Personality traits are in part inherited from our biological parents and can be observed across siblings and other relatives (a pattern you may have noticed in your own family) but are also shaped by the environment. Our personalities are pretty consistent, and obviously some personalities are easier to work with than others (cheerful resilient folks often make easier and more pleasant companions), but the challenging personalities may be more seductive, simply because they are challenging.

A personality disorder occurs when a person has a set of what we call "maladaptive" traits or patterns that interfere with relationships, work, behavior, and functioning in the world. A personality disorder represents personality taken to extremes, so instead of someone being orderly, he is obsessive; instead of someone being shy, she is paralyzed when she is with other people. In the case of narcissistic personality disorder, it is an inability to form deep connections with others, superficiality, and a complete lack of a basic and necessary human quality: empathy.

The Rise of Narcissism

A survey of 35,000 people conducted by the National Institutes of Health (NIH), and published by Stinson et al., estimated that 6.2

percent of Americans experienced symptoms of narcissistic personality disorder, and a far higher proportion of young adults in their 20s (9 percent) received this diagnosis than older adults over 65 (3 percent). This is concerning because these young adults are the ones who are looking to get into relationships, get married, and have children. While some of this research that looks at narcissism in large samples and over time has been criticized for methodology and other issues in how these narcissistic traits are measured, taken together, study findings do suggest that narcissism may be on the rise, and that young adults are the population at greatest risk. Turn on the television, and it suggests that these data are not wrong.

In 2008, Jean Twenge, a professor at San Diego State University and a noted expert on narcissism, along with her co-authors, examined data from more than 16,000 university students across the U.S. and observed a 30 percent increase in narcissism scores in a 25-year period (from the early 1980s until 2006). Interestingly, she notes that these increases are on par with the increases in obesity observed during the same time period. (I find it particularly compelling that narcissism is not being cited as a public health threat in the same way as obesity; I would argue that narcissism is worse—it is not only harmful to the individual but destroys other people as well.)

In *The Narcissism Epidemic*, Twenge and Campbell brilliantly lay out the numbers and the research on the issue, with the simple bottom line: Narcissism is an epidemic and no one is free from its effects. Much like any epidemic, whether or not you get the illness, you are affected. Think of it as a vast flu pandemic—either you get the flu or you end up having to take care of those with it, or do more work because those who are ill cannot do it. In a world in which narcissism has become epidemic, if you aren't a narcissist, then you may be under the spell of someone who is a pathological narcissist, and it is taking a toll on your life. If we look at Twenge's statistics, or the data from the NIH, and if there are more narcissists out there, then you are simply more statistically likely to fall in love with one. And the dice are loaded, because frankly, narcissists are better at winning a mate. This book will break down in detail how you fall prey, how to manage it, and how to avoid it from happening in the first place—or happening again.

Technology appears to incentivize narcissism, offering constant reinforcement of validation-seeking and a steady diet of admiration. Devices, social media, and our chronic drive to share our lives allow people to outsource their egos and remain reliant on the outside world to do what they should be able to do on their own, which is to regulate their sense of self. It is very likely that the disproportionate difference in rates of narcissism between adults in their 20s versus those over 65 is a byproduct of the reliance on technology. The cultural pressure and norms around posting selfies and chronic validation seeking makes many of the behaviors associated with narcissism simply normal in younger adults. These expectations about validation and admiration then bleed into the rest of life. It is hard to engage in listening to another person with empathy if you are waiting for the spotlight to shine back on you. It is easy to fall prey to grandiosity when folks are just a few thousand Instagram likes or YouTube views away from "stardom."

The pendulum has also swung very far in the direction of giving young people a steady diet of "self-esteem" without any substance. In other words, our focus on simply saying "you are great" without recognizing hard and fast accomplishments is not doing young people any favors. If they repeatedly receive a trophy simply for participating, then not only will they anticipate a reward for simply showing up but also their fluffed up self-esteem is not connected to any specific achievement. This is not to say that children have to run fast or get perfect grades to "earn" the esteem of others, but they do need to be clear on expectations for behavior and to experience disappointment. By experiencing disappointment, whether that is hurt, sadness, or simply coming in second, a child learns to lick his wounds, feel a range of emotions, and realize that everything will be okay without a sense of panic. It's easy to tell children "you are great"; it is quite a bit more challenging to pay attention to them, foster their strengths, help them shore up their weaknesses, and meaningfully recognize their growth. The pendulum has overcorrected from the cruel era of rapping a disobedient child's knuckles with a ruler to giving every child a trophy for showing up. Every child should have the experience of being loved unconditionally, supported, and encouraged, but this requires more than a standing ovation every time he or she enters the room. These shifts—in technology, in education, and parenting—are all likely contributing to the steady uptick in pathological narcissism.

Ultimately, in the narcissistic hall of mirrors, our inner worlds matter far less than the digitally enhanced images that appear to provide the narrative of our lives. As long as the picture matters more than the reality, we have a problem.

Our Culture Celebrates Narcissism

Gaggles such as the Real Housewives of _____ (choose a community: Beverly Hills, Orange County, Atlanta, DC, New Jersey, New York), the superficial antics of the Kardashian clan, or the mean-spirited ramblings of judges on makeover/entrepreneurship/cooking/dancing/singing competition shows have become the narrative and town criers for an entire generation. Loud blasts of emotion and invective with little regard for how words and actions affect other people are the norm. We lambast bullies and yet give them endless platforms and attention for harming others. Hours and lifetimes spent acquiring possessions and sharing the imagery with the world have become a cultural zeitgeist that has elevated admiration-seeking and plumage-pimping above everything else. It doesn't matter if you are mistreating others, as long as you look good. Empathy appears to have gone the way of the VCR.

In addition, the acquisition of wealth is helped along by narcissism. Pathological narcissists are often singular in their pursuit of status, power, and wealth, and traits such as entitlement and lack of empathy make it quite simple to act in accordance with the dog-eat-dog ethos of capitalism. That Wall Street wonk with the big bonus and the multimillion dollar condo and house in the Hamptons did not get that via empathy and mutual regard. Our economy rewards the harsh competitor. These traits are not going to be turned off when these folks leave the office. While collaboration and connection can and should be fostered in corporate and competitive economic environments, as long as the perception of the "winner take all" mentality holds sway, it is difficult to push back. However, there is a solid body of literature that suggests that collaboration and compassion make for a wonderful and sustainable business model (unfortunately, the narcissists did not get the memo).

Narcissism has contributed to a culture of illusion. This isn't just about one grandiose person monopolizing a dinner conversation, or vapid television, or over-documented and over-shared lives on social media. We are sliding into a culture that is living in an illusion of grandiosity and a citizenry that has little or no ability to be alone. People can no longer sit quietly, and even when they are ostensibly alone, social media ensures that they do not have to tolerate the transient sense of solitude. The word "no" has become passé. People live to be seen, sometimes even "faking life" in hopes that their "pseudo-life" goes viral.

We value wealth and its associated mythology at any cost; easy credit means that the illusion of a fancy façade, expensive car, and designer shoes can be easily accessed, with potentially dire fiscal consequences down the road. Maintaining the façade becomes more important than understanding why we feel the need for the façade in the first place. We often believe we "deserve" luxury goods, and because we are continuously blasted with these images via all media, there is an illusion that they are necessary and ubiquitous. The belief then becomes the reality. As long as I have the right toys, all is well.

Beauty and youth have become an obsession in our culture. The weight-loss industry is a $20-billion cash cow. Cosmetic surgery is a $12-billion industry, and a $62-billion cosmetic industry keeps us eternally young and wrinkle free. But to what end? More than 90 percent of women report that they are dissatisfied with their bodies, and in an increasingly visual culture, the drive to achieve "perfection" is even more pressured. The post-modern Cartesian riff becomes "I am thin, therefore I am."

The democratization of media means that anyone with a phone can become a celebrity. Our short-sighted focus on self-esteem in children means that everyone gets a trophy, universities and education are "brands" instead of places of learning, standardized tests are used to assess wisdom, and grade inflation is rampant. The tribe has been replaced with followers and likes. Our economy, our bodies, our health, our children, and frankly our psyches are in big trouble.

We have become an unkind world. Insults, mean words offered from the anonymity of a computer keyboard, social isolation, and a focus on "me" instead of "us" dominate our landscape. We often do not regulate ourselves or monitor our words and actions, and meanness, much like narcissism, appears to be more prevalent every day. It now appears that many people are no longer having relationships *with* people, they are having relationships *at* people. As narcissists and narcissism saturates our culture and our population, we are all going to pay, and much of this will be paid for in our relationships.

Relationship and dating shows, such as *The Bachelor/Bachelorette* and *Millionaire Matchmaker,* are just the tip of the iceberg of what has become the "emptying" of the intimate relationship. Dating apps such as Tinder predicate the beginning of a relationship on a simple "right swipe" on a smartphone, and the subsequent hookup culture created by such technology attempts to fast-track intimacy and cut out the process of deeper conversation and acquaintance. Increasingly, we are emptying the connection, respect, and empathy out of one of the most important and healthy of human experiences and turning it into branding, showmanship, and posturing. In the midst of this epidemic and cultural shift into narcissism, relationships have taken the hardest hit of all.

Don Draper: The Quintessential Pop-Culture Narcissist

Sometimes the simplest frame of reference is one that is shared, such as a character in film or television. In my psychologist's opinion, *Mad Men* may be one of the finest television programs ever made—and perhaps that is because it featured one of the best narcissists ever written. If you've watched it, then you will get this, and if you haven't, it is worth the investment. Spoiler alert: Don Draper, the handsome advertising executive, was a classic narcissist.

Simply put, Don Draper is not a good guy. At the surface, when we first meet him, he is a successful advertising executive, husband, and father with a nice home in the suburbs. He is everyman. Within a week we recognize that he is a cheater and a liar and throws wives, kids, coworkers, lovers, and extended family under the bus, sometimes with tragic consequences. While he had some gritty and traumatic beginnings, that doesn't qualify as a get-out-of-jail-free card or rationalize his habitually callous behavior. He was forever a revisionist, constantly edited his life and identity, put his own pleasure and success before all else, and pushed through life with abandon, caring little about the ramifications of his actions, unless they inconvenienced him. Most people transitioned out of his life, but not without him doing a fair amount of damage to their psychological worlds. He had his dark nights of the soul; all narcissists do. He could rarely regulate his emotions, and alcohol, cigarettes, and lots of women were his ways of managing feelings and self-esteem. He walked through the world feeling like an imposter, and he used superficial methods to manage that feeling.

Interestingly, most of us kept watching for years because we thought he *would* and *could* change. Week after week we thought he would find redemption; he could be a faithful husband, a decent father, and an honest person. It reminded us that we get drawn in and transported by a narcissist's vulnerability, charm, and humanity.

Don Draper was a fantastic example of the fact that these guys are actually sometimes really lovely, and so we let down our guard. He would have flashes here and there—of love, of connection, of passion—but at the end of the day, these were fleeting. Far more consistent were his dishonesty, selfishness, infidelity, lack of empathy, Machiavellianism, ambition, and at times downright cruelty. Simultaneously, he brought traits of devilish sex appeal, charm, intelligence, and charisma. Interestingly, even with a fictional character, where it doesn't matter a lick in our lives whether he is good, bad, or indifferent, we still care about whether he can be redeemed.

The last episode was spot-on for someone who studies narcissism. The writers and producers ended it brilliantly. Don Draper winds up, exactly as he should, alone. When he finally has a moment of seeming "empathy" at the very end, hugging a distressed guy who was alienated from everything and everyone in his life, it was the classic narcissistic response. For the first time Don Draper is offering real comfort to someone, but only because he was experiencing the same distress as Draper (not because Draper suddenly became warm and fuzzy). And finally, at what could have been a moment of meditative transcendence, he instead uses that mindful moment to keep forwarding the cause of himself through the mental creation of an inspired advertising campaign. Even the deep moments get spun into the superficial.

Don Draper played with our minds, because sometimes he was downright kind, and there were more than a few situations in which he did the right thing. This is where narcissistic personalities can feel like a confusing menace—it would be much easier if they were cruel 24/7, but they are not. Those kind, connected moments play with our heads and awaken us to the possibility of redemption. The good moments keep us in the game; the bad moments leave us questioning ourselves. The roller coaster between redemption and disappointment is infinite in relationships with narcissists.

So much of the mythology, film, and television in our culture is peppered by these larger than life narcissistic impresarios. They make for great leading men (and women): Tom Buchanan, Gordon

Gekko, King Lear, Faust, the Wizard of Oz, John Willoughby, Miranda Priestly, Dorian Gray—you get the idea. They are fun to watch, not so fun to live with.

Now reflect on every narcissistic character in a TV show, movie, book, or play that we thought might turn a corner and transform, and we may even watch these movies several times in hopes of that moment of redemption (as though the ending might change). Now extend that to the real people with whom we live who are pathologically narcissistic. We tune in to them not every week, but every day, and every hour, thinking (and hoping) they will change. The bulk of what they do is dismissive, disconnected, dishonest, and dysfunctional, and yet they give us enough flashes of "hope" and charisma and fantasy, so we hold out for the ultimate turnaround, or at least the hope that things may become easier. They validate the broken parts of ourselves, they validate the rescuer in us, they validate the concept of "hope."

And it never happens. They give us just enough rope to hang ourselves, to hang around, to stick it out. We throw bad money after good. Most of us were taught the redemptive power of forgiveness through religion, greeting cards, and new-age mantras. We keep turning the other cheek until we are out of cheeks.

But, just like Don Draper, they never change. They never will. Even at the very end, when we hoped they would see the light. And yet most people go back to them, again and again and again. Why?

The facts are clear. Narcissism is here and it is only going to proliferate more. There are too many incentives for it in our world: social media, wealth as a barometer of success, reality TV, and the possibility of going "viral." By definition, narcissism and narcissistic personality disorder are characterized by lack of empathy, entitlement, grandiosity, superficiality, and the chronic search for validation and admiration, and can include other patterns, such as lying, cheating, jealousy, paranoia, manipulation, and interpersonal exploitation. Narcissists are also quite charming, intelligent, articulate, well-put-together, and great showmen. Because relationships tend to be superficial for them, intimacy is a stretch, and as you can imagine, this cluster of traits does not bode well for relationships in the long term. In the next chapter, we will explore some of the most common traits of narcissists, the red flags that you may be in a relationship with a narcissist, and the different types of narcissists and the corresponding patterns in your relationship.

CHAPTER 3

ARE YOU IN A RELATIONSHIP WITH A NARCISSIST?

People speak sometimes about the 'bestial' cruelty of man, but that is terribly unjust and offensive to beasts, no animal could ever be so cruel as a man, so artfully, so artistically cruel.

—DOSTOYEVSKY

This isn't a clinical manual; it is a survival manual. No one can really diagnose someone they haven't met. The one thing you *can* do is reflect on how they make you feel. You can also observe patterns, and it can be useful to have a blueprint with which to understand those patterns. People with narcissistic personality disorder or who are pathologically narcissistic are often experienced as "mean" or "difficult" people, who are very well disguised—the proverbial wolf in sheep's clothing.

The last chapter gave an overview of narcissism and the development of narcissism. It also acknowledged the very real fact that narcissism is on the rise, so there is an increasing probability that you could find yourself in a relationship with a narcissist. So how can you tell the difference between someone who is simply charming and a little self-absorbed and someone who is manipulative, controlling, and completely lacking in empathy? How do you *know,* for sure, that you are in a relationship with a narcissist? This chapter is the longest—and perhaps most important—chapter in the book because it illuminates the most common personality traits of narcissists and the red flags you should watch out for early in a relationship. It will help you identify whether you are currently with a narcissist and empower you to know what to look for in future relationships to avoid getting involved with a narcissist.

QUIZ: IS YOUR PARTNER A NARCISSIST?

Answer "yes" or "no" to the following questions:

1. Does your partner seem cold or unfeeling in the face of your feelings or the feelings of other people, or does he seem to have difficulty understanding the feelings of other people?

2. Does your partner talk about his life, accomplishments, and work in an exaggerated or larger than life way (for example, having an impossibly good job, how he is going to have the greatest of everything)? Is your partner arrogant and convinced of his superiority over other people?

3. Does your partner believe that he is entitled to special treatment in all areas of his life (to receive special treatment from businesses, service workers, friends, and life in general)? Does he become angry when this special treatment is not accorded to him?

4. Does your partner manipulate people and situations to get his needs met with little regard for the feelings of other people?

5. Does your partner become intensely angry very quickly—and usually out of proportion to the situation at hand?

6. Does your partner often think that people are out to get him or take advantage of him?

7. Is your partner able to hand out criticism easily, but does he have a hard time hearing even the slightest feedback without becoming defensive and even angry?

8. Is your partner frequently jealous of you and your friendships, relationships, successes, and opportunities?

9. Does your partner do bad things and not feel guilty about them or even have any insight into the fact that these were not nice things to do?

10. Does your partner need constant admiration and validation, such as compliments, awards, and honors, and does he seek it out (for example, through social media or constantly letting people know about his achievements)?

11. Does your partner regularly lie, leave out important details, or give you inconsistent information?

12. Is your partner an expert showman? Making a big show of everything he does including parties, the car he drives, the places he goes, and the way he portrays his life to others?

13. Does your partner regularly project his feelings onto you (for example, accusing you of being angry at a time he is yelling at you or accusing you of being inconsistent when his life is chaotic)?

14. Is your partner greedy and materialistic? Does he covet more things and more money and stop at little to achieve these things?

15. Is your partner emotionally cold and distant? Does he become disconnected, particularly at times when you are experiencing or showing strong emotion?

16. Does your partner frequently second-guess you or doubt you to the point that you feel like you are "going crazy?"

17. Is your partner cheap with his time or money? Is he a person who will only be generous when it will serve his interests?

18. Does your partner regularly avoid taking responsibility and is he quick to blame others for his mistakes? Does your partner tend to defend himself instead of taking responsibility for his behavior?

19. Is your partner vain and absorbed with his appearance or how he displays himself to the world (for example, grooming, clothing, accessories)?

20. Is your partner controlling? Does he attempt to control your behavior? Does he appear almost obsessive and compulsive

in his need for order and control in his environment and schedule?

21. Are your partner's mood, behaviors, and lifestyle unpredictable and inconsistent? Do you frequently feel like you do not know what is coming next?

22. Does your partner take advantage of you and other people on a regular basis? Does he take the opportunity to ensure his needs are met even if it means inconveniencing or taking advantage of the connections or time potentially offered by you or other people?

23. Does your partner enjoy watching other people fail? Does he take glee in the idea that someone's life or business is not going well, especially when that person has typically done better than him?

24. Does your partner find it difficult to be alone or spend time alone?

25. Does your partner have poor boundaries with other people? Does he maintain inappropriate relationships with friends and co-workers, and keep doing this even when he is told that this is uncomfortable for you?

26. Has your partner ever been sexually or emotionally unfaithful?

27. Does your partner tune out when you are talking? Does he yawn, check his device, or get distracted by papers and tasks around him while you are talking to him?

28. Does your partner become vulnerable or sensitive at times of stress or when things are not going well? Is he unable to cope when faced with significant stressors and become very fragile at these times?

29. Is your partner regularly neglectful or just not mindful of basic communication and courtesy (e.g. letting you know he is going to be late or reflexively saying and doing hurtful and careless things)?

30. Does your partner frequently use his appearance or sexuality to get attention? Is he very flirtatious or does he frequently use sexy banter with people outside of your relationship in his words, actions, and social media posts or text messages?

If you answered "yes" to 15 or more of these questions, you likely have a pathologically narcissistic partner. If you answered "yes" to 20 or more of these questions, then it is pretty much a guarantee. Obviously, some of these characteristics are more problematic than others, and some may cause you more distress. For example, you may have answered "yes" to only a few items, including number 26, because your partner cheated on you. Not all cheaters are narcissistic, but that one behavior may have betrayed your trust in a significant and permanent way (however, it will be rare for a person with an unfaithful partner to have that as the only "yes" on the list). Some of these questions hold more weight than the others when it comes to diagnostic or pathological narcissism. The key questions include 1: grandiosity, 2: entitlement, 4: empathy, 10: admiration and validation seeking, 13: projection, and 18: avoidance of responsibility. These characteristics form the core of narcissism and fuel the dynamics of superficiality and inability to form deep and mutual intimate relationships. If your partner has these key characteristics, many of the other questions on the list will follow. No one will have a partner for whom all of these answers will be "no"—all of us have some of these characteristics—so you may have a sweet empathic partner who just happens to like a very clean car or closet. One snowflake does not make a blizzard and one "yes" does not make a narcissist. However, the more of these you are experiencing with your partner, the more challenging your relationship will be.

The Narcissist Checklist

This checklist will break down each of these points in detail so you understand them. The list below represents a "constellation" of traits derived from diagnostic criteria for narcissistic personality disorder, theoretical writings on narcissism, and existing scales on narcissism. The list is followed by a comprehensive description of each of these indicators, drawn from clinical observations as well as theories and existing knowledge about narcissistic personality disorder. Again, this is not a diagnostic manual—this chapter is designed to help you identify the kinds of traits and patterns you may have encountered in your relationship. Once you determine the traits and patterns, the next step is to learn how to respond to these patterns and this person.

If you are dealing with 15 or more of these traits and patterns with someone in your life, then you are likely dealing with a narcissist (and perhaps even narcissistic personality disorder). The more traits he or she has, the more challenging it is going to be to maintain any kind of healthy and consistent relationship. These traits tie back to the questions you answered, but a checklist may help you quickly focus on the traits in question and understand them in a more specific manner.

Keep in mind: We are all guilty of some of these things *some of the time*. As you review this list and think about your partner, or even other people close to you, think about how "patterned" or typical these behaviors are. Many of us will behave in an entitled or a jealous manner here and there; it is the consistency of these maladaptive patterns that makes them problematic. Some of these patterns can also be adaptive at times. The fact that something is a pattern means that these behaviors occur more often than not. For now, just look at the list, check off the ones that apply most of the time, and then read forward to understand each trait. After you read all of the descriptions, you may end up coming back to this list and revising some of your responses. First, however, check off the ones that are most relevant (these items link back to the quiz as well):

- ☐ Lack of Empathy
- ☐ Grandiose
- ☐ Entitled
- ☐ Manipulative
- ☐ Angry and Rageful
- ☐ Paranoid
- ☐ Hypersensitive
- ☐ Jealous

☐ Lack of Guilt/Lack of Insight
☐ Needs Constant Admiration and Validation
☐ Lying
☐ Everything is a Show
☐ Projection
☐ Greedy
☐ Emotionally Cold
☐ Gaslighting (leaves you feeling as if you are "losing your mind")
☐ Cheap
☐ Never Takes Responsibility
☐ Vain
☐ Controlling
☐ Unpredictable
☐ Takes Advantage of Others (or you) on a Regular Basis
☐ Engages in Schaedenfraude (Reveling in Others' Misery)
☐ Does Not Like to Be Alone
☐ Poor Boundaries
☐ Infidelity
☐ Doesn't Listen
☐ Fragile
☐ Careless
☐ Seductive

It can feel insurmountable when it is all in one list like this. These patterns likely began piling up over time, and many of these traits are interdependent. We will now break these traits down more specifically, so you can get a better handle on them. Each trait will include a detailed description of how it looks, because some of these can take very different forms. In addition, each behavior will feature a RED FLAG section to help you identify patterns early on and hopefully avoid them in the future.

LACK OF EMPATHY

She was struggling to make ends meet, and he had been at best marginally available to her. To an outsider it looked like a relationship of convenience. He knew how bad her financial struggles were and yet would rarely offer to pay or would avoid spending time with her because he did not want to have to pay for a drink or dinner (though he was tremendously generous with colleagues and business interests whom he was trying to impress). He would regularly spend money on other people, but only if he felt they would be useful to him in his career or other pursuits. Instead, he would show up at her house relatively late, after she would have eaten, so he could avoid purchasing her dinner or eat what she kept in the house. One night, he stopped to see her at work, where she was having a uniquely challenging day after a subordinate employee was found stealing money. She was exhausted in every way, and he stuck around her office (even though she had not asked him to) as a way of "supporting her." She did not want to hurt his feelings, so she did not ask him to leave, and she offered for him to sit in her office and wait while she attended to the crisis at hand. He criticized her for her handling of the crisis as well and told her that she was ruining his day with her complaints about work (even though it was he who came to her workplace). At the end of her work day, he suggested that they go out to dinner, and while at dinner he said, "You just wasted my entire day—I expect you to buy me dinner." Exhausted by the day, the relationship, and her many other stressors, she reached into her wallet and pulled out her last $50 to pay for dinner, assuming that he would stop her, knowing her situation. He just sat back, smugly thanked her for dinner, and reminded her how lucky she was to have his support.

Lack of empathy may be the key defining characteristic of the narcissistic person. It is the inability to identify with or recognize the experiences and feelings of other people. Basically, narcissists do not care or understand how other people feel and rarely consider other people's feelings in their actions or words. They will often say very cruel things in an offhanded manner and are oblivious to the pain that they cause with their words. If they aren't feeling something, then it is not happening or it does not matter. If they are sad, then they assume everyone must be having a rough day, and if they are joyful, you will be labeled a "buzz-kill" if you are not operating at the same level of joy (regardless of your current state of mind). While they never offer it up, they crave understanding from everyone else. Emotionally, life with them is a one-way street.

The lack of empathy demonstrated by a narcissist is a mirror that does not look back at you. It can leave you feeling misunderstood, isolated, and confused. The lack of empathy experienced when in a relationship with a narcissist results in feeling unseen, unheard, untouched, un-smelled, and un-tasted. It is literally as though you only exist when you are useful. Of the numerous challenging traits presented by a pathological narcissist, lack of empathy may take the greatest toll on a relationship. It can make communication all but impossible and often results in tremendous frustration for you, after trying every means possible to communicate. Communication is predicated on the other person not only listening but also caring.

Narcissists walk through life assuming that their concerns are of paramount interest to everyone that they meet. As a result, it is not unusual for them to launch into long diatribes about what is happening in their lives or about their own experiences, without any regard for the fact that they are taking the other person's time or without even inquiring about how the other person is doing. Interestingly, after going on at length about their concerns and issues, they will become highly impatient or even scornful when other people share their problems with them. This typically unfolds as follows: You listened to their problems for a long time and offered some heartfelt and useful feedback and sympathy. When you start sharing your story, they yawn, check their phone, start tidying up, look around the room, and tune you out.

RED FLAG: LACK OF EMPATHY

The best early empathy RED FLAG is, in fact, the yawn. Or any behavior that evidences that on a regular basis he is not listening when you speak: picking up his devices, looking around instead of at you when you are speaking, or yawning while you are speaking. It is easy to discount these responses as fatigue, distractibility, or being busy. Those excuses do not fly. If he isn't listening early on in your relationship, he is never going to listen. Watch how he listens; it is often one of the most useful tools for assessing his empathy early on. Without empathy, you are building your relationship on air and not on solid ground.

GRANDIOSE

My dad knows everyone; we are practically royalty in the city where I am from. My new boss drives a Bentley and has a killer house in the hills. He thinks I am such a great guy, and he loves my ideas. This guy also owns venues in Vegas, New York, San Diego, Boston, and Miami—and with my connections, I should be running the club inside of six months. I am okay with starting at the bottom as a server, but I don't intend to stay there. I am going to pitch an idea and line up the top celebrities in the business to headline this event. My boss knows my dad through his older brother, and so he will definitely let me put this together. I am so much smarter than everyone who works in this place, they will wish they were me after this event comes together, and I can easily see doing more events all over the country. It's all who you know.

Grandiosity is a pattern in which a person tends to exaggerate accomplishments, talents, connections/relationships, and experiences. These do not have to be real experiences; grandiose people also tend to maintain over-the-top fantasy worlds. So if they haven't accomplished much yet, they talk about what is coming in the future. For example, "I talked to a guy who knows a guy, who is friends with this billionaire venture capital guy, and I know he is going to want to invest right away." They tend to talk in big language about the places they have been, the things that they have done, and the people that they know. A single "celebrity" meeting will launch a thousand tales.

Grandiosity can also be manifested by a sense of self-importance—a belief that their existence is bigger and more important than anyone else's and certainly more important than yours. A major challenge with grandiosity is that grandiose people often want notable credit and adulation even when they do not do anything. Basically, they want to be recognized (in a big way) for merely maintaining big fantasies. So convinced are they of their impending success that they already live in that "reality."

If they really are already successful in some way—hold a major leadership position, are famous, or have accumulated wealth—then the grandiosity is a permanent fixture, and they will repeatedly boast about their accomplishments, their many possessions, and their extraordinary experiences. Going to their homes and listening to them talk can feel like a tedious game of show and tell.

Initially, it can be sort of fun to listen to these people. They are dreamers; they always have the next big idea, they know the "right people," and they have big dreams and even bigger fantasies. They want partners, friends, and associates that are breathtakingly beautiful, or famous, or fabulously wealthy, because this fuels the fantasy. After a while it gets tiresome because the investors rarely show up, the projects rarely get launched, the books rarely get written, the "fabulous-ness" rarely happens. The "visionary fantasies" at some point have to be replaced with real life, a nearly impossible transition for a pathological narcissist.

But that doesn't daunt them, and they keep talking about the grandiose fantasies. When they do not materialize, they also get frustrated, and the disconnect between the reality and the grandiose fantasy can make the narcissist angry, frustrated, sullen, and prone to lashing out. They become angry at the world for not delivering on the big promises they made to themselves in their heads.

It's also not unusual for them to over-identify with famous, wealthy, or otherwise renowned people. They will presume "important" relationships to be closer than they really are (after meeting a celebrity or other notorious individual briefly at a bar, they talk about it to others as though they are well-acquainted). Narcissists often believe that they can only be understood by other high-status people, and they derive a sense of importance by creating these relationships. On the flip side, as they overvalue themselves, they tend to undervalue others, and it is not uncommon for them to devalue the contributions or accomplishments of other people who, like most of us, are just regular people (especially their partners). It is not unusual for them to neglect friends and family who have consistently been there for years in favor of newly acquired "higher status" friends.

Their fantasies and unrealistic standards preoccupy their everyday thoughts. They live and breathe in a dream world where they will be incredibly successful and wealthy and can spend hours thinking about or researching real estate, cars, and other high-end possessions. They may also get themselves into financial hot water by overreaching to acquire expensive clothing, accessories, and other grown-up toys. You may observe them spending money on club memberships, expensive tables at benefits, luxury hotels, and other means of access to people of "higher status." Grandiosity is also connected to seeking out beauty, either spending lots of time achieving their own standard of beauty or bringing it into their lives via partners whom they largely select on the basis of appearance.

Grandiosity is also seductive and can turn your partner into something "larger than life," so when things are going well, it can feel perfect, but when he turns it off (which he will), it can feel like the sun going behind a cloud.

RED FLAG: GRANDIOSE

This is a book about relationships, and the RED FLAG when it comes to grandiosity and relationships is when narcissists talk about their "great love story" or the idea of an "ideal love." It is so easy to get swept away in this early in the game, but that fairy-tale idealism often means all sizzle and no steak. By turning their romantic relationships into a "larger than life" concept, it often becomes intellectualized and not real. Nothing can live up to that vaunted perfection of the mythical love story, and as a result they are chronically disappointed in their relationships (it is hard to think about dealing with stuff like who is going to buy the toilet paper when you are in a "great love story"; it is difficult to imagine Romeo and Juliet arguing about unloading the dishwasher). In the early phase of a relationship, it can feel mighty special to believe you are in a great love story or that you are termed a "great love." Just be careful when you hear that term thrown about by your partner. While it can be fun to live in a fantasy for a day, love is a long game, and it is far better to be a "real love story," rather than some "pie in the sky" fairy tale.

ENTITLED

Entitlement can be captured in six simple words: *Do you know who I am?* Not a day goes by in the tabloids when the ne'er-do-well son of a celebrity or business magnate behaves badly in a hotel, airplane, or other public place and reacts with the mantra of the entitled: "Do you know who I am?"

But these words are not just reserved for the rarefied space of celebrities, tycoons, and their spawn. Many people out there, particularly pathological narcissists, believe their own hype. One of the women interviewed for this book said that when they met, her husband believed that he was such a gifted musician that he should never have to work and that she and others should support his art because he was a great artist (he is pushing 55 now and never quite "made it" but still expects the room, board, and adulation). Ironically, the women in his life did just that. He never worked a day in his life, and they kept a roof over his head and his entitled self in a sports car. He had no problem accepting this because he believed he *deserved* this special treatment. Another woman shared a story of a narcissistic husband who rarely worked but expected her to take on extra work so they could take lavish vacations to various cities, stay in majestic hotel suites, and order $150 bottles of wine at the best restaurants.

Entitlement is the belief that one should be accorded special treatment, typically without reason or cause. Entitlement also involves the belief that everyone should comply with one's demands, no matter how unreasonable they are. Entitled people do not want to wait in lines, always expect upgrades of all kinds, maintain that they deserve the best of everything, chronically complain if they believe they have received short shrift in any way, believe everyone should cater to them, and believe the rules do not apply to them. They will become angry, frustrated, or even downright confused if their needs are not met on their terms. Remember John and Rachel from the Introduction? This is exactly how John behaved when they were on vacation in Africa.

We live in a culture that fosters entitlement. Our deference to those who have perceived status, to those with wealth, or those with presumed power throws more wood on the fire. Over time, if someone becomes accustomed to people jumping through hoops to please, then it will become expected. As such, not all entitled people are necessarily narcissistic (we will talk about the idea of "acquired narcissism" later in the book). Some people may have slowly "crept" in the direction of entitlement by dint of growing up with wealth, privilege, and access. Because of this, entitlement as an isolated characteristic is not a presumption of narcissism (though it remains a relatively unpleasant characteristic nonetheless!).

Entitlement manifests across so many situations and scenarios, but it is often most visible when a person is dealing with service professionals (wait staff, flight attendants, hotel clerks, sales clerks, attendants in any situation where there are lines or waiting periods). Narcissistic people measure themselves on the basis of how they are treated by the outside world and expect special treatment that is *visible,* such as a first-class seat, a larger hotel suite, or VIP line access, which goes a long way to soothing their fragile self-esteem. Entitlement can result in tremendous embarrassment for the partners of these people, because the narcissist will often rather harshly insult innocent service workers in a public and rather gruesome way. Numerous people shared with me their stories of always trailing behind their narcissistic partner and issuing apologies in the wake of angry, hurt, stressed, and horrified people assailed by their partner's entitlement.

Entitlement goes beyond yelling at a waiter or a flight attendant; it can also impact other significant relationships that can have ramifications for you and your family. For example, the entitled narcissist will believe that obviously he is entitled to special treatment and, by extension, so too is his child. It is not unusual for these folks to wreak havoc with teachers and school administrators, and even when the teachers do attempt to conduct themselves as professionals and not blame the child for his or her parent's bad behavior, it can create a challenging environment for the child and the educators who are working with the child. Obviously, entitlement will also be seen in the workplace and in any other situation where our narcissist wants to be treated better than everyone else.

Entitlement will also impact a person's view of his role in a family or other social group. Narcissists typically expect people to go along with whatever they want or request, regardless of the inconvenience. They will expect their families or close associates to change plans for them, wait for them when they are late, or cancel them altogether. In one case, a father whose career was the governing focus in his family would think nothing of canceling family vacations the night before, because he had a work issue arise (and would insist that the family miss out on the vacation and stay home with him). In short, in the world of entitlement, it's "my way or the highway."

Entitlement can also present as snobbery and arrogance—sneering or looking with disdain at people who don't "do" the right things, wear the right clothes and accessories, own the right car/home/material possessions, have the right job or pedigree, or live in the right part of town. In the presence of people they believe are "less" (which is often most people), entitled people are uncomfortable, dismissive, cold, and rude. It can be highly embarrassing for you as a partner to watch this unfold and quite hurtful for the others involved. It is also damaging for children who are either embarrassed or getting schooled in how to behave like entitled little people who become entitled big adults.

RED FLAG: ENTITLED

Early on, pay attention to how your partner treats service employees; this can be a great early relationship hack for figuring out if you are signing on with a narcissist. Even if it is insecure grandstanding, it is a clear signal. The reason for his bad behavior does not matter. Watch how he treats bartenders, clerks, valet parking staff, restaurant servers, doormen, desk clerks, and if you are observing entitled behavior, it may be a sign of a more global pattern. It is quite likely that he is often overly friendly with people who can "do" something for him (for example, he may engage in the rather distasteful habit of doing things like flirting with the restaurant hostess), but he may quickly react coldly and rudely when his manipulative warmth and flirtation are not met with upgrades and perks.

MANIPULATIVE

In one interview, a woman shared a story about a lengthy marriage that culminated in having her son inform her about her narcissistic husband's affair. The son was so ashamed that he quietly handed his mother a note with this information on it. For this woman, after years of emotional abuse and neglect, this deception was more than she could handle, so she called her husband where he was with his lover and told him she knew (which of course he denied). He begged to come back, he moved back in full time with their kids (she left), and after nearly 15 years of not being any kind of a father was finally taking care of them, cooking dinner, and calling and texting her regularly. She said that she almost caved and returned, because the things he was doing—the cooking, the attentiveness—were what she had hoped for and wanted for years, but after years of bad behavior culminating with such a blatant lie, she didn't succumb. Think about the story of John and Rachel featured at the beginning of the book. Even when she was concerned about what she was experiencing, he would twist and turn it to the point that she felt like the "bad guy" for even expressing her (well-founded) doubts.

Manipulation is a major weapon in the narcissist's arsenal—and is also the major piece of the Dark Triad trait of Machiavellianism. Narcissists are masterful at twisting the situation and working the rules to get what they want. Even more frustrating, they will turn things around in such a way that you may ultimately give them what they want and exhaust yourself in the process. Repeatedly, I observe stories in which the narcissist is superb at spinning his circumstances (for example, "after being abandoned by my father, and how it affected my self-esteem, you have to understand why working would be so difficult for me"), so that the unwitting partner succumbs (for example, working two jobs to protect the manipulative narcissistic partner in hopes of rescuing him).

When a person is so skillfully manipulative, you may find yourself falling into his trap and remaining relatively unaware it is happening. Years later when you connect the dots, the manipulations are as clear as day, but since most of us are not wired to be cynical or to look for trickery at every turn, we often miss it. Narcissists are masters at getting what they want, and because they have no empathy, they may not care what it costs someone else. They deviously use manipulation as a tool to get their most essential needs met, which are typically attention, validation, and status. Nothing gets in their way. Certainly not you.

RED FLAG: MANIPULATIVE

Pay attention to when you feel like you have been "played." It is often something you cannot identify, but it may feel as though you just dealt with a con artist. Early in a relationship, the manipulation is most often emotional ("I had a tough childhood, so sometimes I say things I do not mean" or "I am under a lot of stress, so I blew up—I didn't really mean it") and financial (masterfully getting you to take on disproportionately more financial responsibility, finding yourself spending money you do not have to keep your relationship going and your partner happy, or the narcissist gives you a gift and chronically reminds you about it). Keep an eye out for those patterns, because over time the manipulation can become downright diabolical and leave you feeling nothing short of "insane."

ANGRY AND RAGEFUL

This had to be the most universal theme that emerged across the interviews, in my own clinical work, and in the literature on pathological narcissism. Almost without exception, rage is part of the equation. Whether it was physical violence, yelling, throwing objects, slamming doors, threatening violence, or storming out of the house, it was present in every story I have ever heard about these kinds of relationships.

Let's first differentiate between anger and rage. There are some key differences. Anger is a normal human emotion, a normal response to a specific situation or person, to internal feelings about a situation, or even to memories about something that happened. It is an adaptive response that is designed to protect us and allow us to fight back when we are attacked or perceive that we are being attacked. Anger sits on a continuum, with controlled responses to a threatening situation on one end all the way to uncontrolled rage on the other end. Anger, when expressed appropriately, is useful—it can communicate frustration, emotion, and help people in relationships understand each other. That is not typically what is happening with the rageful anger expressed in the narcissistic relationship. Anger can also be expressed appropriately, speaking firmly and directly with someone, or it can be expressed in a way that is counterproductive, such as hanging up on a phone call, storming out of a conversation, or insulting and name-calling. But because anger is indeed based upon "perception," and by definition, narcissists "perceive" insults and threats to their self-esteem at every turn, then they likely "perceive" anger-inducing situations quite regularly.

Rage is a different animal. It is out of control, ramps up quickly, and can rapidly spin into violence and aggression, abusive language, and fear in those who are witnessing it or on the receiving end. While anger may be a normal response to a given situation, rage is anger out of control and often disproportionate to the stimulus. For people who are narcissistic, rage is often a manifestation of internal frustration. It tends to appear when their fragile self-esteem is endangered. At those times, they feel even more insecure and threatened and want to come out swinging. For most of us, our self-esteem is intact enough that an angry experience comes and goes; for them, all disappointments are extremely personal and threatening because they endanger the very core of who they are.

Rage may be manifested in many different forms: Beyond physical violence and the throwing of objects, it can also be witnessed in disruptive screaming jags, driving in an angry manner that is potentially dangerous (cutting people off, aggressively accelerating), storming out of rooms, and slamming doors upon exiting. Because it happens so quickly, it can catch you off guard and feel even more threatening. It is an emotion that often throws off the balance of the relationship considerably. It is uncomfortable, and you will want to avoid it, so you end up walking on eggshells, becoming anxious and fearful about talking to him about anything for fear of the rapid rageful reaction. Rage gives pathological narcissists two payoffs: the opportunity to rapidly vent extreme and disproportionate anger and a means of controlling the world, since most people are often very "careful" with them. It is not unusual to hear people talk about narcissists as people who need to be "handled" a certain way.

RED FLAGS: ANGRY AND RAGEFUL

The RED FLAG here is obviously not only to watch for inappropriate displays of anger early in the relationship but also to find some of the more visible places to observe "angry" behavior. A great way to get a handle on this? Watch how he drives. Is it erratic? Is he cutting off other drivers, criticizing them, tailing them closely, and cursing at them—or worse? Is he expressing rage in other situations—at service employees who are not behaving as he wishes, on the phone at co-workers or subordinates, or with family members? While he may not pull out the rage with a new partner early in a relationship, observe whether it unfolds in other situations. Rage is rage, and if a person is prone to it, it tends to come out indiscriminately. The idea that a person could be a lion with some and a lamb with others (while a rather romantic fantasy) is unlikely and often leads people to turn their heads when they observe the rage as long as it is not targeted at them. Trust me, it is only a matter of time before you are the target of that rage.

PARANOID

This isn't tin-foil-hat paranoia or "the FBI is monitoring my thoughts" paranoia. This is the kind of paranoia that manifests as the belief that everyone is on the make, everyone is out to take advantage of them, everyone envies them, and this results in walking into many of their interactions with their fists up. They are always looking for the angles and, ironically, often do get "gamed," because they are frequently attracted to those who are even more grandiose con men than they are (which subsequently reinforces their own paranoia). The paranoia can get tiresome after a while, because it can be isolating and challenging to have to listen to it (especially when things in their lives are not going well). Once again, it speaks to the fragile quality of who they are, and the world is divided into those who admire them or those who are out to destroy them—there is little middle ground.

The paranoia can and will invade your relationship space, too. Beyond their paranoid fears about other people in the world, narcissists will also believe that you are likely in on it, too. Most often, the paranoia surfaces as doubts about your fidelity. Initially, it may be accusations that you do not support him and his dreams, that you are cheating on him, that you will make him look bad, or that you are going to betray him. He will always connect the dots in such a way that the picture at the end looks like persecution. If he does not answer the phone for six hours, it is because he was busy, but if you do not answer it for 15 minutes, it is because you are having an affair or you are deliberately attempting to upset him.

RED FLAGS: PARANOID

Start with the modern paranoid "tell": the smartphone or the tablet. He will often protect his phone with obsessive zeal and will have passwords more fiercely guarded than nuclear launch codes. It is not uncommon for him to ask endless questions about whom you are going to see, and where you have been, and to even go so far as to snoop into your electronic world. However, he will offer little transparency into his phones, text messages, and e-mails. If he is guarding his devices like they are state secrets, and at the same time he is chronically asking about yours, pay attention—it may be the paranoia of narcissism rearing its early head. Ask yourself if you really want to live in a police state.

HYPERSENSITIVE

I love to joke around and make light-hearted jabs at my friends, no-ticing little silly things about them, like their messy car or their sloppy outfit. When I met this guy, I would just joke around as usual about the same little things—his cell phone, something in his house—and he would take it so personally and became so angry and sullen. Over time, I thought I was the bad guy, and I became more and more careful about what I said. After a few years, I noticed that I had become very quiet with him, because I was so worried that I would say something that would "hurt his feelings."

While they are careless with everyone else and rarely censor them-selves, narcissists have a keen awareness and sensitivity any time they feel slighted in any way. Even the smallest thing, for example, saying something mildly disparaging about a restaurant they like, can be interpreted as an *ad hominem* attack and be personalized to the point that it is an insult against them. They tend to take every-thing personally but at the same time would never accord anyone else the same sensitivity, awareness, and respect that they chron-ically expect from the world. In that way, narcissists are like "pros-pectors"—they have their eyes and ears pointed in a way that they are chronically monitoring everything that other people say or do and extracting the criticisms or insults. They will even interpret ambiguous situations to fit their constant hypothesis that they are being offended or that something is "personal" (for example, someone shows up late to the narcissist's birthday party because of a sick child, and he or she views it as the guest not taking the big event seriously).

Similar to paranoia, everything gets over-interpreted. If you ne-glect to call him back right away, he will lecture you or criticize you for being insensitive. He will write you terse e-mails but if you respond in kind and point out his lack of sensitivity, then you are painted as not being loving. Because even the most subtle behaviors on your part can lead to him becoming quickly offended, it can leave you feeling like you are living in a glass menagerie—forever afraid to say anything or even give an honest opinion for fear of toppling everything and being left to clean up the mess.

RED FLAGS: HYPERSENSITIVE

The RED FLAGS here are always clear in hindsight. Early in the relationship you likely thought he was being too sensitive, then you may have transitioned to thinking that maybe it was you who was not being nice enough, and then over time you may have become more and more careful to the point of self-censorship. Any overreaction to a "slight," or even observing his reactions to other people and to little things, can give you insight into this phenomenon. The early weeks and months of a relationship can lead us to miss these kinds of clues because we are learning a new person's patterns and rhythms, and this hypersensitivity can sometimes be easy to miss.

JEALOUS

I am not the cheating kind, never have been. With him, all of my friendships were questioned, and he always perceived a threat from old friends or new friends. Even when things in my life were going well, he would be jealous of those experiences as well. But I made a classic mistake: I mistook all of his jealousy for "passionate interest" in me. I figured he was "so into me" that he was afraid of losing me, and I was flattered.

Narcissists have poorly regulated self-esteem, so they are chronically vulnerable. If they are vulnerable then there is the threat that they may get found out, so they often maintain a grandiose exterior. Because they always measure themselves by other people, they also measure themselves against other people. They are chronically reliant on the opinions of others to form their own sense of self and are always comparing themselves, their status, their possessions and their lives to other people to determine their sense of worth and self-esteem (in a way, narcissists outsource their sense of self). Because of this lack of a consistent stable inner sense of self, other people can easily be perceived as a threat (when you become too reliant on something or someone else, it is easy to resent it). The ultimate betrayal in a relationship for them is that they can be "replaced" by someone else and someone better. Mix a little paranoia in there, and you can bet on the fact that they are chronically going to be worried about or accusing you of cheating on them.

Their lack of insight means that they are not aware of how their poorly developed self-esteem leads them to feel vulnerable. In fact, they are not only vulnerable but also need validation *all the time*. So they are also often predisposed to having inappropriate relationships with other people, as well as affairs and one night stands, because it makes them feel validated and admired for a minute. They are also prone to something called projection (discussed later), whereby they place their flaws and questionable behaviors on everyone else. Jealousy is often a great litmus test of whether or not your partner is actually the one cheating; if he starts accusing you of cheating out of the blue, you can bet the farm on the fact that if he is not already cheating, he is likely engaging in some inappropriate relationships that may be ready to veer in that direction. His jealous accusations are often a form of "truth serum" that can give you insight into his bad behaviors.

The jealousy, while it is often focused on cheating partners, also takes many other forms, including jealousy of a co-worker who receives a better office or promotion, a friend who gets a new car or great new house, or a sibling who buys a summer house. The jealousy can consume them and leads them to feel worse about themselves, so they seek validation to offset these bad feelings, which can often get them into trouble and be hurtful for their partner (for example, spending money they don't have or cheating). Narcissists tend to be envious and covetous, like a jealous child who wants the toys other people have and measures themselves and others by these toys.

Monitor whether he becomes jealous of your accomplishments. As long as you are lagging behind him, or he is much more successful (financially, career-wise) than you, then things will run just fine. Your success in any realm—your career, your education, your raise, your promotion—while initially tantalizing (it makes him look good), in a short time will become threatening. Remember, he is a deep cauldron of low self-esteem; if you succeed then you may leave him, or you may soak up the admiration that he wants for himself. This jealousy can lead him to undermine you, criticize you, and minimize your successes. It does not feel good when the one person with whom you want to share your success is the one who berates it.

RED FLAGS: JEALOUS

Pay attention to early and bizarre accusations about infidelity, as well as his covetousness of other people's lifestyles. One theme that emerged consistently in the interviews and observations conducted for this book was the early escalation of jealousy in narcissistic partners. They would be suspicious and ask lots of questions, even sneaking peeks at phones and e-mails, and stalking social media accounts. In many cases, they would limit or forbid contact with friends with whom there could be a possible romantic interest. Jealousy often gets misinterpreted as passion or deep interest. The people I spoke with believed that their new partners "cared" about them, which was why they were paying such careful attention to the possibility of "other people." Provided that you are indeed conducting yourself appropriately in the relationship, this "passionate" jealousy is often a red flag that is the forerunner of even more controlling and isolating behavior.

LACK OF GUILT/LACK OF INSIGHT

I am so sorry; I did not realize that my one-night stand would be so hurtful. I don't know what I was thinking. . . .

Seriously?

When a client told me she was told this, it felt less like an apology than a reflection of her partner's utter lack of insight. While the word "sorry" appears in his statement, the lack of awareness that a careless infidelity could be so painful feels less like contrition and more like clueless. Which pretty well sums it up: Not only are narcissists often careless but also clueless.

Traditionally, lack of remorse or guilt are not part of the definition of a narcissistic personality disorder but rather something more typically seen in psychopathic behavior (as part of the Dark Triad). However, a general lack of insight into the hurt caused by their words and actions and an attendant lack of remorse or guilt are often observed. (If they cannot genuinely get their heads around their misdeed, it is not likely that there will be an expression of guilt, or the apology does not really feel like an apology.) Narcissists will often write off the psychological bumps and bruises suffered by those in their path as opportunity cost; if they get their needs met, they tend not to focus on the needs or hurts of others. Most of us are (for better or worse) wired for forgiveness. If narcissists do rapidly and repeatedly face consequences for their bad behavior, they may shape up a little bit, but our tendency to forgive (especially early in a relationship) can set precedent that can be nearly impossible to shift with a pathological narcissist. (The proverbial "I have created a monster." You didn't create it though; the monster was there all along).

The lack of insight that is observed in narcissism can be frustrating because it is as though they have no idea how they affect other people. Their inability to monitor how they impact other people reflects their childlike selfishness. Children rarely check in with their mothers before they throw a tantrum. Their lack of insight is operating from many angles: They do not observe the impact of their behavior on others, they are disconnected from their inner worlds, they have little empathy for how others feel, and they rarely are corrected or face consequences for their behavior. All of this can contribute to the narcissist's lack of insight, which can make a deep relationship challenging (and day-to-day life incredibly frustrating).

There is something chilling about someone doing something unkind or downright nasty and not feeling any remorse about it. In general, most people do feel badly when they do something wrong or hurtful; it is how our nervous systems are wired. With narcissists, it can sometimes be a matter of degree—they may be only mildly or insincerely apologetic for glaringly bad behavior. This can be destabilizing because you are feeling distressed and upset about something done to you by your partner, and he doesn't see it as a major transgression, or he believes that an apology cleans the slate. It adds to the sense of feeling as though you are "losing your mind" in the relationship, or that there is something wrong with you because you are blowing "out of proportion" something that the other person does not see as a problem.

RED FLAGS: LACK OF GUILT/LACK OF INSIGHT

These can be hard to spot because bad things may not (hopefully) happen early in a relationship. However, look for the level of owner-ship and apology for even small mistakes, such as showing up late. If there is a dismissive attitude toward these slights or behaviors that were unsettling or problematic for you, that could be a har-binger of a person simply not feeling bad or lacking insight when he does bad things.

NEEDS CONSTANT ADMIRATION AND VALIDATION

It felt like he could never be alone; it was always about being with other people. He is very good at what he does and loves hearing it, so being around people would bring him more and more of that admiration. He was constantly on social media, posting pictures of his life and carefully selecting those "perfect" moments. While I would often tell him how talented he is and how great I think he is and support him in what he was doing, I felt like it was not enough coming only from me. He needed it all the time. It was always about putting his life out there and people applauding him. I guess that is why it was hard for him to be alone—he needed props from other people whenever he was awake.

This is a core motivating factor for the narcissist. Narcissists need the admiration of the outside world to survive. They find it difficult to be alone, and when they are alone, they are often mired in social media, which is basically a way to efficiently receive admiration and validation without having to return it. In order to be in a relationship with a person like this, you need to be a one-person cheering squad, congratulating him on his achievements and glories and encouraging him at every turn. Praising him for everything from a promotion to the color of his tie to how nicely he parked the car to the fact that he called you back. It is exhausting.

Social media is the narcissist's mother ship. It is an efficient way to seek admiration, and since it is relatively effortless for the participants in social media to provide validation, narcissists use it like a drug and a weapon. The research on social media is very clear: Social media and narcissism are highly associated. Social media can be a noisy distraction in the narcissist's world, pulling him or her away from the potential depth of live "in-person" relationships and to the easy one-click validation of superficial online worlds. It also allows them to play at their aspirational selves. Many people cultivate a "false self" on social media that is typically the "better" version of themselves. While anyone on social media is guilty of this to some degree, for the narcissist, who does not maintain a well-developed sense of self and cannot regulate his or her own self-esteem, it is a playground in which he or she can focus on the superficial characteristics and false self that attracts validation.

Without the admiration and validation, narcissists' lives are experienced as empty. Validation is the air supply necessary to keep their fragile egos alive. This can also lead to them getting it anywhere they can, and they tend to accumulate lots of superficial relationships. Typically, a relationship of depth would require too much mutual reciprocity for the narcissist (and the other person subsequently gets dissatisfied and leaves), so superficial relationships tend to serve their purposes more efficiently. In the early weeks and months of a relationship, you may be more likely to admire and validate a new partner out loud and often. Over time, as the relationship transitions from passionate to companionate, it can become exhausting, which means that your narcissistic partner will either demand it from you or get it elsewhere.

RED FLAGS:
NEEDS CONSTANT ADMIRATION AND VALIDATION

After a certain age, posting selfies and photographs of French toast on social media may be a bit emotionally stunted. If you observe someone who lives and dies by his social media, who documents the minutiae of life for the reasons of sharing it, or whose moods go up and down on the basis of how many "likes" he gets, this is likely a barometer of his tendency for approval seeking, admiration seeking, and fragile self-esteem. Social media is a great tool to suss out this piece of narcissism early in the game. Keep in mind that not every social media aficionado is a narcissist. It is such a common pursuit, especially for young adults. The research is clear that more time spent on social media is associated with higher scores on measurements of narcissistic traits, but if you have a sweet, empathic, sensitive partner who just happens to like to post pictures of ▼

his French toast, you do not need to throw him under the narcissism bus. It is important that you embed his social media use within the larger context of how he interacts with you and the world. Just be aware: In a new relationship, a narcissist may often get caught up in documenting your adventures together, so it can be easy to get swept away and become a party to the admiration seeking. Is he at the Grand Canyon to actually drink in the splendor of the Grand Canyon, or to get the selfie? Pay attention.

LYING

He often left out the details or would not offer up information, and then I would ask about it, and after the fact he would tell me he was with an ex-girlfriend at a bar but only because I asked. He was really good at giving me pieces of the truth, or holding on to it unless I asked the right questions. A text message would pop up on his phone and often catch him in his lies and "rationalizations." I was never the girl who checks her boyfriend's phone, but it got to the point where just hearing the "ping" of his phone made me feel sick to my stomach. It just meant another lie to me.

Narcissists lie. They lie because it is consistent with many of the patterns we already discussed—lack of empathy, entitlement, grandiosity, and lack of insight and remorse. Lies serve a function: They help us "save face," get out of a difficult situation, and avoid blame. We all lie sometimes, but they are usually minor offenses and ideally do not cause harm (for example, telling your boss you are late to work because you were caught in traffic, rather than because you overslept by 15 minutes). The narcissist's lies tend to take in more territory. Not only do they regularly engage in the innocuous lie (getting stuck in traffic) but also they lie about everything else if it benefits them—and they are coolly efficient at it. Lack of empathy makes you a highly skilled liar.

Lies are complicated for people who are on the receiving end. Most of us, especially when we like or care for someone, assume he or she is telling us the truth. To protect the relationship, we will often turn our head away from the lies, even when the data does not add up. In many cases, we may even take the blame on ourselves (for example, I am being overly suspicious, I shouldn't question what he just said), even when it feels really suspicious and dishonest, just to preserve the relationship or to avoid the pain of doubting someone we love. Many of the people I work with and have spoken with about these relationships said that, over the years, the chronic lying took a terrible toll and left them filled with self-doubt, suspiciousness, and an inability to trust others. Our story of Rachel and John illustrates how the lying becomes a daily pattern and then a lifestyle.

Remember, narcissists are motivated by seeking out admiration and validation to survive. Lying becomes just one more tool in that arsenal -whether it is lying about an accomplishment, lying about an opportunity, lying about behavior—to help them to retain their sense of self and superficial façade. Their lack of empathy and entitlement means that they do not see their lies as weapons that are harming someone else, but rather a rationalization for what they have a "right" to do.

RED FLAGS: LYING

The RED FLAGS on lying are simple. When 2 + 2 equals 5, question it. A good rule of thumb: The longer and more confused the story, the greater the likelihood it is a fiction. Most of us, especially women, and especially when we are in a new relationship, are socialized to give second chances, third chances, and chronically turn the other cheek. We want our relationships to work out (especially if they took a long time to find). The warm "fuzzies" of a new relationship can lead us to forgive repeatedly. Pay attention to when the numbers don't add up and when things do not make sense. Because, over time, lying can take a genuine toll on your psyche and impact all of your relationships and your ability to trust.

EVERYTHING IS A SHOW

He never really worked a day in his life, but I worked two jobs so we could have a house in the mountains, new cars, kids in private school, and despite our financial struggles, he would insist that we take lavish vacations, get $150 bottles of wine, and spare no expense. When the bills came in, he couldn't be bothered, but he always expected the show to go on.

The 50th birthday party on a yacht. The chronic selfies. The edited existence on social media. The perfect holiday card. The perfect façade. If those pictures could talk, they would be saying that the big smiles may not match the real picture. Because narcissists are such expert showmen, other people only see the perfect façade but never the mess behind it. It is bad manners for others to question it. For people in relationships with narcissists, the pictures and the show suggest that everything is perfect (or at least looks perfect). Yet, you may often feel as though you are living in a performance and not in real life. It can also make it harder to rally support from others when you need it, because they see an external reality that is at odds with your experience. Because everyone thinks your relationship is so wonderful and that it looks so perfect, your own experience of suffering or discomfort sometimes feels like it is not valid.

Increasingly, the proliferation of methods to show off our lives to others has lifted "keeping up with the Joneses" to an unprecedented level. In our digitized world, photographs can be repeatedly taken until you get the "perfect" one. Narcissists, who operate solely in a superficial space, thrive under these conditions. Even without the public theater to put this on display, they will tend to spend money they don't have to throw a big show. One place this will sometimes emerge is in wedding planning. Many people I talked with reflected back on their weddings as though they were a "show"—a finely honed production where every detail looked perfect—but the feeling wasn't there. It ended up being the motif for their lives. The various background stories that informed the story of John and Rachel (the picture-perfect wedding in Santa Barbara) all reflected on grand and grander weddings—the day was a perfect prelude to what would end up being a far-from-perfect life.

RED FLAGS: EVERYTHING IS A SHOW

Pay attention to the courtship phase. When it feels like a show, it is easy to get swept away. Narcissists often court hard with larger-than-life gestures, fancy restaurants, vacations, gifts, lots of public showmanship, and they may do it in their own lives in general. If you feel like a player in a production, flattering though it may seem, pull back for a minute and ask the question about whether this big show is genuine and romantic or a show for the sake of a show. If you feel like the big gestures are taking place against a backdrop of lack of empathy, indifference, or unkindness, then think it through. Shakespeare may have said the world is a stage and all of us merely players, but that doesn't need to be true. Life should not be a stage production.

PROJECTION

This is the case of a woman with narcissistic traits who was deeply insecure and would fly into rages when she believed that she was not viewed as the most beautiful woman in the room. Her moods were deeply dysregulated and she would range from being needy to rage-fully angry to tearful under times of stress. She required chronic re-assurance at times of vulnerability. When her partner, who tended to be rather even keeled, was having difficulty with the roller coaster of emotion and with his exhaustion with having to keep reassuring her, she said "I cannot believe what a pathetic man he is. His moods are

*all over the map. He needs to be viewed as the most important person
there is. He is emotional and he is ridiculous. One minute he is angry,
the next minute he is crying. It is ridiculous." Listening to her describe
him was literally like listening to her highlight some of her own emotional challenges. She had no insight into this for herself, yet her ability
to almost precisely project this onto her partner was almost uncanny.*

Accusing someone else of what you are doing or calling out your
flaws and fears in someone else is a psychological trick of the eye
called projection. The person who is cheating accuses his partner
of cheating. The partner who is emotionally unavailable accuses
the other one of being emotionally unavailable. Projection is
called a "defense," or basically an unconscious pattern that occurs
when the person feels psychologically threatened. Narcissistic ego
is always monitoring the world for threats and often finds them.
Then they quickly blame other people for their deficits.

But Projection is frustrating because your partner is accusing you
of doing things you aren't actually doing (if you are, then it is a
different story). But these projections and accusations are not just
about cheating and betrayal; they can be about the narcissist's own
vulnerabilities and weaknesses (accusing you of being overly ambitious when he is ambitious, criticizing you for being unsuccessful
or not making enough money when he is not feeling successful in
that space).

But since most of us are not psychologists (and even if we are),
when we feel hurt about an accusation or insult being hurled at us,
we are not going to take the moment to think that this is "projection" and just let it go. However, projection gives us an interesting
insight. When an accusation is thrown at you that does not fit you,
when it doesn't capture what you know to be true about yourself
or your behavior, mentally flip it back on your partner. He is likely
accusing you of what he is doing or feeling.

RED FLAGS: PROJECTION

Monitor the times when he accuses you of unfounded behaviors or patterns. When that happens, take a moment and step back. At first you will feel as though you are in the *Twilight Zone*, because it is so patently untrue. But once you recognize it as projection, you have been given an opportunity to peer into his mind, thoughts, feelings, fears, and behavior.

GREEDY

He was basically like a mean kid who would not share his toys. It was never enough, and after a while, it was not even clear why he wanted more. I think it was about the win more than the stuff.

We live in a consumerist and materialistic culture. Possessions are the most superficial way for people to show off and validate themselves. Narcissistic folks are often over-focused on money and resources, largely because in our culture (and most cultures) money communicates status, power, access, and ultimately validation—the fuel that fills the narcissistic engine. As such, the pursuit and acquisition of money becomes a simple path to achieving superficial admiration by many. And in our culture, a significant proportion of the very wealthy hold many narcissistic traits, because our economy is set up to reward these traits. Our economic system in many ways is founded on greed, profits at any price, and rating performance on the basis of asset accumulation. Having lots of expensive possessions or money does not necessarily make a person bad. But coveting material possessions, devaluing people who don't have the "right" possessions, measuring people and themselves by their possessions, and stopping at nothing to get the money, possessions, and status is where this can turn dark. Greed and entitlement are often closely aligned—more money means more entitlement—and entitlement implies the belief that one "deserves" more and will not be thwarted in that pursuit.

Obviously, greed can and will affect relationships. If your partner is on a single-minded campaign to acquire high-status possessions, and preoccupied by these objects and pursuits, it can impede the development of a healthy relationship, and you are likely to become one more of those materialistic pursuits (or get lost in the shuffle). It can also be isolating and alienating for others who may start getting bored of the show-and-tell that accompanies greed. In addition, a person driven by greed is more likely to envy the possessions of another person, which can result in friendships and relationships feeling more like "pissing contests" than collaborative and connected.

RED FLAGS: GREEDY

The RED FLAGS here? Look at his relationship with money and possessions. Does the relationship feel like a chronic game of show and tell, always having to hear the provenance of the things he has or the things he wants? Is there constant reference to the car he wants or the labels he has? Does he insult or put down others who have more (or less) than him? Greed shows its hand pretty early.

EMOTIONALLY COLD

When the economy tanked we were broke, and she refused to get a job to help out. I had been explaining this to her for a long time, and when I finally suggested that perhaps our best course of action would be to sell our house and move someplace cheaper, she looked at me with dead eyes, and said "figure it out." There was no way she was giving up her lifestyle. I just started crying, and she walked out of the room.

Narcissists are notoriously shallow with their emotions. They can pull out the hearty laughs and the rage, but when it comes to other bread and butter emotions, such as sadness and happiness, not so much. Being emotionally and empathically unplugged can result in little interest or attempt to radiate warmth with others. This can be experienced as distance and coldness. Emotional coldness can be unsettling. The descriptors that often come up are things like "he has no warmth" or "it's like he doesn't feel anything." That is a hard trait to live with, especially during a time of need. This often occurs in part because of the lack of empathy. Most of us are able to adjust our thermostats to the emotion being shown by another person. If the other person is upset, we adjust so we can comfort him or her. Narcissistic people do not do well with emotion; it requires going deep and feeling their own emotions, which is challenging for them. In addition, they do not have a thermostat, so they cannot adjust their temperature to the temperature around them because they are simply not tapped into it.

To be with an emotionally cold partner often means not being comforted, sometimes during the most difficult days in our lives. I remember a client sharing with me the story of the day her mother died, after an illness of a few weeks. Her partner's first question was to ask her matter-of-factly, "when are we going to the hardware store to pick out the fixtures?" Another woman spoke of talking about her pain in the wake of her grandmother's death earlier that day, and her partner just coldly said that he was busy and had to attend to work. We most acutely experience this phenomenon of emotional coldness when we are going through something difficult ourselves, and the other person offers nothing.

The emotionally cold or distant trait also rears its head during arguments when one person is experiencing and expressing significant emotion and the narcissistic person just checks out and does not respond—or does so in a cold and clipped manner. At such times you may find yourself spinning—and actually feeling as though you are "going crazy"—because the coldness of the response makes it even more difficult to regulate yourself in that moment. The emotional coldness can be confusing for you and may result in attempts to jump through hoops to generate warmth and connection with your partner. I have observed people wearing themselves out over decades, trying to create a fire where there was no possibility.

RED FLAGS: EMOTIONALLY COLD

The RED FLAG here is often a hard one to see early, though some people will note that they observed the coldness early on and wrote it off as shyness (but be careful to not unfairly label shy people as cold). Shy people tend to be shy all the time. Cold people tend to be more detached and distant when real emotion is on the table. In addition, patterns such as disinterest and halting conversation may be precursors to this longer-term pattern of emotional coldness. If you feel like you need to bundle up in this early phase of your relationship, pay attention. It may be the emotional chill in the air. And that is a climate that is not likely to change.

GASLIGHTING (Leaves You Feeling as if You Are "Losing Your Mind")

In the 1930's play *Gas Light*, a husband, in an attempt to drive his wife crazy, keeps turning down the gas-powered lights in the house. When the wife asks why he is dimming the lights, he denies it and says they are no dimmer. Over time, she finds herself going "mad."

Gaslighting qualifies as a form of emotional abuse that involves denying a person's experience and making statements, such as "that never happened," "you're too sensitive," or "this isn't that big a deal." It tends to happen gradually over time, and it leaves you feeling as though you are going slowly crazy. The "gaslighter" uses techniques such as withholding or stonewalling (for example, "I don't want to hear that again"), contradicting (for example, telling you that you do not recall something correctly), and diversion (for example, when you bring up something that concerns you and your partner turns it into something you had said years before or deflects it and describes it as a conspiracy by all of your friends against him). He also minimizes your feelings ("How could you be upset about such a little thing?") and denies events that definitely occurred ("I never did that").

The damage of gaslighting is that it is confusing, isolating, and often results in you questioning your own reality. The doubt seeps into all areas of your life, and before long, your partner seems like the only real thing in your life. Gaslighting fills you with self-doubt, second-guessing, and hopelessness. You may find yourself chronically apologizing and no longer as relaxed and joyful as you once were. Gaslighting is very simply a form of emotional abuse, and because it happens so gradually, it overtakes you from the inside out, leaving you isolated and so confused that you don't even know how to ask for help.

Ultimately, gaslighting makes communication all but impossible. The concept of communication is predicated on the idea that the other person listens and tells the truth. Because the prevailing wisdom is to work on "communication" in relationships, and if it isn't working it is somehow your fault, gaslighting can result in frustration to the point of making you feel psychologically unstable. When Rachel was feeling more and more unsettled about various things in their lives, John's responses often left her feeling like she was literally "losing her mind" because he was denying her reality.

RED FLAGS: GASLIGHTING

The RED FLAG here is recognizing when your reality is denied. HOLD YOUR GROUND. You do not need to take the fight. When you see this happening early in a relationship, step back and realize that no loving person would ever deny your feelings. If you find yourself constantly second-guessing situations or doubting yourself, it's an early sign. Remember that narcissists are masterful at working a system to their benefit—even if it means denying your reality.

CHEAP

He would tell me "you are so lucky to be with me, lots of women would love to be with me," and then this would be his rationalization for why he would not spend money on me. He was saving up for something he wanted (a vintage motorcycle) and did not want to steer off of his goal. And when he finally would spend money on me for anything, he would remind me of it so many times that after a while I hated accepting anything from him, because it wasn't worth hearing a thousand times how much it cost and what a good guy he was for buying it for me or taking me on that trip.

Narcissists live in a world where they are endlessly generous in their own minds. But their generosity is typically designed to make them look good or to use as a weapon down the road (for example, "I took you on vacation, so you don't have the right to feel angry at me about anything"). I often term this "hush money"—I spent money on you, now be quiet. They use their money as a weapon—whether it is a dollar or a billion dollars—and lord it over others. They often feel taken advantage of financially and expect endless thanks when they open their wallets. This is also often a trick they will employ with children, being absent or inconsistent parents but then sparing no expense when it comes to toys, luxury goods, or big vacations. This can be confusing for a child, but it is not easy to manage as an adult either.

There are really two kinds of "cheap" we are talking about here, and they frequently co-exist. Some are truly not generous. They will only spend money to further a goal, which is why they are usually generous during the courtship phase, but then once they have you in their lives, the gravy train stops. They will be downright miserly, or spend generously on themselves and not on others. Or they spend it strategically—on people or in situations that will forward their cause.

On the other side, they use their money and gift giving as a weapon: spending money (which makes them look generous) and then chronically reminding you of the money they just spent (again, the "hush money"). You may become more reluctant to accept their "largesse," because it comes with a price down the road. Their "cheapness" isn't just about money; it is about their space, the food in their kitchen, their possessions, their time, their willingness to pick you up at the airport—there is a miserliness that cuts across everything.

RED FLAGS: CHEAP

Monitor his generosity (or lack thereof) in all areas: not only with money but also with spirit, with time, and with space. If he keeps reminding you how much things cost, or drawing attention to his generosity, or is just plain cheap, remain aware of that. Be mindful of over-generosity of gifts or spending contrasted to an under-generosity of spirit or time. Any fool can open up a wallet and purchase a gift or a dinner; it is something quite different to be there for you, offer you support, or simply listen.

NEVER TAKES RESPONSIBILITY

Narcissists are like Teflon; nothing sticks. They don't take responsibility. For anything. They are master deflectors and try to avoid the blame when lying, cheating, stealing, and everything in between. They make up complex excuses and can rationalize anything. When they finally get called out, they are quick to claim they are being persecuted, though they may be apologetic for a minute. When someone never takes responsibility for anything—words, actions, feelings—it is a challenging if not impossible way to maintain a relationship. Even preschool-aged children are asked to take responsibility for a broken crayon or toys left out. It is not too much to ask for a person to take ownership. But since they are unable to distinguish the boundary between responsibility and blame, narcissists attempt to avoid both. We frequently observe the celebrity or public figure who attempts to neutralize a public gaffe through an anemic apology issued by a well-heeled publicist. Perfunctory "responsibility-taking" can be even more frustrating than complete denial.

By and large they employ denial as a defense here—either flat out denial or circuitous denial—to avoid taking responsibility. This can be experienced as a combination of manipulation, lying, and lack of empathy. Sometimes, even if we are stung by someone who has done something inappropriate or wrong, it is soothing to hear that person take responsibility for it and many of us are able to move forward from that. Don't wait for it. Genuine acceptance of responsibility is very unlikely to be issued by your partner and you can wear yourself out by waiting for it.

RED FLAGS: NEVER TAKES RESPONSIBILITY

Take notice of whether he takes ownership of behaviors or words— big or small. We all make mistakes. Ideally, we also take ownership of our words and actions. When his behavior is problematic but there is no acknowledgment, remain aware of that pattern. Also be mindful as he shares the story of his life. Does he take ownership of past mistakes or missteps? Or does he share his history as though it were blameless and free of any errors on his part? Does he always seem to blame others for any negative situations in his life? Take note if it seems like nothing is ever his fault.

VAIN

He got very far on his looks. They got me, and they got him lots of other women when he wanted them. Even after we split up and his looks had faded somewhat, his appearance plus his charisma meant that he would never have to pay the bills. He would take time out of the day to ensure he ate well, he worked out, and he took care of himself. I on the other hand was running around like a crazy person, dragging the kids to work with me, so he could take care of himself. He not only never offered to help but also he would become angry if we got in the way of his "routine." It's funny, it wasn't just him looking good, it was the house needing to look good, everything looking good.

Perusing a magazine rack, television ad, or social-media feed reminds us that vanity is a national pastime. Pathological narcissism is embedded in vanity in appearance and in lifestyle. Many hours are spent on appearance, trying to look young acquiring the latest labels, the best address, the newest toys, the best façade. The superficiality of pathological narcissism plays well into the trap of vanity. Vanity can be a time-consuming and expensive pastime, and while it may be initially engaging and even attractive, over time it detracts from the relationship.

Vanity and "doing everything for show" are obviously closely related. Vanity tends to be about the personal preening to get ready for the show, but it all boils down to valuing the external more than the internal. In addition, vanity attracts narcissists; they are chronically drawn to beautiful things, people, and objects. Because they are not creatures of commitment, narcissists often become vulnerable to making financial and personal mistakes in the name of vanity. It is easy to become infected by this, and you may even feel that if you do not always bring your A-game in terms of appearance and accessorizing, you may be quickly forgotten.

RED FLAGS: VAIN

Watch his grooming rituals. Courtship is when the peacock ruffles his feathers, but when he is spending more time in front of the mirror and on the workouts, the selfies, and the grooming than on anything meaningful, pay attention. In addition, vanity is often projected onto others, and he may "expect" you to look a certain way. One of the women I interviewed shared how her husband would rarely talk to ▼

her while they watched TV, but when he finally did, it was typically to point out ladies on a bikini-clad TV show and ask her why she didn't look more like them. Vanity projected onto the other also results in a sense of objectification. I spoke with several women whose husbands insisted that they stay in top shape and be impeccably put together all the time (breast implants and all). It took a tremendous toll on these women, who realized that their role in the relationship was more as object than as person. It's easy to get dazzled by something pretty, but don't fall prey to his vanity. Vanity tends to be a short game.

CONTROLLING

He would even criticize me if the flowers in the vase were not "bent" in the right direction.

This is another hallmark symptom of narcissism, and it goes well beyond simply order and control in the environment. It is overarching control over everything related to you as a partner. What can make this uniquely frustrating is that your significant other is controlling you while remaining disinterested in your life. Much like gaslighting, this tends to happen gradually. Many times control initially gets confused with passion or attention—and who doesn't love attention? You may find yourself saying, "He loves me—that is why he keeps asking where I am." Or, "She is just intense and passionate—that's why she always texts me."

Control is often a part of abuse dynamics in relationships; the control culminates to the point where a person feels like she cannot move without asking for permission, and the narcissist uses control to isolate the person. Shame is often experienced by people who find themselves in controlling relationships. Knowing that the obsessive order and control would seem odd or concerning to other people, you may not talk about it with close friends or family.

The most common manifestations of relationship control are a partner monitoring your whereabouts at all times, which can manifest as regular contact to confirm where you are or whom you are with, snooping into your e-mails and text messages, weighing in on your appearance, making recommendations about your career and other life decisions, with little regard for your opinion, and making nearly all important decisions about children, leisure, and major purchases. Control may also manifest in a paradoxical way, with your partner checked out and indifferent but still making demands about the order of the household, schedules, mealtimes, and routines. When Rachel moved in with John, she found herself increasingly constricted, having to keep the house the way he wanted and anxious about a stray sweater. Living under such control can be exhausting.

Demands for order and control can also extend to the environment, and this can surface in demands around how a household is maintained. Narcissists are often obsessively ordered about their belongings, their surroundings, and their cars. Or they just want things the way they want them. We live in a culture in which order is commonly overvalued. Narcissists will take all the time and space they need to the detriment of others. This can look and feel almost obsessive-compulsive and add to the "walking on eggshells" feeling that can pervade these relationships with narcissists. Raising children under these circumstances can be all but impossible. Several people cited how the narcissistic spouse would demand that the children be quiet and clean all the time, never play with toys in common areas of the house, and that the house be impeccably ordered. In a few of these interviews, the children were now grown, and they remain anxious as adults because of the tension in the home about the unending need for order.

This pattern is likely an attempt by narcissists to exert control on their outer worlds. Remember, their internal worlds are lacking, their self-esteem is vulnerable, and they rely on the world for validation. So they will control that internal chaos by externally controlling others. Their vulnerability can also leave them concerned that they will be made to look foolish by you (for example, if you cheated on them) or will lose you if they do not control you (this is a reflection of their grandiose sense of control over everything).

RED FLAGS: CONTROLLING

Are you frequently being questioned about your "who, what, where, why, and when?" It can be easy to interpret this as interest and flattery in the early stages of a relationship. In addition, reflect on whether you are being consulted in decision-making. While it is nice from time to time to be swept away to a restaurant or a surprise weekend away, if it feels like the relationship is happening *to* you rather than *with* you, then those surprising and thrilling moments may be coming at a cost. In addition, pay attention to an obsessive need for order. A clean house is nice, but if his focus on order overrides good manners or is accompanied by abrupt and rude commands, irritability, or a preoccupation with things being just so, look deeper. Does your partner rudely inquire about whether your shoes are clean before you enter the car, or does she berate you for using the wrong towels in the bathroom? Valuing order and rigidity and cleanliness over everything else is a clear red flag.

UNPREDICTABLE

It was like living in a minefield. Unpredictability makes life challenging. Even in the absence of a narcissistic partner, when life catches us off guard—with a flat tire, sick child, or snowstorm—we experience stress. Because narcissists regulate their moods from the outside (external validation), their moods are dictated by the events in their world and the validation they receive from other people. When they have a good day, and things are going their way, it is far more likely to be a good day for everyone involved. When things aren't going well for them, it will be a challenging day for everyone. This ties into their lack of empathy and can make life dicey at best.

Now, obviously, as a matter of degree, this applies to everyone. On days when we receive good news, we are cheerful, and on days when things keep going wrong, we tend to be more irritable. But a primary difference is that our sense of identity doesn't shift. Normally, people monitor and re-monitor themselves, they accept feedback, they titrate their responses, they are sensitive to other people, or they ask for what they want. For example, you may ask for a few minutes or hours to yourself because you are having a challenging day and do not want to lash out at anyone else. The unpredictability of narcissists originates from the fact that they are not only subject to the whims of the world's approval to figure out who they are but also do not monitor how their reactions could make other people feel (nor do they care). It's typically a mentality of: Shoot first, ask questions later.

The unpredictability can result in moods ranging from cheerful grandiosity to cold rage in a matter of hours and sometimes minutes. Sadly, because they require validation from someone they view as "important" and typically devalue their partners over time, your validation is often not enough. Narcissism is a disorder of dysregulation, and because they cannot regulate their emotions, this can contribute to their unpredictability. Many partners of narcissistic people become frustrated because they can never soothe or uplift their partners. As a result, your partner is not the only one at the mercy of approvals from the outside world; now you are at the mercy of their world, too. (I have heard more than one person say that they started becoming afraid of their narcissistic partner's boss, not because they had any contact with them, but because the boss's actions would set the tone for the household.) Many people in narcissistic relationships find that they start becoming more anxious and even less able to regulate their own moods, because they feel as though they are living in chaos—and there was nothing they could do about it, because they were unable to soothe, comfort, or cheer up their partner. Interestingly, because of the narcissist's tendency to blame other people for their difficulties (the Teflon theme again) and engage in projection (described above), they will often blame you for being unreliable and inconsistent, when it is in fact their moods that are all over the map.

Unpredictability may not only surface in unpredictable moods but also in a lack of predictability in plans and in behavior. Again, the lack of empathy means there is little regard for how this pattern of up, down, and all around is affecting the ability of others around them to plan their own lives. It can be infuriating, destabilizing, embarrassing, and expensive to keep up with this mercurial behavior.

RED FLAGS: UNPREDICTABLE

When the cheerful puppy dog you left in the morning is an angry junkyard dog at the end of the workday and starts lashing out at you, pay attention. When you recognize that your partner is unpredictable and it becomes the only predictable thing in your relationship, it may be too late. Dr. Jekyll and Mr. Hyde make for exhausting roommates. Think about whether life on a roller coaster actually holds any appeal.

TAKES ADVANTAGE OF OTHERS (OR YOU) ON A REGULAR BASIS

The technical term that is often used for this is "interpersonally exploitative." In short, because of the singular focus on fulfilling their needs, especially external needs, narcissists will use other people as objects to get those needs met. This can happen in many different ways: getting plum seats to a concert from a family friend who works at the venue, putting you in the uncomfortable position of asking an acquaintance for access to her vacation home, calling an old friend after years of being out of touch to obtain a campaign contribution. In the narcissist's world, other people often do serve literally as objects—a tool to get a job done.

As the partner of a pathological narcissist, it will happen to you as well. As his partner you are the ultimate object, existing to serve his needs. Because you are not in on this secret in the beginning, it can feel a bit depersonalizing—as though you are only valued when you are functional. It can feel manipulative, because your partner may compliment you excessively and then hit you with a difficult request or ask you to make uncomfortable requests of others. What feels so exploitative is that there is no sense of discomfort with making the request, or even a preface such as, "I know this is a big request, but I was wondering if it would be possible if . . ." Or, "we would be happy to pay for the seats/house/ favor and thank you so much for being willing to do this." By its very nature exploitation is exploitative and not collaborative, but you may find yourself feeling extremely uncomfortable as the recipient of it, or when you are asked to do your partner's bidding.

RED FLAGS:
TAKES ADVANTAGE OF OTHERS (OR YOU) ON A REGULAR BASIS

Are you being asked to call in favors, and even when you express discomfort, are you chided for feeling sheepish that it would be an inconvenience to the other people? In addition, pay attention to whether your partner's mood shifts are also correlated to times when he needs things from you. Is he nice when he wants you to do something and nasty or indifferent when he doesn't? When going to the well too often becomes a pattern, or there is little regard for the experience of other people when exploitative requests are made, this pattern may persist and continually leave you in an uncomfortable position.

ENGAGES IN SCHAEDENFRAUDE (Reveling in Others' Misery)

Schaedenfraude is the German word for "being a bad sport." But it is more than that. Specifically, it means the enjoyment or pleasure derived from watching the misfortune of others, taking glee in someone else's tragedy or failure. This is a hallmark of narcissists and can offer a chilling insight into their worlds.

Because narcissists are so envious of others, they also reciprocally believe that others are envious of them. They often do not get pleasure out of someone else's success, especially when they themselves are not happy with where they are in life (which is often because of their fragile self-esteem). This is magnified with their partners; they are rarely able to drum up any enthusiasm for their partner's successes, and when they do, it can feel forced or empty. A consistent theme that arises when I talk with partners of narcissists is their narcissistic partner's utter lack of enthusiasm when something good happens to them and, alternately, their partner's relative satisfaction when things go wrong for them.

This can be quite nightmarish if you are in a relationship with a narcissist who not only does not derive pleasure out of your triumphs but also disparages or mocks them and may even take dark satisfaction in your failures or losses. This pattern over a long-term relationship takes a significant toll. After years or decades of not having successes heralded, but actually disparaged and insulted, many people I interviewed reported a significant decrease in self-esteem over the course of the relationship. Over time, they transitioned from a sense of confidence and excitement about the future to one of self-doubt, discouragement, and even hopelessness. Ironically, they would often receive cheerleading and support from everyone else—friends, family, co-workers—but because their narcissistic partner could not bring it, they felt as if their lives were one long quest for approval (approval they would someday find out was *never* going to appear).

RED FLAGS: ENGAGES IN SCHAEDENFRAUDE

Watch how your partner receives other people's good news, whether it is yours or someone else's. Is he a cheerleader? Or is he ▼

bitter? In the early days of your relationship, narcissists are often able to reflect back your good news, but it may fade over time. Pay attention to how he reflects on the successes of others—with joy and support or with chronic disparagement? When you share a triumph with him does he uplift you (no matter how big or small it is) or does he give you the bum's rush or even downplay it? Does he seem to express satisfaction about others' misfortunes? Does he like watching other people fail? These patterns tend to evidence themselves early because the pattern of envy and insult is so ingrained for a narcissistic person. Remember, other people's successes, especially yours, are often a threat to them.

DOES NOT LIKE TO BE ALONE

When asked why it was so important for him to be famous, he said "so I would never have to be alone again."

Narcissists often hate being alone. Remember, they need others for admiration, so being alone is a challenge for them. It varies, depending upon whether they are seeking out large crowds, one-on-one time, time with family, or time in the workplace, but time alone is not their forte. And if they cannot find other people, you will find them on social media. For most people, being alone means being alone with your own thoughts, and it's a necessary and healthy part of life. However, if your sense of self is shallow, and you rely on others for your self-esteem, then being alone is a grim reminder of that emptiness. This surpasses regular extraversion—yes, some people enjoy being amongst other people, but the inability to tolerate being alone is an issue.

This trait can sometimes lead to tension in relationships, when a narcissistic partner may seek out your company even when you need down time, insist that you do things together all the time, or, conversely, always want to be in large crowds or in large gatherings where he can be chronically validated by others in a superficial way. This particular issue may not be a problem if both of you are content with the social rhythms you have constructed. Your needs may be met in a different way, but you may be on board with the social or interactive rhythms you have.

RED FLAGS: DOES NOT LIKE TO BE ALONE

Is alone time rare for this person? Do you find him calling you every time he is alone to fill in the time and space? Does he chronically need to be with others? Does his phone constantly shake, buzz, ping, and ring because he is frequently in touch with others via text messages, instant messages, and social media posts? If it appears that the "being with others" or "not being alone" piece is obvious, pay attention to that. By itself, this is not a ringer by any means, but combined with other traits it may be a red flag and may also speak to issues that could arise in your relationship. For example, the chronic need to be "out and about" does not always bode well for stages in a relationship that may require more mindful locking down, such as parenting.

POOR BOUNDARIES

There were always lots of female friends around, and interestingly, most of them were single. They tended to worship him, and he rarely introduced me to them. Initially, I thought it was that he was a cool guy who got along with women and had a strong feminine side, and I wanted to be the cool girl who was good with her man's friendships. Over time, it started to feel weird, social media messages felt inappropriate, texts and calls would come in from these women at all hours. Down the line, once we were on the rocks, I met one of these friends, and while we had been in a relationship for years, she said, "I had no idea he had someone in his life."

Boundaries are the lines in the sand that exist in relationships. They reflect social rules of order, culture, respect, and appropriateness, given the other contexts of your life. They can shift over time. For example, snuggle time with a female friend may evaporate once the man enters into a committed relationship. Boundaries are usually implicit and understood by the persons in the relationship. If you are in a relationship, maintaining appropriate boundaries with new and old friends and family is part of the trust, respect, and values within a relationship.

Boundaries are not just about romantic relationships; they can also relate to colleagues, family members, and even strangers. You would not (and should not) walk up to strangers and ask them about their sexual proclivities. You also may not want to invite your parents on your honeymoon. Boundaries are also a dance— and most people are pretty clear on them. Sexy, flirty texts to other people when you are in a committed relationship are not appropriate, and when you have to spell that out, it should give you pause. Many times in new relationships the restructuring of boundaries can be hard work and requires mature and insightful communication. A common mistake is to assume that boundaries will just figure themselves out; they often do not, and hurt feelings are inevitable.

Narcissists are notoriously bad at boundaries. Because they regulate their self-esteem through others, they maintain their relationships to get their needs met and will frequently cross a line and violate a boundary because it makes them feel good in that moment. Because they lack empathy, they do not pause to reflect on how these chronic boundary violations make you feel as a partner, nor do they reflect on how they may be treating the other people in these relationships.

RED FLAGS: POOR BOUNDARIES

Modern technology has turned boundary violations into a day-to-day series of landmines. Whether it is text messages or e-mails from former partners or overly amorous coworkers or inappropriate social ▼

media posts or comments, these kinds of signals are indicators of boundary problems. The beauty is that narcissists are often so reliant on social media that you can glimpse into their poor boundaries rather early in the relationship. The challenge is that narcissists will often minimize their loose boundaries but will also mock you and make you feel like a Puritanical fool or a "stick in the mud" for raising your concerns about these folks ("they are just friends"). If it doesn't pass your smell test, it is probably an issue. In the world of smartphones and easy 24-hour-a-day access to everyone, boundary violations are easy to commit. Listen for those late night text message pings; it may be blurred boundaries, and it can be a slippery slope.

INFIDELITY

He managed to keep another relationship going for years. When a family member finally told me about it, I moved out. After 20 years of marriage, three children, and a lifetime of neglect, working three jobs to support him and his "art," strangely, it took knowing and confirmation of the fact that he was cheating to get myself out of the relationship. When I called him out on it, he said "it's because you weren't there for me."

Narcissists cheat. In fact, I often cite narcissism as one of the primary predictors of relationship infidelity. While not all infidelity is attributable to narcissism, a significant proportion of narcissists do engage in relationship infidelity (and as shown in the scenario above, they are masterful at making it your "fault"). Infidelity can take different forms, and is most often either sexual or emotional (and often both). This can manifest as having a full blown sexual and romantic relationship outside of a committed relationship, a deeply emotional connection that is not yet sexual, or just a one-night stand (or series of one-night stands!). As a rule, narcissists tend to be more prone to sexual infidelities than emotional ones.

Infidelity is a glaring extension of the boundary violations. The lack of empathy, the entitlement, the grandiosity, and the constant need to get their desires met often culminate in affairs. Their need for admiration and novelty is so vast that they are wired to be unfaithful—affairs are typically characterized by excitement, flattery, and superficial grandiosity. The lack of empathy can lead them to want the "proverbial cake"; they may keep their steady relationship with you and cultivate other needs outside of the relationship. It's a coward's move.

The rules do not apply to narcissists, and they can rationalize a morally questionable situation into a love story, because they are "so special" and deserve to "feel alive." They live in a fantasy world, and whether it is one-night stands or long-term affairs, they believe these relationships are their due. And because they are empathically nonexistent, they do not grapple with the usual moral demons a healthy person would face when being unfaithful to a committed partner. These infidelities can take any number of forms: frequent attendance at adult entertainment venues (for example, as observed in the vignette about John and Rachel), one night stands during business travel, or long-term relationships.

Many people spend a lifetime recovering from infidelity. It is a fundamental breach of trust, and when it occurs repeatedly, it can result in major psychological fallout, including depression, anxiety, and health difficulties. Do people make mistakes? Of course. And one episode of infidelity is not a diagnosis of narcissism. Combine it with the chronic problems with boundaries and the other patterns cited above and it is more likely that the infidelity is embedded in pathological narcissism. As a rule, infidelity is careless, unkind, and sloppy. At a minimum it is a wake-up call that the committed relationship has likely reached its expiration date.

RED FLAGS: INFIDELITY

If, early in the relationship, you have observed this pattern or your partner's behavior is strongly suggestive of it, then take pause. If he confesses to a pattern of cheating in the past, take a deep breath. ▼

As much as narcissists may say "I learned my lesson and will never go there again," it is rarely a one-time behavior and may happen on your watch, too. Finally, watch other boundary-violating patterns: maintaining close relationships with past flames, taking time away from your relationship in favor of one-on-one time with others, and social media behavior. Do not fall into the "cool chick" trap. If it makes you feel uncomfortable, say something. If the behavior does not change, then re-evaluate.

DOESN'T LISTEN

The TV was on loud, most of the time. Early on I would try to talk to him; I don't know if he could hear me over the TV. The only time I knew he actually knew I was speaking was when he would tell me to stop talking so loud because he couldn't hear the TV. Some of our biggest fights would come from the fact that I always assumed he was listening when I was talking to him, so days or weeks later when he would claim I "never told him" something, I felt like I was losing my mind. I then realized he never heard me in the first place—he had been tuning me out for years.

As psychologists we often make the distinction between "hearing" and "listening." One can be viewed as a straight audiological and perhaps neuropsychological phenomenon—a sensory ability to detect sounds, and then comprehend those sounds as words and language. That's not what we are talking about here. Obviously narcissists can hear, and they do hear *and* listen when it matters to them. Most of us assume that when we speak, the other person is listening, but with narcissists this is often not the case.

That assumption, that the other person is listening, can create a fair amount of confusion in the early phase of the relationship with the narcissist. Because you assume he was listening, it can be confusing when he claims to not have been told something (because he did not listen initially). It literally feels "crazy-making." It can also feel isolating. It is not interesting to have a one-sided conversation, to say something and not be heard, or alternatively to have someone talk at you with no ability or interest in listening to your response. You end up feeling like a sounding board that is not allowed to "sound." It becomes a metaphor for the entire relationship with the narcissist: to feel like an object that only exists when you are necessary (almost like a tool in a toolbox—only useful when there is a job to be done). No one listens to a hammer or a screwdriver. They use them when they need them, and then they put them away when they are done.

RED FLAGS: DOESN'T LISTEN

Pay attention to the cadence of the early conversations. Narcissists can actually "play" at being good conversationalists early in the relationship. They will ask interesting questions, and you will answer them. Their response, however, will often reflect that they are not listening, and it will typically steer the conversation back to them. They can engage in the polite niceties of your day, but their responses will reveal that either they were not listening or simply do not care. If your conversations feel more like "parallel" play—two people dancing separately, rather than waltzing together—then *listen* to that. No one wants to spend years of their lives being unheard.

FRAGILE

He was arrogant, until his "art" was criticized. He would become really sad, and just sort of hang around all day. It would take him a few days to get out of that funk. Sadly, at those times I sometimes saw that beautiful baby-faced boy I remember falling in love with.

After this long list of traits, this is the one that feels like it does not belong. While most narcissists come off as arrogant, sometimes life does not comply with their wishes, and at such times, there can be an obvious vulnerability. Narcissists cannot regroup well after a crisis, such as losing a job. They genuinely feel fragile at these times and look fragile. This pattern can throw off many people—and particularly you as their partner. In the wake of something shameful or difficult, they turn into someone you feel you can actually help or reassure. Just as soon as you become accustomed to their neglect, lack of empathy, and overall arrogance, the ground may shift to this place of vulnerability, and it can be confusing and destabilizing for you. It won't last. Once the dark time passes, your self-absorbed, controlling partner will return.

RED FLAGS: FRAGILE

This may be one of the most difficult traits to identify early on, because this is one that is not clear when it first occurs. Most people in a new relationship are not going to harshly judge a person's vulnerability in the face of criticism or bad news. Early in a relationship observe your partner's reactions when things go wrong, and particularly when he is criticized. If your seemingly "confident" partner becomes weepy, vulnerable, dependent and needy in the face of any critiques or downturns, make a note of that. But this is indeed tricky because nearly all of us will become more vulnerable or downcast when we are criticized. If your partner quickly transitions from grandiose to withdrawn and vulnerable when things in his life are not going as he hoped, that too may be an important signal. If you initially meet a narcissist during a vulnerable phase, it can be even more confusing if over time he returns to grandiosity. This pattern of fragility or vulnerability may initially be experienced as dependent and needy. Sadly, this red flag is often one that only gets figured out backwards.

CARELESS

He would plan dinners out with colleagues and admiring co-workers at restaurants I had been dying for us to try. He would build weekends away at the end of his business trips, not invite me, and not tell me until he was calling me from the beach. I don't know if he was forgetful, rude, or just plain stupid. No matter how many times I would tell him that this would hurt, and he would apologize profoundly, he would just do it again. It was like that movie Groundhog Day.

A key difference between narcissists and psychopaths is that psychopaths will sometimes set out coldly to hurt someone. Narcissists often hurt people through their carelessness. Obviously, this is embedded in the entitlement and lack of empathy, but carelessness implies a lack of mindfulness and a lack of "self-monitoring." A mindful person typically looks ahead and considers how his behavior may impact someone else; he may sometimes still engage in the behavior, but he takes that moment and may also learn from his careless error.

Carelessness can often be experienced as neglect. Little things like messages left unanswered, questions left unaddressed, or simply not noticing you can build over time. It accumulates like a heavy weight, and neglect can sometimes be more painful than attentive cruelty. It may be experienced as a negation of your existence or experience.

The carelessness of narcissism may be one of the most confusing and destructive patterns because there is a profound lack of awareness. It tends to be a habit and a pattern of bulldozing through life that can be hard to address, because they make messes and other people (including you) clean them up. Relationships require mindfulness, and carelessness can slowly erode the soul of a relationship. An endless cycle of carelessness followed by apologies gets tiresome.

RED FLAGS: CARELESS

Late to dates, does not return phone calls, forgets to show up, agrees to two events at the same time. Early inconsiderateness can give a glimpse into what may become a permanent pattern of carelessness. Is he mindful? Does he communicate clearly? Does he attempt to anticipate your response or ask you how you feel about something? Carelessness is a pattern that sets in very early, and the ▼

tendency is to excuse someone for their early carelessness, writing it off to absentmindedness, busy schedules, or miscommunication. Carelessness is a slow burn, and something that becomes more apparent over months and years. It can be experienced as an internal alert system that you develop that helps you prepare for the chronic disappointment that this relationship will regularly deliver.

SEDUCTIVE

It wasn't even like he was that handsome, he was sexy, there's a difference. When it was happening to me, it felt like it was happening only to me. Over time I realized this is who he was, and he kind of did this with everyone. It was always winks, nods and nudges—in person, on his social media, even in his text messages to other women. When I would call him on it he would minimize it. It was pretty awful because I would sometimes watch him at a party talking to another woman and you could see that she was being seduced by him, as though I did not exist. I realized that it was his power, and he used it.

Theodore Millon, a noted personality theorist, divided narcissistic personality disorder into subtypes, and one of them was identified as the "amorous" subtype, characterized by being seductive and exhibitionistic. Many narcissists (both men and women) use sexuality as they would any other tool—to get what they want and to get attention. Because boundaries often do not matter to them, and they enjoy being the center of attention, seductiveness and excessive flirtation are frequently observed. Their focus on appearance, vanity, and superficiality all contribute to this pattern. It is often their seductive and exhibitionistic ("showy") qualities that draw people in, and this may be manifested by a man who shows off his beautiful face and body and who speaks in suggestive language or a woman who plays up her physical assets through her style of dress or may conduct herself in a very sexualized manner. This type of pattern definitely attracts attention, and in the moment can be very exciting and obviously, seductive.

RED FLAGS: SEDUCTIVE

Do they dress to the situation or is it over the top? Look for suggestive or provocative style of dress, language, or attention getting appearance and behavior. This can often be something that is reflected on after the fact, because the courtship phase of a relationship is often characterized by fluffing up our feathers and looking our best. So pay attention to the style and the situation. Are the words and style out of context (e.g. wearing revealing or inappropriate clothing during a children's school event or a professional or somber occasion)? Sexy, flirty fun is expected (and enjoyable) in a relationship, but when the seductiveness becomes a lifestyle and crosses the line to being flirtatious or too sexualized with other people your partner meets, you may want to pay attention.

Not All Narcissism Looks the Same

Narcissism, as with any "descriptive label," often fails to capture the nuances of individual human beings and experiences. A key issue with narcissistic personality and narcissistic personality disorder is that it does not always look the same. Theoretical, clinical, and empirical work on the diagnosis of narcissism unearths different "subtypes"—and these are often driven by the "traits" you may have checked off above.

Here are the most common "patterns." They often look quite variable and are sometimes nothing alike. It may be why you can meet two different pathologically narcissistic people who behave and make you feel very differently. Each subtype will feature the KEY traits that often comprise this particular pattern to help you determine if you are in a relationship with a specific type of narcissist. Not every key trait may be present, but these are the types of narcissistic traits that are most likely to be observed.

THE DARK TRIAD NARCISSIST

These are the folks who are downright *mean*. Not only will they violate moral and ethical codes but also legal ones as well. They can be dangerous and terrifying. Because they feel little remorse or guilt for their behavior, it can be quite chilling to be with them, and certainly to be their partner. However, these "Dark Triad Narcissists" are often quite successful, and their "legal or ethical transgressions" may take the form of corporate malfeasance (for example, Bernie Madoff), sexual improprieties, or downright brutality. Because of their frequently ostensible success, power, and wealth, they are often quite skilled at attracting partners, and their partners can find themselves psychologically hollowed out before the relationship is over. The Dark Triad Narcissist is a grim reminder of the seductiveness of wealth and power, and the fact that everything comes with a price.

KEY TRAITS

Grandiose, entitled, manipulative, zero empathy, angry and rageful, paranoid, little remorse/guilt, jealous, validation-seeking, lying, emotionally cold, irresponsible, vain, controlling, unpredictable, take advantage of others, poor boundaries, infidelity, doesn't listen, careless, seductive.

THE CONTROLLING NARCISSIST

Narcissists are often controlled and controlling by nature, but many are also disengaged. The controlling narcissist is the person who is controlling most of the time, more concerned with accountability than empathy and connection. They will often bring this hyper-controlled persona into the workplace, expecting everything and everyone to be "just-so." When they are in charge, they are tyrants, and it is quite typical for them to be "workaholics." They are often inflexible about matters of organization, appearance, and public image. Their over-focus on order and control can sometimes feel obsessive-compulsive. They can also take quite a toll on their children, requiring nothing short of perfection, and grinding their children into the ground with demands of excellence, ambition, and performance, but with little support, warmth, interest, or empathy. Interestingly, these Controlling Narcissists may not always be cheaters, because they are so wedded to a certain sense of "how things should be." If fidelity is part of their moral order, they may not go there.

Initially, partners are often confused by the Controlling Narcissist, because, if anything, they appear "over-engaged." They will provide input and be solicitous about everything from your appearance, your work, or your whereabouts—and if they have the resources, they may expend them on creating a certain "look" for you. It can feel like *Pygmalion* or *My Fair Lady* with your new partner purchasing clothes, jewelry, and other accessories to costume you (and it is easy to get pulled into the creepy *Pretty Woman* fantasy of becoming someone's dress-up doll). This form of attention is so culturally reinforced in our mythology and media imagery, that it is often initially interpreted as romantic and passionate interest. As it devolves into the need for updates on who you are with and where you are, demands for sex, conversation, companionship, and lifestyle—all according to their schedule—it starts to feel less like *Pretty Woman* and more like Pretty Scary. It is a slowly suffocating situation, but because they are seemingly attentive to the "details" (but are rarely actually listening to you), you slowly recognize you are a prop in their lives, and it can become especially difficult to disengage.

KEY TRAITS

Grandiose, entitled, manipulative, zero empathy, angry and rageful, paranoid, hypersensitive, jealous, need validation, putting on a show, vain, controlling, unpredictable, does not like to be alone, doesn't listen.

VULNERABLE NARCISSIST

This is an interesting group, and in some ways the most challenging, because they do not look like classical narcissistic personality disorder at first blush. Elsa Ronningstam, psychologist at McLean Hospital and Associate Clinical Professor at Harvard Medical School (and author of *Identifying and Understanding the Narcissistic Personality*), is one of the leading international experts on narcissistic personality disorder. She has expertly characterized a subgroup of narcissists as "shy narcissists" and describes them as interpersonally and occupationally restricted. Basically, they appear somewhat shy or socially awkward and are not likely to be as defined by their career status. They tend to be more sensitive, vulnerable, socially restrained, and plagued by shame. This type of narcissistic personality will typically be self-critical and be afraid of failing. In addition, they are highly sensitive to the criticism of other people. Because they are so full of shame, they hold back from other people, and that leaves them feeling isolated—and even longing for connection to other people.

So if they are all of these things, where does the unpleasant narcissistic part surface? They are not the grandiose blowhards, nor are they entitled—traits that are easy to observe. Instead, they tend to be shallow, detached, envious of others, and unskilled and unable to communicate with or take care of other people. They do not come off of as "mean" or even unkind, rather, they lack the depth of empathy needed to identify the needs of other people and then respond to them.

This is a tough pattern to discern, and even skilled psychologists and psychiatrists may have to reflect on this one for a while (it often looks like depression). If this is your partner, you may become aware of this pattern over time through the absolute sense of isolation, neglect, and disconnection that unfolds. Your partner may frequently put himself down and sometimes respond to positive feedback, but, in general, he is chronically self-critical and may seem neglectful or dejected most of the time. It is a heavy cloud under which to live.

KEY TRAITS

Little empathy, hypersensitive, projection, emotionally cold at times, envy, fragility, careless.

THE NEGLECTFUL NARCISSIST

All of the subtypes can also share this quality (except for the Controlling subtype, though the Controlling Narcissist may be neglectful of your hopes and aspirations). The Neglectful Narcissist often evolves over time. They are frequently drawn to new people and new experiences and then tire of them relatively quickly. Initially, they may be quite engaged, but after they have had their fill, they typically move on to the next thing. They can also be dishonest and careless, have their fun (even if it involves boundary violations or other improprieties), and then apologize and attend to your feelings after the fact, or tell selective truths about what they did without you.

Because they cannot (and do not want to) maintain the initial level of energy they brought to an earlier phase of your relationship, once they disengage it can be extremely frustrating for a partner. They may run hot and cold, interested at some times, and then off on their own path at others. If you are involved with such a person, you could easily find him taking a week-long business trip and leaving you and the children at home, and then coming home and heading out to go golfing with friends. It is a careless and frustrating pattern. This pattern really brings home the idea that you may serve as nothing more than an object in his universe, attended to when you are useful or pleasurable, and then mentally put aside when other, more interesting things emerge. This pattern can also find you experiencing gaslighting and projection, so when you call him out on his patterns, he will either take a stance of defending himself, painting you as neurotic, or engaging in self-shaming or self-critical blather about how he is just not "good enough" and maybe he does not deserve you (this is one of their better tricks because it then forces you to soothe them at exactly the time when you are feeling vulnerable).

KEY TRAITS

Entitled, little empathy, need validation, lying, projection, gaslighting, emotionally cold, cheap, never takes responsibility, unpredictable, takes advantage of others, doesn't listen, careless.

Narcissism is a complex set of traits and patterns. As you can see, some of these traits as standalone characteristics do not mean much, but altogether they add up to something incredibly challenging. Hopefully, you now have a clear sense of the most common characteristics, behaviors, and patterns of narcissists. Remember, if your partner exhibits 15 or more of the traits on the checklist, you are likely in a relationship with a narcissist. Odds are that you figured out a long time ago that something is "not quite right" and have been struggling with your relationship for some time. If you are in a relationship with a narcissist, you may be wondering how you fell for this person. Don't berate yourself. Smart, successful people fall for narcissists every day. Why? Because narcissists by their nature are often incredibly charming and brilliant. On the surface, they are often the "best get" in the room. The next chapter will explore the seductive traits that may have attracted you in the first place to help you clearly understand your vulnerability to certain types of personalities. By understanding why these narcissistic traits are so attractive, it may give you more power to understand how to manage the relationship you are currently in, or avoid falling for these traits and patterns again.

CHAPTER 4

HOW DID YOU GET SUCKED IN?

Often it is the most deserving people who cannot help loving those who destroy them.

—HERMAN HESSE

nce you are in, and your relationship stops making sense, the frequent questions are:

- ▶ How did I get here?
- ▶ Why did I choose so badly?
- ▶ What was I thinking?

Don't be so hard on yourself. Narcissists are magnetic and highly skilled at attracting people. Most of us will be drawn in by one at some point in our lives.

It can't be all doom and gloom. If you review the long list of attributes that are often observed in narcissism, it appears that the only missing elements are horns and a forked tongue. Obviously, that cannot be entirely clear or correct, or most people would never be drawn in. While the red flags, narcissistic traits, and the "danger signs" are powerful (and everything makes sense in hindsight), the "seductive" traits are even more powerful. These seductive traits are the ones that block our ability to detect the red flags, play into our vulnerabilities and egos, and result in us being pulled in so deep that making changes can feel all but impossible.

The Seductive Traits

These are the characteristics that drew you in when you first met. What usually draws you in when you meet new people? This pretty much nails it. And since narcissists tend to have most of these traits, particularly early in the game, it's easy to see how these often serve as the proverbial "lipstick on the pig." Some of the classic "magnetic" traits of narcissism are as follows:

- ► Experts at winning "the game"
- ► Charismatic, Charming, Confident
- ► Intelligent/well-informed
- ► Attractive/well-put-together
- ► Passionate and creative
- ► Articulate
- ► Great branding
- ► Visionary

Carrie Haslam and Tamara Montrose, researchers at Hartpury College in the UK, published a paper entitled "Should have known better: The impact of mating experience and the desire for marriage upon attraction to the narcissistic personality" in the journal *Personality and Individual Differences*. They capture it beautifully when they say "narcissistic males do not make good romantic partners." They attribute this to narcissistic men's propensity for manipulation, game-playing, infidelity, and their inability to commit. In the short term, the goodies that male narcissistic partners often bring, especially status and resources, can make them seem like more attractive partners at first blush.

Sadly, Haslam and Montrose also found that women who wanted to get married were more attracted and attractive to narcissistic personalities than women who did not desire marriage. Thus, women were drawn to precisely the men who were not built for long-term commitment and those very men pursued them. The traits of the narcissist, such as career success, authoritativeness, and the implied status that accompany these traits, may have drawn the attention of marriage-minded women who could not (or perhaps would not) see the darker traits that would evidence themselves down the road—and make a satisfying and collaborative marriage all but impossible. Or as Haslam and Montrose note, "whilst the narcissistic male is not good marriage material, it can be seen why he may appear to be so." The fact is women and men need to retrain themselves. Instead of the flashy charismatic guy who is confident and "hot," you may do better by paying attention to the quiet rumpled guy in the corner. Instead of the attention grabbing woman in the center of the action, consider the kind lady with the serene smile.

As you may recall, when the more "problematic" traits were listed and defined in the previous chapter, they always came back to the same issue: fragile ego and poor self-esteem as well as the constant search for validation. The traits listed above often originate from the same place—narcissists work on the outside because there really is no inside. And it is difficult to search for validation if you don't have the bait to attract it. Cultivating traits such as appearance or charisma is a great way to obtain "external" validation, a handy psychological shortcut. Narcissistic people have a well-honed ability to assess a situation so they can quickly get their needs met. That often requires being able to "work a room" and possess traits, such as charm, that help that along. The bottom line, at least among men, is that being narcissistic ups your desirability to a new partner. And that is the dangerous paradox: The very trait that is most likely to draw you in is the one that will ultimately be your undoing. Narcissism is basically the flame that draws in the moth.

PLAYING BY THE "RULES"—AND WINNING

This game may be one of the reasons you find yourself in this situation. There are more than a dozen books with the word "Rules"
in the title designed to help people find and capture a partner. A
variant of "the rules" has existed since Cinderella (leave behind a
shoe, and then make him work to find you).

The basic premise of the "rules" is simple. I am going to give the
gendered version of this, because 99 percent of the time the rules
are pitched to women.

- ▶ Make him work for it.
- ▶ Play hard to get.
- ▶ Don't be overly available.
- ▶ Vary between being dismissive and overly attentive.

The overarching premise is that if he has to work for it, there
will be greater buy-in and he will be more likely to commit to you.
And the sub-rules include the following: insist on/allow him to pay
for dinner and purchase you gifts, don't have sex on the first date,
don't get back in touch with him too quickly, wait him out until he
calls you.

This has of course spawned a new level of anxiety. *How long
before I call/text him? I really like him and want to say thank you,
but then I won't be playing hard to get. Am I supposed to be dismissive after the third date or really nice?* It's a game, and there
is a whole legion of dating coaches out there who will hold true
to their messianic message that it is indeed a game and should be
played as such. Because, of course, nothing would feel better than
the idea that I "scored" my life partner on the basis of "gaming"
him. Let's now link this back to narcissism.

The rules work beautifully with narcissists because they love
a win. And having to work for it means a win. It pulls the "get
acquainted" process off of deeper connected qualities and processes, such as intimacy, empathy, and mutuality, and turns it into

superficial posturing (which plays upon a narcissist's strengths). The narcissist is happy because he is plotting how to get the win, and the recipient is happy because she used manipulation and psychological sleight of hand—playing hard to get—and got the guy (thus getting her money's worth out of the rule book she purchased). In addition, because many narcissists are in possession of the kinds of resources that play into the rules (they can afford to pay for expensive restaurants and gifts and show up in the right car, wearing the right shoes), they are a perfect "mark." Another built-in advantage of the rules for a narcissist is that these rules are predicated on the person being pursued (usually the woman) having to spend days at a time not getting in touch with the narcissist, which works out nicely for the narcissist since he is so disengaged, so he gets his break and he gets the girl.

The whole "hard to get" game forces the narcissists to play at being nice for longer than they usually do. They can't ignore you as easily (because they want to win you over), they are focused on the win, and may not seem initially neglectful or uncommitted because they are committed to the game (do not confuse this with being committed to the relationship or to you as a human being). This can result in a big mess. Because you are postponing the inevitable.

What happens when the game is over and you find yourself in a relationship with this person? What happens when you are looking at each other over glasses of chardonnay, after he puts his phone down long enough to notice you are there?

Making him "work for it" means that you don't clearly observe the neglectful narcissistic patterns early enough and may find yourself in too deep to easily escape once you recognize these patterns. The rules delay the inevitable. If you play it clean—just be you, reach out when you want to reach out, expect kind treatment, don't allow yourself to be dazzled by the hot new bar/restaurant/nightclub/gift/first-class seats—then you may glimpse the problematic patterns, such as grandiosity, lack of empathy, entitlement, and coldness early enough to get out with less difficulty.

Many times the "gaming" and the "rules" become more compelling than actually noticing who it is you are trying to win over. The harder they are to capture, the harder you will work for it, with little regard for the fact that this narcissistic partner and all of his trappings are actually turning the search for a committed partner into a Machiavellian merger. Games may be flirtatious fun in the early days of courtship, but they are not nearly as interesting when you are trying to raise children, manage daily stressors, and build a real life together. The challenging part of playing "games" is that they have to be maintained—once you set the tone, you are sort of stuck with it. Do you really want to spend the rest of your life playing hard to get? Do not turn the early phase of your relationship into a game, because when that is the bait, you won't catch commitment.

THE 3 C'S: CHARISMATIC, CHARMING, CONFIDENT

We met at an outdoor music festival. I was single at the time and just having fun and enjoying all of the attention. He was handsome, successful, had lots to say, and even a little bit shy, but we caught each other's eye and remained with each other for the rest of the festival. I immediately felt at ease, and clearly lots of other people enjoyed his company, too. He has always been the center of attention in every group he is in, and at first that was kind of exciting. But over time, I realized that it was always about him. Dinners with groups of people felt like a show—with him telling stories about his life and everyone listening. The charm was fun at first, but over time it was definitely not enough.

The 3 C's of the narcissist—charisma, charm, and confidence—are magnetic traits that have been created and honed over many years. People with narcissistic personalities were taught at an early age that perception may actually be more important than the real you, so all of their energy goes into developing the traits and qualities that others see, rather than developing their sense of self. As such, people with narcissistic personality are knowledgeable about what they do and what they care about—this can be manifested by a fancy education, lots of knowledge about a specific area (for example, music, sports, art), and they are willing and able to share this information. Most of us value knowledge and assume smart and clever people are capable of lots of good things. In the anecdote about John and Rachel, John was heavy on the 3 C's and they drew Rachel down the rabbit hole. Charm can be highly seductive, charisma can light up a room, and confidence can be comforting.

In the best of worlds, the 3 C's are embedded within a person who is fully formed, inside and out. Many people who are confident, charming and charismatic are also people of depth and interest, empathy, and kindness. Charm, charisma and confidence by themselves are not enough; they need depth to balance them out. These traits draw us in, for good reason, but a new relationship requires walking that challenging tightrope between being open and also remaining aware.

NARCISSISTS ARE SMART

He was the smartest man I have ever met, and that is saying a lot as I am a pretty smart woman. He is well-read, self-made, and can hold a conversation with anyone. He is incredibly successful in his career. I have to admit, I noticed red flags early on because he was very controlling, but his intelligence kept things interesting so I stuck it out. Unfortunately, he could also be really arrogant and sometimes people felt insulted by the things he would say, including me. He can be so condescending and this can take a toll on our child. Sometimes his intelligence starts to feel like a weapon.

Intelligence is a complicated concept. When we hear it, most of us think about people who are often termed "book smart"—who know facts, have completed higher levels of education, and can hold their own with other well-educated and smart people. Obviously that is only one part of it, and intelligence can also manifest as being knowledgeable about specific areas like professions and hobbies, such as the law or fishing or the arts. It can also be a potentially "dangerous" trait since an intelligent person may know how to get what they want from others and may anticipate the angles before other people do. Intelligence can make a strong first impression, and intelligent people can appear confident, a highly attractive trait. The bottom line? Smart is sexy.

Narcissists are smart, which is why they are so skilled at getting what they want. They will often put the time into cultivating their knowledge about a topic or obtaining a sophisticated education. Intelligence and accomplishment are considered attractive traits in our culture. Slick intelligence is initially alluring, and it can be exciting to be with someone who is smart and talented with a good career, whom you imagine will be able to contribute financially to your future home/family and carry on intellectual conversations. Unfortunately, those conversations may be few and far between once you really get to know a narcissist. Because they are so self-involved, they are more likely to ignore you or talk at you than with you.

When I asked people what initially drew them into their relationship, many of them highlighted the extreme intelligence of their partner. Intelligence in the narcissistic person often serves as a coat of armor. Initially, it may make them more intriguing, and can often keep the relationship interesting in the long term, however, it can also be wielded with tremendous arrogance. Over time, the intellect and the knowledge can feel cold and distancing, and their intelligence frequently becomes a weapon with which to insult you as a partner. We presume intelligence and wisdom to be the same thing—they are not. It is not a slam-dunk that intelligence will translate into the wisdom of compassion or empathy.

NARCISSISTS LOOK GOOD

Physical appearance is often one of the first things that attract us to a person. Narcissists can be extremely attractive; they use their clothes, bodies, faces, and hair to maximize their assets and make sure they are noticed. They may not have been blessed with genetic good looks, but they will take what they have and enhance it. If they were born with good looks, it can be a curse, because they learn at an early age that their appearance often opens doors more quickly than anything else. If a person learns that his appearance is his strong suit, it can foster the kind of superficiality often observed in narcissism, or make the attractive person an easy "mark" for a narcissist, since the narcissist tends to prefer attractive partners and be flattering. The trait of vanity was highlighted when we were discussing the red flags, and many people who are narcissistic keenly monitor their appearance. This can include high-end clothing, impeccable haircuts, sculpted and toned physiques, and even surgical enhancement.

Psychiatrist Alexander Lowen reflects on the role of appearance in narcissism. He makes the important distinction of looking good versus feeling good. Much of our culture is focused on looking good, with little reflection on whether our weight loss, body building, and wrinkle eradicating is translating into inner serenity or sense of well-being. Lowen argues that the narcissist wants to put forth a physical appearance (for example, making wrinkles disappear and denying the impact of gravity on breasts and bellies) that does not belie any signs of worry or experience, as though he or she does not want life to touch his or her appearance. For narcissists, vanity goes beyond simply looking good; it is one more symptom of their general denial of their real lives, their real feelings. Beauty can draw us in, but it is also a trait that should be carefully considered as it gives us little insight into what is underneath it. As long as a person relies on his façade, he is vulnerable.

However, outer beauty is a key element to early attraction. The most attractive person in the room gets the attention, and in most cases I have worked with, the narcissist was extremely attractive, which often led the other person and the world in general to excuse many bad behaviors. Over time, all the beauty in the world will not compensate for the cold reality of being in a relationship with a narcissist, but as an early hook, it is incredibly powerful, and most people will acknowledge that it was the trait that drew them in and kept them in, especially in the seductive early days of the relationship.

PUTTING ON A PASSIONATE, CREATIVE SHOW

The following is a question that often arises when people reflect about getting sucked in: "If a person lacks self-esteem, how can he look confident?" Here is where the grandiosity comes in to play. Much of it is showmanship: The curtain goes up, he plays the part, and the part is to "look confident." Just as a good actor can play any role, the emptiness of the narcissist allows him to behave in ways that are inconsistent with his inner experience. When we are not feeling confident, most of us do not look confident because our inner worlds are reflected in how we appear to the outside world. This is not the case with narcissists—they are experts at hiding their vulnerabilities and putting on an act.

In the interviews I conducted for the book, and in hearing from clients with whom I have worked, I specifically asked the story of "how they met their narcissistic partners" and the key elements of their initial attraction. Two themes were typically highlighted: "they were extremely attractive" and "they were creative and passionate about their art or their work." When people are passionate or excited about their work or interests, it shines out of their face. The passion and the excited energy are almost infectious, and you can find yourself getting caught up in the wave of it. Let's face it, not everyone is enthusiastic about what they do—there are many people out there who just punch a card and work for a salary. Meeting someone who is excited about work, a hobby, or a cause can be uplifting and even stoke the flames of your own interests and passions. In that way a passionate new partner can feel like a muse and an inspiration. Many times the passionate interest is presumed to be a depth that will also be reflected in depth of connection, emotion, and insight. Meeting a person who is passionate about his or her work is wonderful, but take the time to ensure that passion and deep interest cut across more areas than simply their own work or interests.

ARTICULATE

A person can be termed "silver-tongued" or poetic or just "having a way with words." This falls under charisma, and they can be smoother with a compliment or even well-asked questions than most people. They may also be able to speak about a variety of issues knowledgably. This quality is incredibly engaging and can often result in some really interesting early conversations that can leave you wanting more. Is every narcissistic person articulate? No. But it is often a quality that is so elegant and intoxicating that many people will reflect back on how this quality drew them in and kept them hooked for a long time. In hindsight, many people interviewed for the book reflected on the fact that the articulate quality of their partner was wonderful initially, but then they realized that over time they felt like they were listening to a lecture or a TED talk rather than actually being engaged in a conversation.

WHAT'S YOUR BRAND?

We presently live in a world where people are often viewed as "brands"—defined by possessions, addresses, the places they have visited, the things they have achieved. Key branding variables can include the type of car you drive, where you live, the university you attended, your profession or job title, awards you have received, the places you have traveled, the status of your family. These variables can be head-turners; a Harvard degree or a law partnership, a fancy home, the right neighborhood, a grown-up toy like a boat or a beach house, a fat wallet, or a Maserati can often excuse a lot of bad behavior during the early phase of a relationship. Branding is quite "magnetic" and often draws a person in and lends the narcissist tremendous credibility, solely on the basis of the myth of the brand with little regard for his behavior.

So much of the courtship ritual in our culture is based on "branding." Most dating websites and relationship-advice books break relationship-seeking into a "list" of variables that significantly skew towards external characteristics or requirements, such as jobs, salary, address, religion, height, weight, hobbies, and eye color. Dating websites, Tinder, and social media rarely inquire about feelings, empathy, or an inner world. The narcissist is not wired to do that kind of inner work, and in a world of external valuation, they play a great early game. By the time most people awaken to the emptiness, neglect, coldness, detachment, and disconnection of the relationship with a narcissistic partner, they are often too invested and will keep working at it and destroying themselves in the process. You may have also become rather accustomed to the material comforts that come with this relationship.

Branding also plays into the fairy tales and expectations of our society. Our narratives around relationships are often focused on external attributes: what he does, the size of the ring, the places you travel, what he looks like. It's easier to "sell" an ostensibly successful, wealthy, or attractive new partner to your family and friends than it is someone who may not have the titles and the "brand" but who is kind, gentle, and respectful. A standing joke I have with others in my field is that if the protagonist in *Fifty Shades of Grey* had been an unemployed hot guy living in his mother's basement, odds are that she would not have succumbed to degradation and hanging from his ceiling.

WE'RE OFF TO SEE THE WIZARD . . .

People with narcissism are impresarios—they are showmen and often quite inspirational. It is so easy to fall under their charismatic sway and their vision. In that way, they often feel like cult leaders (cult leaders are notoriously narcissistic and employ their charm, charisma, passion, and vision to draw large groups of people close and then control them). In his book *Dangerous Personalities*, Joe Navarro lays out the traits of cult leaders, and while they exert their influence on a wider stage and scale, their techniques are experienced just as profoundly by individual people in narcissistic relationships. When you look at cult leaders and impresarios, such as Jim Jones (Guyana), Marshall Appelwhite (Heaven's Gate), Warren Jeffs (the polygamist cult leader), and Bikram Choudhury (disseminator of Bikram Yoga, also known as Hot Yoga), you observe that they draw people into their orbits through the usual narcissistic traits of grandiosity, arrogance, and control but also that they often ply their influence through sexuality, offering "magical" solutions, and communicating that they are somehow chosen or special. It is this "visionary" piece that can encourage people to destroy their lives to come into the inner circle of these cult leaders. In fact, the victims of these hypnotic people will often feel "guilty" or "ungrateful" for not embracing the cult leader's willingness to draw them close.

While most pathological narcissists are obviously not cult leaders, this visionary, almost magical element can be what draws individuals into relationships with narcissists. By being with someone who talks so much about being special, it can leave you feeling special.

It's an Old Story

The story of how you got into a relationship with a narcissist began long before you ever met your partner. When we choose a romantic partner, or are enraptured by someone new, some ancient scripts and themes are activated for us. One pattern that arose repeatedly with my clients and in the interviews I conducted for the book was that the vast majority of people who wound up in a relationship with a narcissist had at least one narcissistic parent. Having a narcissistic parent is an early manifestation of a phenomenon termed by some as "co-narcissism." Alan Rappoport describes this as unconsciously adapting to and supporting the narcissistic patterns of another person. He argues that this pattern starts in childhood, with the child having to adjust and calibrate to the narcissistic parent.

Narcissistic parents are not tuned into their children, and the narcissistic parent largely views the child as an object with which to satisfy his or her needs. Narcissistic parents will be overly indulgent and intrusive about some things and detached and uninterested in others. Children in these situations often believe life is unpredictable and strive hard to please "unpleasable" and distracted parents. If you grow up like this, you learn that you are valued for what you did, but only if it was aligned with your parent's wants and needs. It can be a confusing way to grow up and also the perfect set-up for accepting narcissistic behavior as "normal" and then tolerating it from a partner or in other close relationships. One could argue that a person with narcissistic parents may even seek out these kinds of relationships.

Odds are that if you are in this kind of relationship, you may have had a narcissistic parent, or perhaps a parent that you felt you had to impress in order to get attention, regard, or love. You learned early in the game to please others, to do whatever you could to suit the needs of others, and to deny your own needs in the name of your parents or other significant caregivers. Narcissism then starts to feel familiar and, in a twisted way, almost comforting.

In addition, another theme that often gets highlighted in the partners of narcissists is "self-esteem"—the idea that only a person with low self-esteem would choose or stay with such a partner. Not true. First of all, self-esteem isn't all that it's cracked up to be. Self-esteem is a tricky term that means many different things. Interestingly, sometimes people with "high self-esteem" are often full of bluster and bravado but can lack insight or self-awareness. (Certainly, our modern culture of parenting, which involves giving trophies to every child and shielding them from every disappointment, is contributing to an ongoing culture of self-esteem without substance). Those labeled as low self-esteem are sometimes less likely to pound their chests and talk loudly about their accomplishments, but they also tend to be more careful in their social interactions. So perhaps these people with "low self-esteem" who put up with the narcissistic partner's carelessness and neglect are just a little less likely to cut and run, and because these folks with low self-esteem tend to be more self-reflective, they may be more likely to be circumspect and forgiving with their partners, which to the outside world makes them look like a narcissist's doormat.

These are complicated relationship patterns, and sometimes it may be traits such as compassion that draw people into narcissistic relationships. A simple write-off to "low self-esteem" can oversimplify this nuanced landscape. I do think that many times people who choose narcissistic partners are often less aware of their own inherent value as a human being (and this can be because of their family history or other life experiences), but other factors, including culture, religion, societal pressures, and expectations, may also contribute to their decision.

The Myth of Chemistry

The myth of "chemistry" not only explains why people get into these relationships initially but also why they last. In some ways, it makes no sense. If you put your hand on a hot stove, you get burned. Thus, you never put your hand on the hot stove again. This simple lesson does not seem to apply with narcissists; despite getting burned, you keep putting your hand on the stove.

Chemistry is the modern, but also traditional, buzzword in relationships. Open a magazine, relationship website, or watch any form of media, and the headlines will be about finding chemistry, keeping chemistry, or creating chemistry. Chemistry implies magic and alchemy—human fireworks that have been extolled in poetry, literature, music, and film. Chemistry and "magic" can become the rationale for moving across the globe, taking major risks, and turning your world upside down.

Dr. Pamela Regan, author of *The Mating Game* and renowned relationship scholar, has observed that the literature on attraction is pretty clear: This thing we call "chemistry" may actually be "familiarity." We are in fact wired to prefer the familiar rather than the unfamiliar (familiar = safe, unfamiliar = scary). It is for this reason that we often continue making the same relationship mistakes over and over again. If you come from a world and a childhood in which you had to keep doing things to win over your parents who could not be won over, then you are going to find yourself a partner who treats you the same way. It is familiar. You may be jumping through different hoops than when you were a child. But you are still jumping through hoops.

In *The Mating Game*, Regan notes that neurotransmitters (which are in fact chemicals, so maybe that is the "chemistry") also play a role in passionate love. She cites the work of renowned anthropologist and relationship researcher Helen Fisher, who observes that passionate love is associated with high levels of do-pamine and norepinephrine and low levels of serotonin. In some studies, people who were in the early phase of "falling in love" had serotonin levels comparable to those with psychiatric disorders, such as obsessive compulsive disorder. A study by Fisher and her team using a neuroimaging technique called functional magnetic resonance imaging showed increased activity in dopamine-rich areas of the brain when those in love saw a picture of their beloved. So while there is some chemistry (and this may explain why we feel like we are "going crazy" when we fall in love), this still raises the question of why we keep returning to the same patterns, especially when those patterns are not healthy. These initial neurotransmitter bumps don't tend to stick around for long.

So let's look at the idea of familiarity. Long-term relationships are about patterns. We fall into interaction patterns that repeat themselves and are not amenable to change (in couple's therapy we attempt to change patterns in communication, expectations, and behaviors, and it can be difficult to accomplish). If a relation-ship is healthy and involves partners who listen and empathize, then most of these long-term patterns are healthy and continue to promote and sustain the well-being of the people in the relation-ship over time. Maybe the relationship will need a tweak here and there to clean things up, but by and large it will work. Partners in these healthy relationships cooperate, collaborate, communicate, and create mutually beneficial outcomes. Over time they grow and evolve.

This mutually beneficial pattern is not going to take place if you have a narcissistic partner. Just like in any relationship, the interaction patterns repeat over time, but in this case, the broken patterns repeat. These broken and dysfunctional patterns then erode at your health because they are not beneficial for you (they *are* beneficial for your narcissistic partner, however). Because these patterns are so familiar (they may be consistent with how you grew up), the familiarity keeps you in the game. We like familiarity—even when it hurts.

People in these dysfunctional relationship cycles with narcissists become aware that their relationships are not healthy. There are lots of flare-ups and even moments when they feel ready to get out, but typically they get sucked back in. An oft-cited reason for why they return to the narcissist is "chemistry." Their defense for going back to their narcissistic partner is that "no one makes me feel this way" (to which my typical retort is "thank goodness, given how bad you are feeling"). Or they talk about the chemical "draw." Because there is no real rational reason for signing up for ongoing maltreatment, people who keep going back into these relationships will base their decision on something more metaphysical, such as chemistry. This so-called chemistry is likely familiarity, not just the familiarity of the relationship but also the familiarity of being treated badly in a relationship—an ancient familiarity that resembles early patterns in their lives.

On the flip side, I have frequently observed that for too many people, upon meeting a potential partner who is kind, attentive, empathic, requires little validation, and is respectful and compassionate, the complaint is "we have no chemistry." It is pretty clear that the so-called "lack of chemistry" that so many people may feel with that nice man or nice woman is simply a lack of familiarity. Lack of familiarity with the idea that quiet, empathic, and kind can feel good. Lack of familiarity with not jumping through hoops, or fixing the other person or rescuing them—it is not familiar and it is therefore written off as "lack of chemistry."

In my experience with people in narcissistic relationships, especially the on-again–off-again roller coasters, chemistry is often touted as a reason for putting up with the abuse, for going back, for staying in, or for getting in. Chemistry becomes the mysterious excuse: "This is once-in-a-lifetime magic, that is why it is so complex"; "No one has ever made me feel like this before"; "It's the best sex I have ever had"; "He makes me feel alive." When I hear these grandiose platitudes, I become concerned, because what I hear next is often lots of peaks and valleys—and dramatic shows of emotion. And hurt.

A particularly enticing characteristic offered in the narcissistic relationship is the chronic sense of rejection. The sense that you are always on the verge of being shown the door. The rejection may be the familiar rejection of your parents. The dynamic of having to please all the time and run around in circles to get them to notice you, or never feeling like you are enough, is familiar and it likely started young. When that familiarity gets turned on in adulthood by a rejecting partner, it is strangely comforting—like a moment of déjà vu—which can make it feel almost magical. That old song of rejection is so familiar that we cannot get it out of our head. It is irrational, and because it is "magical" or chemical, the irrationality gets romanticized.

Many people make many big mistakes in the name of chemistry. Enduring ongoing poor treatment in a relationship is the most common. Reflect back on your most "chemical" relationships. They go in one of two directions. Either they were (a) very familiar—perhaps narcissistic rejection that was similar to what you experienced with your parents—or they were (b) very forbidden, a smack back at your parents of origin—an act of rebellion—but you were still making a choice in response to old patterns. Either way, it wasn't really chemistry but either familiarity or rebellion. It can take a few rides at the rodeo with a narcissist to let go of this myth of "chemistry" in favor of the reality of respect, comfort, empathy, and kindness. It may not be butterflies and palpitations, but those symptoms are more likely the activation of ancient (and likely dysfunctional) scripts, rather than something timeless and magical (despite what the poems and dysfunctional love songs say).

For those of you who are Jane Austen fans, think about *Sense and Sensibility*. Marianne Dashwood falls for the narcissistic, handsome, and opportunistic John Willoughby, and after fate lends a hand and she loses him, she quietly falls in love with the kind and steady Colonel Brandon, whom she originally found boring and stodgy. Sometimes the good guys and gals get their opportunity once a person has already been through the wringer with a narcissist. After a person experiences the scorpion's sting, the comfort of a kind person can become a soft and loving place to land.

Pop culture and love songs, in particular, can contribute to our belief that love is all about chemistry and insanity. *Crazy, Crazy Love, Crazy Little Thing Called Love,* and *Crazy for You*. Love songs are never called *Sane, Respectful Love, Reasonable Thing Called Love, Circumspect about You, Let's Be Mindful,* or *I Love Mutuality*. That "crazy," new, special, unique, all-encompassing, obsessive, distracting feeling is exciting and makes us feel alive. Crazy passion is fun, unforgettable, and poetic. However, if it devolves into disrespect, don't use chemistry or craziness as an excuse for enduring it.

If you are fortunate, (and I mean very fortunate), you get the chemistry (or the magic, or the bolt of lightning) AND the collaboration and mutuality, too. Chemistry does not mean you are in a relationship with a narcissistic partner, not at all. Some people really do have that deeply connected and exciting feeling with a partner who treats them well, as well as the comfortable familiarity of companionship. They got it right and they are a combination of wise, lucky, and may simply come from a place where they looked for a connected and respectful partner. It is when you are enduring careless, neglectful, unkind, and disconnected words and behavior from a partner, and falling back on "chemistry" as the rationale, that you need to take a long hard look at the idea of chemistry as a factor that may be imprisoning you in a one-sided, narcissistic relationship.

Jackpots and Unpredictability

A great way to understand how you were pulled in is to reflect on the magic of a slot machine. You can witness hypnotized hordes mindlessly pouring in hard-earned cash in hopes of a jackpot. Sound familiar?

Slot machines suck us in because they are unpredictable. Slot machines are on a variable reinforcement schedule: Because it is not predictable, it is sort of exciting and you fall into the trap of *maybe this time.* . . . Behavioral psychologists will tell you that it is the hardest type of reinforcement pattern to break. You don't know when they will pay out, but when they do, it can be BIG. It is usually small, but the little payouts keep you in the game. Simply put, slot machines run on hope.

Sometimes after 40 pulls with no payout, a person sticks it out because they think number 41 will be the winner. This is powerful because we do not know when they will pay out, and because the potential for a big reward is there, we stick it out—often to tremendous financial cost, wasted time, and other opportunities missed (because we were too busy waiting for the slot machine to pay out). Imagine a slot machine that consistently paid out, and every fifth time you pull the handle, you get a dollar back. That is going to get boring fast, even if you break even or come out a few dollars ahead. If you know the slot machine will give you five dollars after every fifth dollar you put into it, you will play it for about five minutes.

What does this have to do with your relationship? Everything. Relationships with narcissists are the ultimate intimate slot machine. They sweep you off your feet (as they do), and you envision the big payout with them. And, especially early on, you get enough small and big jackpots (the guy is attentive, he takes you on a vacation, he introduces you to his friends, he buys you gifts, he talks about a future) that you know that the triple jackpots are going to show up in a moment. So you keep putting money into the machine and overlook the fact that for each super lovely thing he did there were dozens of disappointments and dismissals (in other words, times when you put the money in and nothing came out). But those occasional payouts keep you coming back to the machine.

You keep thinking, *this is it, this day (this slot pull), he gets it now, he will never cheat again, he will be nice to my friends, he will be on time, he won't lie, he will help me with the kids, he will support my new career idea, he will listen, it will all work out.* So you stick it out. After all, you already put so much money into this machine (emotional energy), it has to pay out. You aren't going to walk away, because what if the next person comes around and pulls the handle and hits the jackpot (the next woman he dates get the engagement ring)? A slot machine that pays out consistently every time you put money into it might get dull, perhaps like a kind, empathic person who is always there for you. It may not be about big jackpots after all, but rather about loving mutual regard, which is in fact the greatest jackpot of all.

A slot machine is a machine, and by definition it does not have empathy and does not recognize what you need or what you are asking of it. People are supposed to. Unpredictable reinforcement, not getting rewarded or even recognized most of the time, but getting it some of the time, and the hope for more, keep people in.

Unpredictability is hypnotic and seductive. Remain aware of that before you succumb too deeply to a sucker bet.

The Back Story

Another common way to get trapped in a narcissist's web is through his or her back story. Because they are manipulative, narcissists know how to spin a tale that will elicit your sympathy, make you want to help them, and also make it harder for you to criticize them or express your disapproval regarding certain behaviors. Common excuses include:

- He had a tough mother who ignored him and was depressed.
- Her father abandoned the family when she was 12.
- Her dad had affairs and her mother never got over it.
- His father was a drunk and a psychopath.
- His first wife cheated on him with his best friend.
- Her boyfriend was killed in a motorcycle accident.
- It's his culture—men are never accountable in his culture.

These are all great causes, sad stories, and likely to be true. These sad stories of yore can often become the ultimate "get out of jail free card." People write an excuse around the back story (and we will talk about narratives later in this section). The narcissistic partner's back story is frequently cited as a reason you kept trying to fight for the relationship. The back story often left you wanting to "rescue" him and to fix his past.

The history of the narcissist, which is often littered with complex family histories, can lead you to write excuses for decades. It also leaves you jousting at windmills. Remember, the past no longer exists; you can't beat it back. But when you have an "explanation" for his bad behavior, you can push back on the explanation, and try to address it, which is easier than pushing back directly on the bad behavior. You keep writing excuses instead of addressing the behavior that is taking a toll on you. Quite often you feel that he is "misunderstood." As his partner, you have heard more of his story than most, and as a result, when your friends berate you for putting up with your partner's bad behavior, you often fall into the belief that your partner was misunderstood. This belief can leave you feeling more protective of him, and fighting harder for your relationship than before.

Many times, knowing that factors from the past may be shaping current behavior, we feel guilty about taking a hard-line stance on bad behavior. In one case, a woman had a husband who was extremely controlling and insecure. His father had abandoned the family in a very public way. The husband wound up becoming successful and wealthy in his chosen profession, and as such was often able to "purchase" fidelity and loyalty from others. He monitored his wife's comings and goings around the clock. Whenever she felt like she couldn't tolerate it, she would re-frame it as "his insecurity, caused by his father's abandonment, and he must be afraid I will abandon him," so she endured this obsessive behavior, because she wanted to show him that she would never abandon him. Playing armchair psychologist was a noble attempt to understand the chaos in which she was living, but in the process it took a terrible toll on her and her health.

It plays into the rescue fantasy of "if I could just love him enough, and he could see how *good* my love is," then the tragedy of mom, dad, first wife, mean ex-girlfriend will evaporate and he will turn into the sweetheart I glimpsed in the early days of our relationship together.

The Shifting Sands

Narcissists are, by definition, unpredictable. This can be why you were drawn in (because they always lead with their strong suit) and why it all becomes very confusing very quickly. Once upon a time (when he was trying to win you over), it was about the seduction, and he would get it right. Gifts, phone calls, lists of music that made him think of you, weekends away. It is gratifying for him because you enjoy this (and he does as well), you are grateful, you praise him, and you believe that while it may not be larger than life for the rest of your days, it will be loving and attentive. And then it is not.

The shift from attentive to disengaged can be hurtful and confusing. It can often lead you to fight harder to bring back the "good old days" of your early courtship. Again, most people have much more excitement in the early days of the relationship, but then that trails off into more quiet routine companionship but still remains attentive. Passionate love is not sustainable, or as Pamela Regan notes, people would die of exhaustion and neglect everything else in their lives if they attempted to keep the passionate love phase of the relationship operating indefinitely. Over time it transitions into companionate love, which is gratifying, mutual, and healthy. With a narcissist it really can shift from "game on" to "rain delay" in a matter of weeks or months. At this point, you may find yourself becoming shrill, naggy, and feel almost dependent, as you try to get him to notice you.

Another shift is that narcissists often start looking like the Greek god Janus—with two faces. There will be the face they show to the world—still the cool, hip, happy, successful guy—and then the grumpy, discontent, irritable, moody guy who comes home from work full of complaints. The dynamic then becomes figuring out ways to please them, praise them, appease them, soothe them, and have the happy partner at home, too. What is even more destabilizing is that everyone sees your partner as a great, exciting, fun person, because they are getting that different version. It can make it hard to not only drum up support and empathic listeners but also can leave you doubting yourself because you cannot be the only one who sees the "mean" partner.

It is not uncommon for relationships with narcissists to be "on again, off again." His behavior can become so intolerable that it reaches a fever pitch, and you step back. Sometimes, there is a precipitating event—an affair, too many missed school plays, an argument about your work, or just the piling up of neglect. He leaves, you leave, or you kick him out, but he soon realizes that other people aren't putting up with his bad behavior, so he comes back. For you, after a few weeks of being free from the neglect and lack of empathy, and all the rest of it, you forget, and then return to that compassionate place of remembering how hard "abandonment" is for him or reflecting on your chemistry together, and you take him back.

And the cycle begins again.

The Culture of Narcissism

We cannot let our culture off the hook. I strongly believe the developmental theories of narcissism explain the lion's share of the "why" of narcissism. But there are enough people who do not have these origins who still end up in this narcissistic place. Culture is the gasoline that fuels this fire. Narcissism is a socially useful trait. Unlike agrarian societies, industrial societies don't really require that much cooperation; you do your job, you make your money, and other people don't have to matter. In a world where success is largely indexed by the size of a house or the size of a bank account or the power of a job title, narcissism becomes reinforced and external characteristics are developed to the detriment of internal ones. We do little in terms of our educational system around values and ethics, spending more time on SAT preparation or standardized tests than teaching the difference between right and wrong. The one-sidedness of interacting with an electronic device or a social media site means that we can use a smile "emoji" to communicate emotion and logoff mid-conversation. An entire generation is growing up with less and less emotional reciprocity with live human beings and a subsequent lack of having to deal with real emotions with real people in real time. We tune into television programs that lay out lavish lifestyles or attention-seeking rather than the quiet accomplishments of ordinary human beings. The corporate models in the global economy value profit above all else, including human rights: entitlement is rewarded, empathy becomes inefficient, and the trait of narcissism becomes societally valued.

The narcissism that develops via our steady cultural diet of "more, more, more" or that may evolve in the face of wealth often feels like "acquired narcissism." Making money in our culture is facilitated by narcissism; free market capitalism is not built on empathy. Surviving in a corporate structure and excelling in a competitive market is fostered by the myriad traits included in narcissism. In fact, one might argue that while narcissism may create short-term success or success for the individual alone, the erosion of relationships and betrayals of trust ultimately are not good for organizations or people, and these narcissist leaders often lead their organizations (and themselves) right into the ground. Does this mean that all successful people are narcissists? Absolutely not. Are the probabilities higher? Yes.

Paul Piff, an assistant professor of psychology and social behavior at the University of California, Irvine, has conducted a series of studies in which he basically found that people who are higher on the social or financial hierarchy are more likely to cheat, lie, and behave in ways that could be viewed as unethical. Interestingly, he observed that drivers of luxury cars were more likely to cut off other drivers and not yield to pedestrians. His work and similar lines of research suggest that entitlement, wealth, and lack of empathy hang together, and that the wealthy are less likely to face consequences for their unethical behavior. (This does not bode well for courtship since the rich guy often gets the girl but is also more likely to behave unethically). In addition, once wealth is acquired, so too is privilege, and a certain ease in getting through the world. Chronic exposure to a first-class world and the expectations that accompany it are likely to result in entitlement and some grandiosity. Social graces, compassion, and manners become less of a requirement to get your needs met, and people are hired to meet the needs of the wealthy. As such, acquired narcissism may also bleed over into intimate relationships with less mindfulness about things like feelings and being present.

Then there is the larger issue of culture itself. Around the world, different cultures socialize people differently. Whether this occurs through a caste system, which arbitrarily labels people as "better" or "worse" on the basis of birth and family, or differential valuation of people on the basis of gender or skin color or sexual orientation or economic status, culture can shape this significantly. This is often most pronounced as a function of gender in many cultures. Patrilineal and patriarchal cultures (power and name handed down through men) reward men simply by dint of being men. This is pronounced in certain cultures, for example India, much of Asia, and the Middle East, in which the entitlement of gender can result in little insight among men who operate on the basis of a presumed superiority, which the culture has reinforced from the day they were born. This generally does not work well when these men are removed from their cultures of origin and placed in more egalitarian cultures in which anatomy does not always translate into respect, and their entitlement and lack of empathy can be experienced and interpreted as narcissism. In Latin cultures, the concept of "machismo" has a similar flavor, and Latina women have said to me that what they once labeled "machismo" may actually be a culturally maintained narcissism.

The temptation is to let someone off the hook when it is a by-product of culture. That's a fine stance, but if you are the partner of someone who originates from a culture where his (or her) status in that culture permitted the development of narcissistic characteristics, writing it off to culture does not necessarily make the unkind treatment you receive any easier.

A student of mine recently debated with me and asked, "Wouldn't narcissism be valuable from a Darwinian perspective?" Basically, asking the question, "Isn't it a useful trait?" Yes, it is. To a degree. The simple Darwinian win of getting a mate and reproducing is going to be maximized for people who have "more." We human beings have evolved a bit beyond our primate cousins. A purely evolutionary view does not account for what we know about the value of authenticity, self-regulation, discipline, loyalty, and community. But the student had a good point—from an evolutionary perspective, the narcissist actually has the best plumage and appears to be the best mate. Carrie Haslam and Tamara Montrose's research suggests that the reproductively promising traits demonstrated by the narcissist make them very tempting. But in our big evolved brains, the feathers only last so long, and we want something more from our partners than food, a nice cave, and more babies. Once the feathers are folded up or have fallen out again, there is no more plumage, and we come to find out there are also no feelings, empathy, or respect.

So whether it is a combination of negating early environments, lack of mirrors, power imbalances, a skewed culture, culture of origin, or evolution, knowing the origins of narcissism can be helpful (though not that helpful after the fact). Understanding the back story may provide a context, and perhaps even some compassion toward your partner. Yes, our pasts do define us, more than we would like, or as Kierkegaard has said "Life can only be understood backwards; but it must be lived forwards."

Narcissistic Supply

I am not enough. Most of us are not comfortable with ourselves. It is a sad statement on how we are socialized. Perhaps it is an adherence to codes of conduct that reward us for being self-effacing (for example, *pride goeth before a fall*). Most people tend to lack that ability to exhale and say "I'm just fine." As such, we often feel we need to rationalize our existences, usually by doing something that feels "important." Our inner worlds are devalued, because others cannot directly observe them. Bring home straight A's, good; spend time thinking about how to solve a problem, not useful unless it yields something. Now, for most people, this lack of comfort with themselves is just a few little neurotic things (I tend to be shy, I wish my hair was longer), but we settle into ourselves and are okay with that. However, many people remain "do-ers." Doing things to make up for their belief that they themselves are "not enough."

This can be damaging in the relationship space, because a healthy relationship should not require that much "doing." Or whatever "doing" there is comes naturally. Collaboration, respect, mutuality, shared values, and kindness are not really activities or tasks—they are ways of being. However, too often if we aren't "doing" there is a risk of boredom; this is particularly pronounced in younger people. In the early phase of a relationship, courtship is characterized by "doing"—gift giving, devising creative dates, finding new restaurants, and just discovering a new person. With time, in the presence of mutuality, the need to "do" starts fading away, and the day-to-day beneficence of a relationship kicks in. Ideally.

In relationships when your partner is not engaging in a mutual way, and you feel that the only way to keep the relationship afloat and to keep your partner content is to keep *doing* things—stay fit, look good, clean the house, make his life easy, buy her things— then that becomes your pattern. In addition, you may need to be yet another bringer of admiration into your partner's life telling him, "you are so attractive/smart/successful/sexy/cool/awesome."

All this stuff you need to bring, day after day after day, can be labeled *narcissistic supply*. It is as though you are a cargo ship, delivering supplies, ranging from validation to admiration to groceries day in and day out. Think of it as a cargo ship that keeps coming into the harbor. The tough aspect of narcissistic supply is that for the narcissist it is never enough. The narcissist is like a bucket with a hole in the bottom: No matter how much you put in, you can never fill it up. The phrase "I never feel like I am enough" is the mantra of the person in the narcissistic rela- tionship. That's because to your narcissistic partner, you are not. No one is. Nothing is.

So you keep accumulating narcissistic supply and bringing it to your partner. For months, years, or decades. It is exhausting, but it gives you something to do—and that is often what keeps you on the hook. The erroneous belief then becomes, *If I deliver enough supplies often enough, then all will be well or things will get better. If things are not going well, then I will deliver more supply.* In the process of doing this, you stop taking care of yourself, and you yourself become narcissistic supply and become depleted, wracked with self-doubt, and ultimately exhausted. This cargo ship tends to be a one-way venture, delivering imports into a port that offers no exports, and your ship leaves the narcissist's harbor empty time and time again.

What is even crueler about the concept of narcissistic supply is the fact that over time it gets stale. Like food in a warehouse. After years or decades of providing it, your narcissist may start looking for other suppliers. These may be family members, friends, mistresses, flirty co-workers, or underlings in the workplace. As your supply gets stale, you will often feel that no matter how much you do, the fresh new supply that other people bring is judged as somehow "better" by your narcissistic partner. It can be a harrowing feeling after doing it for years, and then having it dropped in favor of others (or if your supply is devalued or not welcomed in the same way it once was).

Psychologically healthy human beings nourish themselves from the inside. They do not "need" supply, and other people in their worlds should not be in the role of having to serve them that way. By thinking about it in terms of narcissistic supply, however, you may get some insight into why this relationship has been so exhausting for you as well as your partner's tendency to look outside of you to get his needs met. It is never enough.

The Narrative

People love telling stories. It is what we do, and it may be the most ancient of human pursuits. We tell them, we watch them, and we read them. In some ways, we need them.

Narratives become dangerous when they start running our lives or act as a barrier to seeing a truth. Every day, dozens of times per day, we write narratives about our lives. These narratives become the way we organize our worlds and are also the things we tell ourselves to get through our days. In that way, narratives can sometimes be a tool for coping and a way to extract meaning from challenging situations. Take a moment and reflect on the narratives you have written in your life—about your childhood, your career, your relationships, and yourself.

The challenge of narrative is that it can sometimes distract us from the authentic truth of a situation. An oft-cited "folk wisdom" is that "people tell themselves what they need to hear to get through the day." That is a simple way of saying that you take the facts and knit them into a bearable story to survive. The narrative can be how you use a narcissist's back story to take him off the hook. How you rationalize the bad behavior in the name of the beautiful lifestyle you have achieved. How you truly believe that in your fairy tale a single kiss will transform the frog, and the beast will finally be appeased. You write a narrative around a happily ever after (once he retires, once he gets the promotion, once the kids are grown) that never materializes.

Narratives can also explain how you got in, why you stayed in, and what you may do next. They reflect the traits that drew us in, they account for myths and misconceptions, such as chemistry, they account for the "rescue" fantasy (more on this in Chapter 6), and they allow us to make sense of the challenging landscape of the relationship with a narcissistic personality. The greatest challenge comes from taking an honest look at your narrative and allowing new ideas into that narrative.

The most dangerous narratives are those that are fictional, or an attempt to connect dots that create a distorted picture. I have repeatedly heard people say, "I think I fell out of love with him long ago, but I just love the *idea* of this relationship." As you write or reflect on your narrative, figure out how much this is about the person and your true regard for him versus the entity called this relationship. It can be quite easy to love and fight for a relationship— it's a place to hang your hat, to call home, an image to the world, a shared future—but because it is an "entity," it is also easier to gloss over its faults than when you are talking about an individual person. A relationship can become a "higher order" construct, like religion, that we adhere to and rarely question. Many times, people simply want the relationship, and the narrative becomes about the relationship rather than about their partner (because if your partner is pathologically narcissistic, it is not a pleasant narrative). However, if you focus on the relationship, then it is easier to make the relationship about events, places, activities, possessions, and other inert factors that you can view from a distance and that cannot reject or hurt you. In that way, a narrative can imprison you because you get stuck in the hopeful fiction and an unrealized future.

Armed with the knowledge that your narcissist will never change, how does that impact your narrative? What does that mean for how you think about it? What does it mean for staying? For leaving? The remainder of the book will focus on the two scenarios: staying and leaving. There is no right answer—and it may change and shift.

The Book of You

Each of us has a *Book of Me*. I have a *Book of Ramani*, my sister has a *Book of Padma,* and you have a *Book of You*. Our Books are the story of each of us, our personal gospel. If such a book existed, it would lay out your preferences, fears, vulnerabilities, hopes, wants, needs, values, and world view and provide another person with information on how to understand you (imagine being able to hand it over on the first date!). One person may acknowledge that after a fight she needs to be held. Another person might need to take a walk. Yet another may be terrified of being alone.

Imagine if you could read the *Book of Someone* and then make decisions accordingly? In life, it doesn't work like that (thank goodness). The early period of a relationship is when we become acquainted with this *Book* of _____. The early weeks and months (and even years) are when we learn how our new partner responds to stress, anger, and fear, we learn their vulnerabilities and strengths, and we teach them the same about us. The challenge is that too often we edit this book in a way that makes us look "better" or different than who we really are (because too many people want to be someone different than they are and eschew all of their fears and vulnerabilities). The fact is, sometimes our books are misunderstood, and no matter how hard we try to explain it to another person, he doesn't get it (like that difficult book you had to read in 10th grade English). Or he doesn't want to read it closely enough to understand it. We are all guilty of doing this at times. Most of the time, when I have worked with couples or talked with couples, the people in the relationship will acknowledge that their partner does not always "get" their book or that they chronically misinterpret it.

The challenge is that not everyone is transparent about their books. This is usually for reasons of shame or fear of rejection (if she really reads my book, then she will run away). Many times people will not even engage in the self-reflection of familiarizing themselves with their own books. In some ways, the book of the narcissist is pretty clear to an outsider—*I am grandiose, I am controlling, I am not going to listen, I lack empathy*—but a person with narcissism is also a distinct individual and will have personalized fears, vulnerabilities, habits, and strengths. The difficulty is that we try to edit the other person's book, or ignore it outright (for example, if you know your partner does not like attending social events where he is unfamiliar with other people, why would you be surprised when he is downtrodden or irritable after such an event? You know what the *Book of Him* says, why would it change?).

In a healthy relationship, you edit and modify your own books when you bring someone into your heart or life. You may start to watch football, begin hiking, get a puppy, change religions, move, or become more patient. You also learn that there are some "no-fly" issues for your partner, and adjust your behavior accordingly—and ideally your partner does the same. It's a gradual process of learning, compromise, and growth. And sometimes you cannot align your books enough (for example, one person wants a child and another does not) and it can mean the end of the relationship.

While *Should I Stay or Should I Go?* is meant to be a survival manual for the territory of the narcissist, it is also meant to be a wake-up call. Are you willing to awaken an honest rendering of your *own* book? What does your book say? How do you respond to love? To stress? To fear? To hope? What are your needs and wants? What are your vulnerabilities and what are your strengths? What do you expect from your partner? From a relationship? From life? What is your partner's book? What patterns has he already shown that have given you a clear look into the *Book of Him (or Her)*?

Take the time to explore the *Book of You* and be honest about it. Can your needs be meaningfully met in this relationship? What are you willing to edit out of your book to make this relationship work, and are there things you cannot change? Then think about the book of your partner. You already know what his book says, if you are willing to be open to it. To have an honest relationship, you have to start by being honest with yourself about your own book and your partner's as well.

Here is the bottom line on how you likely got in, and why you remain in: A person with narcissistic traits or narcissistic personality disorder is a human being. If they were truly ogres, you wouldn't have gone in. You may be sorting through the wreckage of it all, or still trying to figure it out. The humane and humanistic thing to do is to see your partner as a "whole" person. That *does not* mean, however, that you have to be his social worker or savior. You are not responsible for his histories, and you cannot rewrite them. For your own health and well-being, do the compassionate thing and recognize him as a whole person. However, for your own sanity, don't try to fix him. Now it is time for next steps: figuring out what to do. The first step in the process is recognizing how the narcissist in your life makes you feel. It's important to acknowledge if you regularly feel anxious, unsettled, depressed, or hopeless. The next chapter will help you to sort through those feelings and will illustrate some common patterns you may find yourself engaging in, such as making excuses, isolating yourself from others, or constantly fearing disappointment.

CHAPTER 5

HOW DO THEY MAKE YOU FEEL?

One can be the master of what one does, but never of what one feels.

—FLAUBERT

isting narcissistic traits is a way of characterizing *another* person. It's a description, and if someone spent enough time with the narcissist, he or she would observe the same patterns. The far more important checklist is the one that relates to you—how does the narcissist make *you* feel? Obviously, qualities such as entitlement, lack of empathy, grandiosity, neglect, and rage are not necessarily positive traits, but ultimately, in a relationship, those traits are only meaningful in terms of how they impact you. What is also significant is that your feelings likely overtook you gradually, which can often be why they are so challenging. Different people will be affected by narcissistic traits in different ways.

Common Feelings in a Narcissistic Relationship

The types of feelings that most often arise in a relationship with a pathological narcissist include the following:

- ▸ Feeling "not good enough"
- ▸ Self-doubt and second-guessing
- ▸ Chronically apologetic
- ▸ Confusion and as though you are "losing your mind"
- ▸ Helplessness and hopelessness
- ▸ Feelings of sadness or depression
- ▸ Feeling anxious and worried
- ▸ Feeling unsettled
- ▸ Anhedonia (not being able to get pleasure out of life and activities that once gave you pleasure)
- ▸ Feelings of shame
- ▸ Mental and emotional exhaustion

This can result in patterns that overtake you slowly and over time, and we'll explore those patterns a bit later in the chapter.

The concept of "mission creep" is relevant here. Mission creep is a military term, referring to unplanned changes that may occur in a military attack that result in an unplanned and longer-term commitment than originally anticipated. This can occur in a narcissistic relationship. The changes may not happen on the first date, or sometimes even within the first year; it is a slow, gradual process that creeps in and takes over. If their detachment, coldness, and neglect occurred from the very beginning, you most likely would not have remained in it. Because creep is a relatively glacial process and the wear and tear on your feelings and behavior happens gradually, you adjust to it and find yourself in a longer-term and more conflictual battle than you had intended. When a person is in a narcissistic relationship, she often learns to slowly start shutting down her feelings and emotions. It makes sense. Your feelings are being negated by your partner, or at least not being acknowledged (and sometimes even doubted), as such, the only way to keep the relationship going is to deny those feelings or at least to numb them. Narcissists are masters of projection (denying their own feelings or behavior and projecting it onto others), and this can often leave you experiencing their emptiness as well.

Many people, especially women, tend to "over-take" responsibility in certain situations, especially emotional situations. If this is your tendency, you will likely "take the blame" for conflict and will then endeavor to be the one to manage the situation, often exhausting yourself in the process. In a relationship with a narcissist this can manifest as trying to "fix" everything—*if he isn't happy, I will work harder to make him happy, I will keep the house cleaner, myself thinner, the kids quieter. I will be better.*

THE GOOD ENOUGH PARADOX

I tried everything: I talked more; I talked less. I constantly cleaned the house. I got rid of friends he did not like. I cooked. I stayed thin and got to know his friends. But yet, it always felt like I was being tested. Honestly, I now see that I really did it all, but the minute, the minute something was not perfect, that is what he would notice. It was never "thanks for everything you are doing," but rather him noticing what I did not get right. I wasted so much time and energy trying to be "perfect" and anticipating what he would want.

We are socialized to believe that if we work harder at anything, we will succeed. Study harder and get the grades, work harder and get a promotion or a raise, weed the garden every week and more flowers will grow. It's satisfying to believe that our effort will translate into results, and in many areas of our lives it does. The one area it often does not is human relationships, and the one area it will *never* work is in a relationship with a pathological narcissist. This presumption of "if I am *better*" can destroy a person in a narcissistic relationship, because it is never going to be enough. The "if" will never yield results.

The feeling of "I don't feel good enough" is the mantra of the person in a narcissistic relationship. Because obviously if you were "good enough" then your partner would be satisfied and would pay attention to you, and he would be present, emotionally available, and empathic. Since those behaviors are not happening, it must be because you are somehow lacking. The idea of "good enough" or conversely "not being good enough" is a theme that is almost universally acknowledged among people in relationships with narcissistic partners. Think about it. If you keep trying harder and harder to please someone and never really can, or can only succeed for short bursts of time, it can leave you feeling inadequate. After all, if you are expending so much effort and not achieving your goal (of pleasing your partner) then you must be doing something wrong or lacking something. Interestingly, most people don't initially recognize that perhaps it is their partner who is unpleasable.

We are all good enough. In fact, I would argue we are all more than enough. The idea of not being "enough" is usually driven by forces outside of us. When someone says, "I am not good enough," my response is, "For whom?"

"Good enough" is a feeling that plagues many people from childhood. If you have a narcissistic or distracted parent, you are left with the question of "how can I win them over?" If the child can't win over the parent, or is only valued when he or she is validating the parent, that script of "good enough" can get stuck. This can set you up for a lifetime of hoop jumping in order to prove that you are indeed good enough, fast enough, pretty enough, or smart enough.

The dynamic of "not good enough" is often experienced as inadequacy and a sense of self-blame. It surfaces in the belief that if you had certain characteristics, your partner would be satisfied. This can lead many people in narcissistic relationships to push themselves to extremes: losing weight, getting cosmetic surgery, maintaining a youthful appearance, buying new clothes, keeping the house impossibly clean, setting up luxurious vacations, making elaborate meals, purchasing expensive gifts for their partner, pursuing high status jobs or positions so their partner will value them, or purchasing a larger home than they can afford. Basically, it can result in doing things to satisfy your "unsatisfiable" partner, in hopes of getting over the hump and feeling as though you are "good enough." Many people who have been through narcissistic relationships will say that they literally gave everything they had to the point they could not try anymore. This carries a tremendous toll for the giver, who will often give of themselves to the point of exhaustion, physical health problems, loss of friends and family, and even their own sense of self. Many will recall turning into someone who they no longer recognize in order to cater to the endless needs of their partner—on a grail quest to feel like they are "enough."

Always remember, because the narcissist is empty, it will never be enough. It's not that *you* are not enough—*nothing* is enough. As we noted in the discussion on narcissistic supply, the narcissist is like a bucket with a hole in the bottom. No matter how much you pour in, it will just pour out. It will never be enough. You are more than good enough (hokey as that may sound). If you are spending a life with someone and it feels otherwise, then the *relationship* may not be enough.

THE DILEMMA OF DOUBT

The narcissist works from the inside out and this is why, over time, confidence erodes and doubt creeps in. When you are attempting to relate to someone who rarely listens or feels or cares (fundamental characteristics of a human relationship), and who regularly questions you, then you begin to question yourself. The belief that you cannot change the situation can also drive self-doubt.

It is very challenging to embrace the central message of this book – that the narcissist will never change. Intellectually, after reading these pages, you may even understand and agree with this premise, but emotionally, the rescue fantasy is often so embedded, culture can be so powerful, and love so blind, that despite knowing this, you will still persist in the futile pursuit of waiting for the narcissist to change. You may even be able to clearly observe these patterns in other people's relationships, but believe that you and your relationship are going to be the exception. As a result, you may keep trying but nothing will change. If you work hard at something and get no result, it is easy to believe that it is because of something *you* are doing (or not doing). At one level, trying various strategies can give you a sense of control, but over time it can also fill you with a sense of doubt. That doubt quickly starts to jump into other areas of your life—work, friends, family, and life in general.

CHRONICALLY APOLOGETIC

One of the patterns that accompanies self-doubt is frequent apologizing. In general, apologies are designed to be issued when you have committed a wrongdoing, even if it is not intentional (for example, *I am sorry I am late*). However, another use of the apology is to acknowledge the disappointment of the other (for example, *I am so sorry it is raining on the day of your golf game*), with full realization that you were not the cause (obviously some situations cannot be your fault—you didn't make it rain). In that case it is not an apology as much as an empathic reflection. However, narcissists are so chronically entitled and easily disappointed when anything does not skew their way that the tendency by others to apologize in their midst is constant. The "empathic apology" starts to turn into a chorus of your doubt; you begin to apologize more and more, largely because you find that you cannot satisfy your partner, and because his life is not always going to turn out the way that he wants.

CONFUSION/LOSING YOUR MIND

It is so weird. Sometimes he is so attentive—taking me away, telling me he loves me, asking me to stay at his place every night of the week. Other times he is so distant and distracted, not returning calls for eight hours at a time, making plans and never consulting me. I just wish it was consistent so I knew what I was getting. When it is distant, it is awful and I can see leaving, but when it works it is great. It is

*confusing, because just when I relax and see the potential, it changes
again to being cold and distant. It also affects my behavior and makes
me anxious—since I never quite know what I am getting.*

The confusion caused by a narcissistic partner is often directly
a by-product of their inconsistency. Many people whom I have
spoken with have said, "Listen, if he was always distant, then this
would make sense and I would know my plan of action." But to be
with someone where you feel connected one moment and then ut-
terly distant, sometimes within the span of a day, can be confusing.
To hear the words "you are the love of my life" and have him sit
down and plan a life with you and simultaneously be secretive
about you with friends and loved ones, or be unwilling to support
you in your hopes and aspirations, can be unsettling at best.

This can happen for several reasons. The emptiness of the narcissist often means that they are only focused on whatever is useful
or interesting to them at the moment. If at that moment it is interesting for them to tell you they love you, they do. It's not really a
long game to them, and when the next interesting issue comes up,
they attend to that. The objectification of others—viewing other
people as objects useful to his needs—can also play a role. When
you are the only thing in the room, or the most interesting thing
in the room, then the narcissist's charisma and charm can leave
you convinced that you are his everything. The problem is that this
is typically superficial regard, and that superficiality results in inconsistency, and emotions for the narcissistic person range from
intense to detached on a regular basis. This vacillation between in-
tensity and detachment can be observed in the narcissist's relationships with people (acquaintances, friends, family, and partners),
work, and experiences. A healthy relationship should feel like a
safe harbor in your life. Life throws us enough curve balls in the
shape of money problems, work issues, medical issues, household
issues, and even the weather. Sadly, a relationship with a narcissist
can be one more source of chaos in your life, rather than a place of
comfort and consistency.

HELPLESSNESS AND MENTAL HEALTH

Martin Seligman, a professor of psychology at the University of
Pennsylvania, developed a construct called "learned helplessness."
Learned helplessness is the idea that over time, when a person is
forced to repeatedly endure unpleasant or aversive situations from
which she cannot escape or which she cannot change, she becomes
unable (or unwilling) to avoid these ongoing aversive situations,
even if she can escape. Basically, if you learn you can't change or
avoid something, you put up with it, even when the time comes
that you can get away from it. Seligman and others believe that
this is due to both conditioning and learning. The person has
learned that she cannot control the situation and so she doesn't
even try to avoid the painful situation. The early work in this area
was conducted using animal studies in which Seligman and other
researchers observed that dogs that were not permitted to escape
shocks (from which they would normally instinctually run away)
over time passively accepted the shocks and did not move, even
when they were able to. In that way, they passively gave in, accepted their discomfort, and didn't attempt to change their fate.

Learned helplessness can place a person at risk for apathy and
depression and the belief that nothing she does will ever make
things better. Learned helplessness also has tremendous implications for why people stick it out in damaging relationships with
narcissists. If, after years of trying to communicate with someone,
to connect with someone, and to be heard by someone, nothing
happens and you are never heard, then over time, there will be the
tendency to stick around and passively accept your fate.

The argument could be made that a person in a relationship
with a narcissist is not truly "stuck" and could escape (unlike the
dogs in Seligman's research or a prisoner in a jail cell). However,
our early narratives and histories can contribute to a sense that a
relationship is forever, no matter how badly you are treated (thus,
in essence, mentally you cannot escape). Or there is the message
that if you work hard enough, and love your partner enough, that

you can turn the tide. Societal pressure tells people to "stick it out," or people live in fear that another partner won't come along. These assumptions can create "mental prisons" that can lead us to perceive that there is no escape and that we just have to accept our situation, or that nothing we do will ever improve it.

An interesting pattern that helplessness often creates is the use of e-mails in relationships. Obviously e-mails are the modern *billet doux*, and many lovers use them to send information and content as well as messages from a distance, poems, and words of passion and love. However, the other pattern is to use the e-mail as a way to express strong and conflicted feelings. I call this the "e-mail litmus test," and it is often a sign that your frustration and helplessness in being unable to communicate with your partner has devolved to a point where you have to put it down in writing, because he never listens to you, and somehow getting it down in writing may make it more clear.

In addition, because narcissistic personalities tend to be far better debaters and combatants than the rest of us, your well-rehearsed request for communication can often be pushed back and debated so skillfully that you wind up feeling like the bad guy. Narcissists, with their rather shallow emotional worlds tend to argue from a place of logic, something that can be frustrating if you are having an emotional argument (which is what many arguments in relationships consist of). In a logic-versus-emotion smackdown, logic always wins (logically), but that does not mean the issue gets resolved, and the person who is experiencing emotion during the argument is often left feeling foolish. So you write a loving and clear e-mail that is a literary and poetic wonder, because you just want to get it down and not be interrupted or debated.

When I hear about these e-mails from patients, I recognize that they are an emblem of their frustration and rarely achieve their goal. More often than not, the narcissistic partner will respond with only a short response of a few words, not respond at all, or respond to the most damning parts, and the thoughtful request or plea may simply turn into one more opportunity to experience their rage. There is no back door when someone does not or will not hear you—the e-mail may be cathartic for you, but expect no miracles. Your better bet is to write it and send it to a trusted friend. Or cast it off to sea, or burn it—just do not send it to your narcissistic partner. I have read dozens of these e-mails over the years from a variety of clients and friends. I have never seen one work. The helplessness is part of the territory, and the e-mail is a symptom but it is not likely to be a solution.

When the helplessness persists, it can descend into the far darker place of hopelessness. Hopelessness can be associated with many unhealthy and even dangerous behaviors and feelings, including depression and anxiety, withdrawal from responsibilities (work, household) and other people, unhealthy behaviors including eating badly, cutting back on exercise, irregular sleep habits, dangerous coping methods including drugs and alcohol, nonadherence with medications or lack of follow up with medical recommendations, and in extreme cases suicidal thoughts and/or behaviors. In more than half of the people I interviewed and have worked with over the years, hopelessness was a big part of the picture of a long-term relationship with a narcissistic partner, and I observed patterns including extreme weight gain, drug abuse, depression, suicidal thoughts, and even long-term psychiatric hospitalizations. Narcissistic relationships destroy people from the inside out, and these outcomes can ruin people's lives.

SADNESS, DEPRESSION AND ANXIETY

While the feelings and symptoms of depression and anxiety experienced may be due to the helplessness engendered by the relationship, these feelings can also be generated by the ongoing lack of emotional reciprocity and mirroring in the relationship. Depression is a complex disorder, but the hallmark symptoms of depression—sad mood, lack of pleasure in activities that are typically pleasurable, feelings of worthlessness and guilt, social withdrawal, poor concentration, changes in sleep and appetite—are all patterns observed in people who are in relationships with narcissistic partners. In some cases these will be low-grade symptoms that detract from overall quality of life, and in some cases they evolve into a full-blown depression that requires clinical management. The helplessness induced by the narcissistic relationship can place a person at risk for depression, and depression can also sap a person of the energy or mindset needed to face down the challenges of a narcissistic relationship. It is also easy to sink deep into this hole of depression and not seek out help. Depression is an illness that responds to treatment; do not view this as a burden to be endured.

In a similar vein, symptoms of anxiety, such as chronic worry, a sense of tension, self-doubt, restlessness, fatigue, and even physical symptoms like headaches and muscle tension are also observed in people who are in difficult relationships, especially when they feel they cannot fix it or nothing is working. When anxiety is on full throttle it can feel like panic, which can include racing heart, difficulty breathing, dizziness, and a feeling that something terrible is going to happen. Like depression, extreme anxiety is also very amenable to treatment and management, and does not have to be accepted as a part of life. The lack of a strategy, or the failure of the strategies you have used to address the challenges in your relationship with a narcissist, can be frustrating and leave you with a wide range of psychological symptoms.

FEELING UNSETTLED

No matter what I said, it was always wrong. No matter what I did, it was too soon, too fast, too little, too much. It reached the point where I was spending an inordinate amount of time composing a sentence to make sure it came out right. Then, after a little while longer, I just became anxious about seeing him, knowing that it wasn't IF I would say something wrong, it was WHEN. It's interesting—I was never in that much of a rush for those close to me to meet him. I think I knew they would be on to him. I was unsettled from the beginning, but I had been looking for a relationship for so long and having little luck. This one was sticking around, but lordy did it come with a price. I don't think I exhaled for the entire relationship.

Think back to concepts such as gaslighting, self-doubt, and "going crazy." Being with a narcissist is unsettling. They tend to fight dirty. They are inconsistent. Being with a narcissist is indeed like "walking on eggshells" (though many would argue that it is like "walking on broken glass") and it can be unsettling to be in a relationship with someone who is so disconnected. In John and Rachel's story, the slow-growing head of steam as she became more and more unsettled in the relationship was clear. For her, "something did not quite feel right." Many people I have spoken to describe this sense of being unsettled as feeling like they have a "pit in their stomach," and a chronic sense of impending doom. Things are always going wrong, there is always an argument, there is always one more disappointment. The unpredictability of these relationships can also be quite unsettling. Maintaining a constant sense of foreboding and gloom is not unusual in people who have survived a trauma. Interestingly, many people in narcissistic relationships describe a similar phenomenon.

ANHEDONIA

A key symptom of depression is something called "anhedonia," or the inability to derive pleasure from activities that typically give you pleasure. This can include work, hobbies, family and children, and daily activities. People who feel anhedonia often liken it to living life in black and white, and they feel no motivation to do anything. This sense of anhedonia is also often glimpsed in people who are in relationships with narcissists, because they feel as if "why bother?" The relationship can become so preoccupying and unsatisfying that other things in life lose their luster as well.

SHAME

There are few human emotions that lead to more bad behavior than shame. Shame is a core conflict for the narcissist—and it is an ancient one. Many times shame has early origins for them, and from a deep psychological place, their morally questionable and insensitive choices may be a response to an internal sense of shame. In addition, they cannot endure feeling shamed, so when they do something "shameful" or inappropriate and get called out on it, they often respond with extreme rage or even more bad behavior.

But shame for the other person in the relationship can often be operating in a different way. Most of us have enough insight to recognize that there are certain things in our lives that may not look optimal to the outside world. Sometimes we do things about which we are not proud, and we take ownership, learn from them, and move forward. At other times we hold back from the outside world because we do not want to be judged, or perhaps we are ashamed. A mild example of this may be touting the benefits of a healthy lifestyle to everyone, but then eating unhealthy foods on the sly. We may not order that burger in front of friends but perhaps do it alone. Because we are slightly ashamed.

The shame you may feel in a relationship with a narcissist is often something that you experience over time. You, your friends, and your family become aware that your partner's words and actions are not okay. This may happen because you share feelings or stories with them about your relationship, because you endure things that don't feel good, or because they observe these things taking place. It can feel shameful to recognize that you are being treated badly. This shame can also raise concerns about being judged for remaining in such a situation, or not addressing it, and as people in narcissistic relationships often do, you may also want to protect your partner. You may feel "ashamed" that he is being judged harshly on just a subset of his behavior (at this point you are being treated badly twice: once by your partner, and once by yourself as you attempt to work through the shame of the situation). The shame then bombards you from multiple angles: shame about putting up with bad treatment, shame about not having enough of a "backbone" to leave, shame about being perceived as weak, shame about how your partner is perceived by other people, shame about your bad choice. That's a lot of shame.

The problem is that this shame can then start leading to a more dangerous pattern—withdrawal from other people. If you feel ashamed about your relationship or how your partner is treating you, then you may not even want to have idle chitchat with friends and family who will ask you basic questions, such as "how are you and your boyfriend doing?" Lying is the "tell" of shame; if it was not shameful, you would tell the truth. But for most normal people with a conscience and an autonomic nervous system, lying does not feel good. So it becomes easier to avoid having the conversations, not wanting to explain yourself and your relationship. This becomes tricky, because for many people in relationships with narcissists, social interaction with people outside of the narcissistic relationship is so important, because it may be their only source of kindness, mirroring, and an empathic ear. When the shame leads to social withdrawal, it isolates you and leaves you more vulnerable to the emptiness of the narcissistic relationship.

People don't like bad feelings like shame. So what do we do? Like most things that don't feel good, we avoid them if we can. How do we avoid them? By not talking about them. That is another contributor to the social withdrawal and even the withdrawal from other important and useful spaces like psychotherapy. Having to talk about these feelings means that you have to *confront* them. The armchair therapists amongst your friends are often going to tell you that you do not need to put up with this and that you should just leave. As the title of this book indicates, it isn't always that simple, and for many reasons, leaving may not be an option. As such, the shame in these instances can be worse. You do feel ashamed, you don't like how you are being treated in your relationship, you don't feel like you can leave, you don't want to be told to leave, and in the midst of this confusion, you may cut yourself off from the world even further.

MENTAL AND EMOTIONAL EXHAUSTION

This is absolutely exhausting. I have never put this much effort into anything. I can't think. I can't sleep. I used to be such a fun and happy person. Now I feel exhausted all the time. I want "fun me" back.

These relationships are exhausting. Because most people in these relationships do not understand what they are experiencing, they spend most of their time "trying to figure it out." People in narcissistic relationships also find themselves having the same conversations and arguments OVER and OVER again. Finally, the patterns (as you are about to read about) never change. So people in relationships with narcissists will say "this doesn't feel fair" or that there is a chronic "double-standard." It is easy to spend lots of time obsessing about these feelings, and that means you are wasting mental bandwidth that you could be (and should be) using for other things. This exhaustion is real, and many people in relationships with narcissists will report that they are tired much of the time, are not as mentally sharp, are not keeping up at work and school, and are dropping the ball on other important responsibilities.

The Patterns

Given that the relationship makes you feel bad, you may attempt to avoid feeling this way (we do not like to feel bad, so typically we try to avoid bad feelings when possible—especially when they are chronic). It can help to reflect on some of your patterns, in order to achieve some insight into how you have been managing all of this. These "coping" patterns allow the broken narcissistic dynamic to remain in place. These are solutions you have developed over time to help survive this relationship, in response to the feelings we have discussed above. Some of the most common patterns include:

- ► Making excuses, including lying because you are ashamed but also are protecting your partner

- ▶ Difficulties with decision-making
- ▶ Frequently apologizing ("I'm sorry" becomes a mantra)
- ▶ Chronic fear of disappointment, which can translate into a fear of making plans or voicing hopes and goals
- ▶ Social withdrawal, avoiding other people and sources of support
- ▶ Numbing your emotions; this can include eating, drinking, spending, using drugs, and over-exercising

Do any of these patterns sound familiar? If you find yourself stuck in many of the above patterns, and your partner possesses the narcissistic traits that have already been laid out, then it is even more likely that you are in a relationship with a narcissist.

MAKING EXCUSES

You may find yourself making excuses as a way to neutralize the shame that you are feeling in this relationship or as a way to put a better face forward—not just to the world, but to yourself. Excuses are an extension of the narratives we already discussed in Chapter 4. Any story can be told many ways; the same story can be turned around to make the villain look like a hero. Your relationship is an investment—an investment of your time, your resources, and your emotions—and it may involve children, other family members, and finances. There is a lot to "protect," so making excuses for your partner's bad behavior becomes protective. Rachel found herself doing this regularly with John: *He's a doctor, he has a busy schedule.* It is easy to do initially, because you may even believe those early excuses: *He is busy, he is tired, I must not have been communicating as clearly as I could have been.* Over time, the manufactured reality of the excuses becomes your only reality.

There is a difference between making excuses and "being understanding." Many times I have had clients push back and say that they are not making excuses, but rather they are trying to keep perspective and understand that their husbands or wives or partners have had a difficult day and maybe are not at their best today. Obviously, that is true in part, empathy means recognizing and responding to the feelings and experience of another, as such, monitoring your responses to the feelings of another is good empathic hygiene. However, *making excuses* reflects a pattern over time, not just one bad day at the office. Making excuses involves taking similar facts and telling a story that denies your feelings while protecting your partner's. And it is a pattern that happens repeatedly, to the point that you believe the excuses more than your own feelings. Understanding is a two-way street—a street made up of compromises shared and offered by both of you. Making excuses is a strategy for surviving a lack of empathy and a long drive down a one-way road.

FIXES: MAKING EXCUSES

Be mindful and catch yourself. Take a moment and reflect on the situation at hand; before you make an excuse, think about why this happened. Be empathic, recognize both sides, but stop and catch yourself before you make an excuse.

Start keeping a record of them. On any given day, it is easy to make an excuse for someone's less-than-acceptable behavior. For example, let's imagine that you are dealing with a non-communicative partner who is chronically late. Your list of excuses may look like this:

Day 1: Late to dinner, never called. Excuse: Late meeting he could not step out of.

Day 2: Late to child's soccer game, texted afterwards. Excuse: Traffic leaving downtown.

Day 3: Would not sign documents that the two of you need to submit. Excuse: He is tired because he has a big deadline at work.

Day 4: Cancelled dinner with your out-of-town friends. Excuse: After a long week, he does not want to be social.

▼

Looking at the excuses in this example, some are practical and real but some are you anticipating difficulties in his life. Yes, sometimes a long week makes things difficult, but do not make the excuse for him. Big deadlines happen, but a signature does not take long. Sometimes we make excuses for other people, because it is easier than having to directly communicate and actually deal with their wrath and anger.

DECISION-MAKING DILEMMAS

Many people get into and stay in relationships with narcissists because of self-doubt. In addition, self-doubt will develop and grow while you are in a relationship with a narcissist. Several dynamics may play into this: being second-guessed by your partner, being ignored by your partner, or being mocked by your partner (and often all three). The self-doubt will undercut your ability to make a decision. If you doubt your ability to do something, or even your own feelings, your confidence will be eroded, and if your confidence is eroded, it will be challenging to make a decision.

William James once said "There is no more miserable human being than one in whom nothing is habitual but indecision." Indecision is an unattractive and inefficient trait. It can be quite painful to slowly become indecisive over time, or to remain decisive in some areas of your life (for example, at work) but then be plagued by constant indecision in your relationship. The inherent self-doubt that colors the relationship with a narcissist, his unpredictable behavior, and his disconnection from you (and everyone else) implies that you are often sapped of the confidence and consistency that are needed to make a decision. Narcissists themselves are often quite indecisive, because they spend their lives hedging their bets, waiting for the next best thing, and rarely committed to anything but themselves.

Being indecisive is exhausting, it is inefficient, and it can result in difficulties in your household, with your children, with your loved ones, and in your jobs or volunteer activities. It can also leave you feeling badly about yourself and augment your existing feelings of self-doubt. Because you spend much of your time in your relationship second-guessing yourself, you are going to do that in other places in your life as well (especially over time).

As you master the moving parts of a relationship with a narcissist and begin to understand how this is impacting your decision-making abilities, you will get a better handle on your waffling and perhaps start to regain command over your decision-making again. Your doubt is likely inserted in you from the outside, from your partner, and from your confusion within your relationship. The indecision comes from the same place. By observing how the doubt infuses you from the outside, and drives the indecision, you can journey back to a place of conviction.

FIXES: DECISION MAKING DILEMMAS

Trust your gut. You have likely stopped doing this a long time ago (when self-doubt gets sapped, so too does instinct). While your instincts aren't *always* right, they often are, and if your relationship with a narcissist is turning every decision into a convoluted mess—ask any kid who is taking a multiple choice test—your first guess is usually your best one.

List out pros and cons. This is an old tool but a good one. Your self-doubt may diminish your ability to engage in focused and sharp decision making but listing out pros and cons can be a way to break down the decision making. But let's add a twist to this. Many times you are clear as day about the right thing to do but realize that your narcissistic partner may not be on board, so you may want to add a third column to your pros and cons list—and that may be labeled "fears." Fear of how your partner will react, or how he may undermine your decision. By remaining aware of your fear, you may be able to recognize how you are blocking your own decision-making powers.

FREQUENTLY APOLOGIZING

I'm sorry. I wish I could invent a linguistic identification app that would record the number of times per day a person says "I'm sorry." I would be willing to bet a tidy sum that the people who say it the most are in relationships with narcissists. As we have clearly established, nothing is ever enough for the narcissist. When nothing is enough, there is often a tendency to apologize. (It is almost as though every apology you issue is "I am sorry for not being enough.") Narcissists often have their ears and eyes trained toward the negative elements of their worlds and toward disappointment and betrayal. As a rule, if you look for something, you find it. An example might be instead of a narcissistic partner saying "hey, thanks for making dinner, I know how busy things have been for you lately," you get "we're having pasta again?" In the second instance your response is more likely to be "I'm sorry."

Obviously some apologies in life are genuine and necessary. If you misspeak, say something unkind, engage in an insensitive behavior, or make a mistake, an apology is a highly appropriate response. An apology is an appropriate acknowledgment and should also be a call to arms to remain aware and to avoid committing a similar transgression in the future. It is likely that your apology ratios are way off—and that the number of apologies you are issuing for "real" errors are far fewer than those you may be issuing to appease or defuse your narcissistic partner.

Fear can often underlie these apologies you are issuing. The simple "I'm sorry" may actually be "I'm sorry, please don't overreact." Or "I'm sorry, please don't let this ruin the rest of our weekend." Or "I'm sorry, please don't rehash the other times I made mistakes in the past." The apology then becomes a bit of a preemptory strike. Since narcissists do not manage disappointment or inconvenience well, your apology may be self-protective. Finally, because narcissists rarely take responsibility for *anything*, and deflect everything (including their own feelings), your apologies are likely a function of spending time with someone who never takes ownership, leaving you in the position of apologizing for both you and your partner. Overall, the narcissist's emptiness, lack of empathy, and general lack of warmth can mean that even the slightest foible, oversight, or mistake raises fear in you, anger in them, and they are rarely able to see the big picture. Until that apology app gets invented, you will have to monitor this yourself.

FIXES: FREQUENTLY APOLOGIZING

While there is no apology monitoring app, you may have more data out there than you think. Review your texts and e-mails to your partner. How often do you see "I'm sorry" in there? If there are more than a few in the ones you can find, then take a look at the function they are serving (appeasing him, avoiding a fight, or genuine apology?). Take a look at your patterns.

Mindfulness matters here as well. When the temptation to say "I'm sorry" kicks in, pay attention, and start thinking about generating alternative and more productive responses. Instead of apologizing in the face of your narcissist's disappointment, acknowledge his experience. In the example of making dinner and being criticized for another night of pasta, instead of apologizing you can acknowledge their experience say, "yes, I know it is repetitive, but it was an easy fix on a busy night." This response recognizes the issue and contextualizes it without your contrition. Save your apologies for true transgressions, and watch those "I'm sorry" responses. Break the cycle of appeasing the beast.

FEAR OF DISAPPOINTMENT

By definition, a relationship with a narcissist is disappointing. Because they are not oriented to the needs of others, their choices usually only reflect what works for them. When their choice is aligned with yours, that's a good day and everyone wins. It becomes a bit of a coin toss, which means that at least 50 percent of the time, you can plan on being disappointed.

If your life with your partner is plagued by regularly scheduled disappointment, it can be difficult to make plans, either short or long term. Even making a dinner reservation becomes an emotionally laden roll of the dice. It is even more difficult with long-term decisions, because routine disappointment can leave you believing that the world is unpredictable and it becomes challenging to voice dreams, aspirations, or long-term plans. The prevailing theme in your life can become "why bother?"

The regular disappointment can take the wind out of your sails. It can be a roller coaster to become excited about something that never ultimately comes to fruition. Disappointment can also extend to other issues. It can be quite painful to become excited about sharing an idea or an aspiration only to have it met with indifference. This disappointing reaction can lead you to retreat and shelve your idea or categorize it as "ridiculous" or not worth pursuing. Think about how many times you had an idea or aspiration ridiculed or at least ignored by your partner, how many times you gave up as a result, and how many lost opportunities that may represent.

Obviously, disappointment is a part of life. Sometimes it rains on game day; sometimes things don't work out. But when disappointment becomes a regular part of your world, and is facilitated by a partner who regularly makes careless decisions or doesn't even support your attempts at launching something, this can result in holding back and missing out on the enjoyment of life and the setting of long-term goals and hopes that can fill life with meaning, purpose, and hope.

FIXES: FEAR OF DISAPPOINTMENT

Don't be afraid of disappointment. This is a bit of a cognitive fix. Disappointment may not feel good, but it will not kill you. It happens, and sometimes when it happens, people have a tendency to become glum and start viewing the world quite negatively through a "woe is me" lens. Since disappointment is part of the landscape with a narcissistic partner, and it is hard to ever really adjust to it, it is useful to stop giving it so much power. The tips below also help defuse some of the emotional power of disappointment, but start by not fearing it so much. Disappointment is a great way to learn grace and to let things go.

Sometimes the best offense is a good defense. Have a B-team or a B-plan. When you can, fill your life with rich wonderful experiences on your own, and be prepared to enact some of these on your own. Many times people will get disappointed because their partner will not want to see the movie, so they miss the movie and there is nothing else to do. Prepare to see the movie alone, with a friend, or have another activity planned. It can be deflating to want to do something with your partner and then have to do it alone or with a friend (that sunset drink cruise may seem romantic but could be a different kind of fun with a friend). Admittedly, this can be tiring, because you may end up double planning on some nights, but at least it gives some element of security if you are planning around a narcissistic partner.

SHUTTING THE DOOR ON OTHER PEOPLE

People in relationships with narcissists are notoriously isolated. As already discussed, this is often due to shame and fear of judgment. This is a psychologically dangerous pattern. It is likely that very few emotional needs are being met in your relationship. If you isolate yourself from the only other place where connection and mutuality can occur—namely other people—you will be cutting off a fundamental human need. The self-doubt that arises from being in a narcissistic relationship can also make you start feeling less confident and "worthy" in *all* of your relationships.

Your social isolation works quite nicely for your narcissistic partner; he may even be the one who wanted it. He may have shared negative opinions or insults about your friends and families, or he may have perceived the disdain with which your loved ones view him. The more socially isolated you become, the more the skewed reality with your narcissistic partner becomes your *only* reality. You lose the sounding boards who can calibrate you back to recognizing your worth, who remind you what empathy looks like, who provide perspective, and who engage with you in the mutual and reciprocal way human relationships should operate. Social support and social networks are good for our health and our well-being. To lose them, especially when you are living in the psychological desert of a narcissistic relationship, can be uniquely challenging.

Isolation can underlie many of the themes we are already discussing, particularly indecision and self-doubt. Like so many of the patterns, the isolation takes place gradually over time. It's not as though everyone is still in your life one day and gone the next. It can be subtle—saying no to a night out with friends, spending holidays away from your family, avoiding having people to the house so they don't witness your partner's behavior, not wanting to hear your partner's criticism about people close to you so you slowly cut them out of your life. In some cases, your craving for social contact can become so deep that you may be thrilled to go to work to have contact with colleagues or welcome the simple pleasure of a child's soccer game, because it means a brief chance to talk with other parents.

This isolation can take months or it can take years, but very often, you will slowly lift your head and see that you are in an empty room. If you realize that you have begun to withdraw from your friends and family, take small steps to reconnect.

FIXES: SHUTTING THE DOOR ON OTHER PEOPLE

The simplest one is don't shut the door. You do not have to share with them the difficult details of your relationship or even talk about it, but the healthy loving companionship of empathic people can be more curative than almost anything at this point. Reach out to the tried and true family and friends who have always had your back and who can listen without judgment. These types of interactions can help fortify you and give you essential support and remind you how communication, reciprocity, and mutuality work in a relationship.

Make a lunch date with a friend or commit to spending a holiday with your family, even if your partner does not accompany you. As you will see later in the book, having outside relationships is critical to your survival and happiness—whether you choose to stay or go.

COMFORTABLY NUMB

When we use things like food or alcohol to cope with our hurt or our feelings, we are managing our feelings from the "outside in"—in essence, numbing them. It is a common approach by people who feel sad, anxious, hurt, and helpless, and it distracts from the situation and the feelings. When you are in a narcissistic relationship, it is easy to escape to this place. Living a life of not being heard can be extremely painful, and managing that pain through any means available is not unusual. The list of "unhealthy" quick fixes includes:

- ► Food
- ► Alcohol
- ► Drugs
- ► Cigarettes
- ► Spending

However, some of the ways we numb ourselves can actually be hidden in more virtuous "packaging" and can also be quite powerful:

- ▶ Work
- ▶ Exercise
- ▶ Housecleaning and chores
- ▶ Staying frenetically busy with kids, family, friends, life

Many times when you are this busy, it is as though you are a bee, buzzing from one activity to the next and never coming down, so as to avoid the challenging relationship in your life and the feelings associated with it. Numbing can become a one-stop shop for not having to think about what you are living in. From time to time, it is an understandable short-term strategy. Obviously, drinking too much is not a viable or appropriate long-term strategy. However, activities like working around the clock may look virtuous to the world, but they also mean delaying the inevitable: facing your feelings and your situation. Feelings are like too much water behind a dam—the dam will hold for a while, but when it breaks, the towns will be washed away.

However, feelings can't actually be numbed. It's like putting on perfume to cover up not taking a shower for days; you still smell funny. And the feelings are still there. Over time, no matter how much you engage in numbing or masking of feelings, you will end up experiencing deeper and more destructive things like fatigue, mental dullness, sadness, doubt, and disconnection. Instead, try to honestly access your feelings and find healthier ways of coping with them. Later chapters of this book will give you the concrete strategies you need to help you work through some of these feelings.

FIXES: NUMBING YOURSELF

Instead of numbing and distracting, another approach is to integrate mindful meditation approaches into your life. Mindfulness has numerous payouts for a person in a narcissistic relationship, as it allows you to be self-reflective, pause before you go down the same ▼

dark alleys with your partner, and end the cycle of rumination. In addition, if you are going to "distract," attempt to do it in ways that permit self-care and connection: exercise outside or with friends, prepare and share a healthy meal, go to movies and museums. There is a difference between numbing a feeling and taking care of yourself. Self-care can strengthen your sense of self and your resolve so you can take care of yourself. Whether you stay or go.

Most people do not want to talk about these feelings of self-doubt, depression, anxiety, shame, or helplessness because it means it may be time to face the music. This book is about facing the music—and reminding you that there are always two paths available: staying or going. You may choose one for now, and then choose another later. Allow yourself to recognize the choices so you can feel your feelings, but don't feel pressured to take steps one way or another. Most important, this book is about new approaches and strategies that allow you to experience these feelings, meet your own needs, and prepare you for the consequences of any decision you make, instead of living in denial or suffocation.

This chapter was intended to encourage you to reflect on how this person has made you feel—a very personal experience—and the things you have done to manage these feelings (including not managing them). At this point you should be pretty clear on what a pathological narcissist is, how they make you feel, and why this happened in the first place. The next step is to figure out what to do.

CHAPTER 6

IT'S TIME TO LET GO OF THE RESCUE FANTASY

In fairy tales, the princesses kiss the frogs, and the frogs become princes. In real life, the princesses kiss princes, and the princes turn into frogs.

—PAULO COEHLO

et's take a look at *Beauty and the Beast*. Originally a French folk tale, it has been tweaked over the years and ultimately Disney-fied. But it is a timeless story that sheds tremendous insight into the culturally universal myth of rescue and redemption that has imprisoned scores of people in narcissistic relationships.

A lovely young gal named Belle (or some variant of pretty) lives with her merchant father (and in some versions with two selfish and greedy older sisters). When dad's fortunes fail, he heads out to manage some business issues, and while the greedy older sisters ask him to bring back fancy clothes and jewels from his travels, Belle asks only for a rose as their garden has died during their hard times.

Dad gets lost in the forest, stumbles on the beast's house, and the beast hooks him up with clothes, jewels, and food. Dad also takes it upon himself to pick a rose from the garden. This incenses the beast, who accuses the merchant of stealing one of the most prized possessions in the house. The dad tries to explain that it is a simple gift for his youngest and most beautiful daughter, and the beast then says the dad can have the rose but must return.

Belle, being a supportive daughter and taking blame for the rose, goes in her dad's place and the beast keeps her prisoner. The story varies in terms of how it goes down for her at this point, but basically he lavishes her with gifts and allows her to live in luxury—food, wine, jewels, clothes—but the catch is that she is imprisoned (control). The beast is prone to *rages* from time to time, but Belle senses that with kindness and support he will come around (rescue fantasy). In Belle's fantasy, she copes with this suboptimal state of affairs by imagining that she is living in the castle with a handsome prince who is imprisoned somewhere in the castle, and she remains convinced he will show up and rescue her.

The beast, in an unusual show of kindness, allows Belle to leave for a brief period of time to visit her family with the promise that she will return in a week. And he gives her some objects to take with her, including an enchanted mirror that allows her to observe what is happening in the palace during her absence. After the one week passes, she doesn't return, because her sisters make her feel badly about leaving her ailing father. But she feels guilty about breaking her promise to the beast, and she looks in the mirror. When she looks in the mirror, she sees that the beast has collapsed from disappointment and abandonment, and he appears to be fading away.

Belle rushes back to the castle and finds him suffering and dying. She leans over him, crying, acknowledging his kindness and hospitality, and apologizing for not returning when she said she would. She leans over and kisses him with genuine love, in the realization that he is vulnerable and lovable despite his beastly exterior. And voila! He transforms into a handsome prince. The rages disappear, and he is loving and kind. He explains that a witch cast a spell on him years earlier, a spell that could only be removed through the love of a pure, good woman.

The castle also magically transforms from a state of disrepair to pristine, and Belle and the Prince . . . lived happily ever after.

If only a class action lawsuit could be filed against the perpetrators of this tale. What does this rescue fantasy mean for you? Are you still holding onto some form of hope that your narcissistic partner will turn into a prince? Do you think that with enough love, attention, and perfection you can somehow change him? If you are caught up in a rescue fantasy, don't expect a happy ending.

The Rescue Fantasy

Without exception, with both men and women, the rescue fantasy is what has kept narcissistic relationships alive year after year. Hope keeps the ship afloat, because once the hope is gone, there is nothing left to fight for. Hope can be real, and it can be an illusion, but in most cases it is a little of both. The gaslighting dynamic mentioned earlier is a critical brick in the rescue fantasy. Issues such as self-doubt, guilt, fear, and the prevailing fairy tale that "if you love someone enough, he or she will change" are what can lead people to spend *decades* fighting for these relationships. Every day becomes a new opportunity to "get it right," "to try harder," and when you look at the typical relationship books, they are about communicating *more clearly,* being *more loving,* and making *time* for your relationship. All of this is lovely advice, *only if the other person is noticing* or listening!

Kierkegaard noted that "Love is the expression of the one who loves, not of the one who is loved." The challenge is that when this expression is not met with any reciprocity, and in fact the opposite, it can be exhausting and demoralizing. The rescue fantasy is embedded in the public consciousness. In addition, if you grew up with parents who needed rescuing or if you found yourself in an early caregiving role (for example, your parents were not available to you in any consistent emotional way, you actually did have to care for an ailing or impaired parent, or you had to care for younger children to a degree that you missed out on elements of your life), then it is easy to think that more love is better. If you do more, if you care more, if you love more, then you will get more back. It's not that linear, and while that may apply in a factory—work harder, make more widgets—it does not work in relationships, least of all with a narcissist.

When you remove that option, the option of "try harder and your partner will notice," it can leave you angry, confused, and frustrated. People will live in a place of futility in their relationships for a very long time. In just about anything else in their lives, most of the people I have spoken with were clear, "If I had been this frustrated for this long in *anything* else, I would have quit the job, ended the friendship, stopped speaking to the family member, or simply just quit." Something about close relationships keeps us in even after all of the evidence tells us to run.

The rescue fantasy is in our DNA, and the rescue fantasy allows the beasts in our lives to get away with too much. We are a culture that *loves* the redemption story, and many people want to be the savior. Although this relationship may have eroded away at your self-esteem, your self-worth, your decision-making abilities, and filled you with a lifetime of doubt, you still keep chipping away at it. Love is a redemptive experience, and when experienced by healthy people, it can open them up to possibilities within themselves, facilitate growth, and provide strength at times of adversity. It is an essential piece of the human experience, though we do focus too much on love "out" versus love "in." This is not about bashing love.

The challenge arises when you are in a relationship and are enduring all of the unhealthy patterns we have been discussing. If you hold true to the belief that your love, giving, and support will *change* your pathologically narcissistic partner, guess again. Personality patterns tend to be pretty entrenched—and the rules of rescue do not apply. It is also quite likely that you keep switching strategies. For a while you try supportive, then loving, then withdrawing, then quiet. From a research standpoint, that makes sense; you try several strategies, gather the data, and figure out which one works best (and odds are no single pattern will work since the narcissist is so unpredictable; it's like trying to win at roulette). But since the end game—holding out for your partner to change—is not achievable, you are not likely to see a change. So you are stuck in a pattern of throwing lots of stuff at the wall to see what sticks. Odds are nothing is sticking.

Vulnerability and Rescue

Temporary shifts in your partner can be confusing. For as psychologically disconnected as narcissists are, under some conditions—severe stressors, a major loss, fear—they will listen, they will buck up, and they will walk the straight and narrow. Narcissists, contrary to popular wisdom, can be quite vulnerable. And those vulnerable moments play perfectly into the rescue fantasy. Obviously, it is not terribly interesting to try to rescue a grandiose, arrogant, entitled person. But when that same grandiose, arrogant, entitled person feels threatened, and then vulnerable, at that moment you may actually feel useful. The narcissist will often draw you closer at those times, relying on you for reassurance and support, and it may even feel normal and connected for a while. These vulnerable moments can resurrect the rescue fantasy. Then in weeks, months, and sometimes years, they slide back to their usual dynamics. Vulnerability is a part of the complex and nuanced clinical picture of narcissism, and it can be those episodes of vulnerability that often keep partners in the game for years and even decades longer, thinking "He cried, he's different." Nope. Same song, different key.

The Challenge

This raises the idea of "challenge." It's odd and somewhat disturbing that people would view relationships as places of "challenge" or something to win. That may simply be a sad byproduct of a competitive society, or a Darwinian echo of getting the "fittest" partner. The idea of having to win over the "unwinnable" narcissistic partner can be initially embraced as a challenge. If you could win over this detached person, it would be a testament about you as a "winner" or a "savior." You alone will be the one who can rescue him. Obviously, that is an unhealthy stance to take in an intimate close relationship. But many of us are competitive, and a challenge may keep us on our proverbial toes. In fact, an entire industry of dating coaches and dating books is based on premises that liken courtship to *The Art of War*. In our culture, the courtship is couched in terms of "challenge," and because narcissists play this game better than anyone else, they often score a hat trick in the courtship phase, which hooks and blinds you.

The concept of a challenge may be initially appealing, but this will work over time only if your hard work actually results in consistent and mutual regard. For example, you do something nice for your partner and it gives you pleasure, he notices and appreciates it, and so does something nice in turn, and before you know it, this is a pattern. A perfect *pas de deux*. But it can sometimes take years or even decades of trying to please the narcissistic partner before it dawns on you that this is a one-way street. You will do, and do, and do, and do. In the beginning he might reciprocate, and then he likely never will again. After the challenge has passed and you are firmly locked down, the mutuality and reciprocity will have passed as well.

Just as it's dangerous to get caught up in a rescue fantasy, it can be equally harmful to let the challenge of winning him over keep you invested in the relationship. You will find yourself feeling endlessly frustrated and will begin to experience those feelings of depression, anxiety, and self-doubt that we discussed in the previous chapter.

So what is the only approach that will work when all other avenues have been exhausted? After the couples therapy was either rejected outright or yielded nothing? After the 20 relationship books you bought on communication and love gave you nothing? After years of keeping the house clean, the kids quiet, the body in shape, the bank account full or well-managed, your needs unmet, and nothing changed? It's painfully simple but also challenging to execute because it requires a rewrite, a re-rendering, a reboot, and a reframe. And the best part is that it requires nothing from your partner—this is entirely within your control. It is the most unromantic piece of advice you will ever receive:

Manage your expectations.

We'll explore this suggestion more fully in the next chapter. For now, one of the most crucial points to remember as you move forward is that you absolutely 100 percent need to let go of the rescue fantasy. If you don't, and you decide to stay, it will only destroy you, bit by bit. So now that you know the beast is never going to turn into a prince, what if you choose to stay anyway? The next chapter will provide you with some helpful tools for making your life easier if this is the route you choose to follow.

CHAPTER 7

SHOULD I STAY?

*When we are no longer able to change a situation, we are
challenged to change ourselves.*

—VIKTOR FRANKL

I t is a complicated question in this kind of relationship. And
it is a highly personal one. But it all emanates from one central premise.

They are not going to change.

This section of the book is focused on managing the relationship if you elect to stick it out. There are myriad reasons a person
may decide to stay in a relationship—children, finances, shared
businesses, religion, culture, fear, health issues—and they are all
important and real factors. The fact is, you may simply be in love
with this person, and that is okay. If you have those feelings, you
are not going to want to leave. The agony many face when they are
in a relationship with a narcissist is that they are enduring a difficult situation but, besides leaving, can think of no other solution.
And they have no intention of leaving. That double-bind can lead
to a deep sense of confusion, helplessness, and imprisonment. Why
do we stay in these relationships? How can a person stay and lift
some of the discomfort?

To reiterate an earlier point, if you are in a relationship that is physically violent or in some other way placing you and/or other dependents at risk, that is a different issue. In such a case, involving domestic violence advocates and other institutions to ensure safety is an essential course of action. This section of the book takes on the day after day, year after year neglect and bad behavior a person encounters in a narcissistic relationship, but it is not designed to address situations of acute danger. Resources at the end of the book provide guidance for people who are in physically dangerous situations

Everyone may have opinions, but the right answer resides within you. Especially when people are married, the prevailing wisdom is to "fight" for it, unless conditions have devolved into something so toxic that they are insurmountable. These toxic situations can sometimes be obvious, such as physical abuse, verbal abuse, financial abuse, drug and alcohol use, or repeated infidelity. Under these conditions, you may have supporters who will encourage you to leave. The fact is, if the damage a narcissist does to a person internally and psychologically was physically apparent on their faces and bodies, people would be calling 911. The slow and subtle changes caused by the narcissistic relationship such as disconnection and self-doubt may result in internal war wounds that may not be as obvious to others, and it may be more challenging to drum up support. Whether you have support or not, staying or going is ultimately your decision. If the decision for now is to stick it out, keep reading.

Narcissists Don't Change

Obviously, there are certain human patterns that are difficult to change, such as habits and addictions, but because of the direct impact of these patterns on the addict, at some point that person will likely attempt to change (and it may take a few cracks at bat to get there). Narcissism often works for the narcissist. Because it is a personality pattern, it is not amenable to change. In addition, we live in a culture that supports and celebrates narcissism, social media is a hall of mirrors that provides constant validation, and wealth and grandiosity are key indicators of success. When the world is supporting them, their needs are getting met, they do not think there is anything wrong anyhow, and they are unable to see, hear, or feel the needs of others, the likelihood of change is close to zero.

Keep in mind, that as we said in the rescue fantasy, narcissists can be quite vulnerable, sometimes oscillating back and forth from grandiose to fragile. In the moments of vulnerability, you may even feel useful in your relationship with him, comforting him and encouraging him, which he will soak up until he no longer needs you or the encouragement. It is at these vulnerable times that the narcissist may actually be willing to seek out therapy, but the results of therapy may not benefit you as his partner.

What About Therapy?

In case you needed a reminder, your narcissistic partner is not going to change. There is virtually no evidence of good treatment outcomes in the literature on narcissism. I have attended numerous lectures, workshops, read papers, books—anything I could—just waiting for the punch line for the riddle: How do you successfully treat a narcissist? The punch line never came.

As a psychologist, it is probably not good for my bread and butter to acknowledge that there are some human patterns that cannot change. This is one of them. A review of the treatment literature on pathological narcissism and narcissistic personality disorder reveals that there is little evidence of any good, consistent, sustainable treatments for narcissistic personality disorder. Dr. Joel Paris, a Professor of Psychiatry at McGill University and author of numerous books on personality disorders, even suggests that unless the therapist is careful, therapy may even foster narcissism. Evidence of improvement has been suggested in a handful of case reports, but at the end of the day, hard core, pathological narcissists are certainly not going to change spontaneously, and even if they get into treatment (to which they are typically resistant), there is not much evidence that it will make a difference and definitely not in the long term.

Obviously it is not good business for us in mental health to say we cannot address this problem. (That's like having a repair shop with a sign out front that says "we can't fix your car.") However, we are still not entirely clear on how to measure narcissism, because the research is still evolving. But at the end of the day, the literature shows virtually no evidence that a narcissist can be "treated" or that his or her behavior and communication "changed" in any kind of significant or permanent way. A real challenge is that treatment studies rarely follow people out for years and years, and some studies do show some improvements in variables such as self-reflection as well as behavioral changes for a few weeks or months after therapy, but long-term maintenance of these changes are unlikely (as they are unlikely with most disorders) without ongoing therapy.

Research on treatment of narcissism and narcissistic personality disorder suggest the value of something psychiatry professor Elsa Ronningstam terms "corrective life events," and interestingly, these do not necessarily come about through treatment but simply by life happening. These corrective events can help manage the narcissists' need to maintain grandiosity, arrogance in their relationships, and their sense of disillusionment. Basically, she argues that having these corrective relationships might steer the ship a little differently. For example, if a narcissistic person can have experiences that show that his or her usual maneuvers of grandiosity, arrogance, and entitlement can be challenged by actually achieving excellence on his or her own (thus pushing back on grandiosity) or having a consistent corrective relationship (thus pushing back on entitlement and arrogance), or disillusionment experiences that allow him or her to grow some humility and let go of some of the grandiose self-concept, then there can be some significant shifts in the narcissistic persona.

My main concern here is that this may play into the rescue fantasy that your unending love can be that corrective relationship experience. It may, but it probably will not. Much of this may come down to timing, and it may just be the alchemy of entering the narcissist's life at the right time for the corrective experience to unfold. Timing is in fact luck, and trying harder cannot make that luck. As you keep trying harder and harder to be that "corrective" person, it may also take a toll on you (and when the "corrective" experience does not occur, it can leave you blaming yourself). These spontaneous shifts and corrective experiences are more likely to take place in people whose pathological narcissism is less extreme. What may be more likely are brief shifts in some of these patterns, with most patterns sustaining. However, the good news is if you do decide to "stay," there is some possibility of some subtle shifts that may make things more bearable.

A final note on therapy and narcissistic personality: It is my firm conviction that narcissistic personality disorder does its greatest harm in close, intimate relationships (for example, marriages). Many people have narcissistic bosses, colleagues, siblings, friends, and neighbors. These are not easy situations, but they do not have the impact that a romantic partner would have. The primitive and emotional nature of a close personal relationship means that the lack of empathy, the rage, the distance, the control, and the inconsistency have tremendous power in shaping the life and the inner world of a person in a narcissistic relationship. Close relationships can activate the best and the worst in us, but the deep emotional demands of an intimate relationship are out of reach for a person with narcissistic personality disorder. Therapy typically cannot make a person less superficial. In addition, the narcissistic personality often takes advantage of the close relationship and just drains it of life slowly and over time.

A major focus in marital therapy is on acceptance and commitment, a powerful and important way to think about marriage and committed relationships. Without acceptance, an intimate relationship cannot thrive. We are not perfect, and to move forward into and maintain a mutual, respectful and loving relationship, acceptance is an essential (and often challenging) part of the holistic view of a committed partnership. This focus on acceptance, however, can become dangerous when one of the partners is narcissistic. Adhering too tightly to an acceptance model often leaves partners in narcissistic relationships feeling like they are not trying hard enough, that they are "quitters," or that they are not forgiving people. This is a slippery slope of self-blame and perpetuating broken cycles. Once it is clear that you are in a relationship with a pathological narcissist, I actually do encourage acceptance, but I prefer to think of it as informed acceptance (that they will not change, that there is no rescue fantasy) that will move you from a place of self-doubt and self-flagellation into a place of self-worth and self-valuation that will prepare you to make the healthiest decisions in a manner that is not blind, but rather wise. This is not about viewing your partner as a monster, but perhaps *accepting* the complex landscape of narcissism and making decisions accordingly.

As a result, even when a person with narcissistic personality disorder is in therapy, and even if some changes are made and observed by friends, family members, or co-workers, the impacts are not felt as profoundly in his close intimate relationship. These changes are usually VERY unlikely to jump the rails into their intimate relationships. The emotional demands, the empathy, and the consistency that are required by a close relationship are out of reach, and the small behavioral changes a narcissist may make may potentially soften the blow, but the blows will still occur. Behavioral changes may make some aspects of your daily life easier, but the emotional emptiness and superficiality is much harder for a narcissistic personality to shift, and those are the factors that can take a toll on a relationship. So now instead of being chronically late to dinner and then ignoring you, therapy may yield a narcissistic partner who is now on time to dinner and then ignores you. However, the being on time may be enough for you—only you will know that.

Other Diagnoses

Personality disorders such as narcissistic personality disorder often co-occur with other mental illnesses, particularly depression and substance use disorders. Older research by Ronningstam suggests that nearly half of the people with narcissistic personality disorder also had a diagnosis of depression, 25-50 percent had a diagnosis of a substance use disorder, and other commonly observed disorders co-occurring with narcissistic personality disorder included bipolar disorder and eating disorders. People with substance abuse disorders also have high rates of narcissistic personality disorder. This takes a complicated clinical situation and makes it more complicated. And it may also make it harder for you to leave.

It really is no wonder that people with narcissistic personality disorder so often become addicted to drugs and/or alcohol. Since they cannot regulate their self-esteem or emotions and rely on external validation to maintain their identity, drugs and alcohol become one more external "tool" to help them do this. It is a superficial quick fix that can quickly spin out of control. A relationship with an addict is a challenging situation and can test a relationship to an extreme degree. Many of the characteristics of drug/alcohol use are similar to those seen in narcissistic personality disorder: denial, lying, projection, and general selfishness. It can make these traits even more fortified and difficult to manage if a narcissistic personality is also an addict. Their poor judgment, boundary problems, and violations of trust can be even more pronounced when they are intoxicated, and it can also amp up their rage and overall challenges in managing any of their emotions.

Given that narcissists can often be quite vulnerable, again, because their self-esteem is so fragile and reliant on the judgments of other people, depression is not a surprising part of this picture. At times when they are depressed, especially for men, it is quite possible that their mood will be even more irritable than usual, or they will become more withdrawn, and seemingly more focused on themselves. Their focus on superficial characteristics, such as appearance, and the problems with regulation can also combine to result in disorders, such as eating disorders, in both men and women. Bipolar disorder, however, is the most severe of the disorders that can often co-occur with narcissistic personality disorder. The peaks and valleys of mania and depression, and the overlapping symptoms, such as grandiosity and entitlement, can make their symptoms far more intense and disruptive.

Drug and alcohol abuse, depression, bipolar disorder, and eating disorders are all manageable disorders. It may take some time, and often a combination of medications and psychotherapy, but the research suggests good treatment outcomes. So if you treat depression or alcohol abuse in a person with narcissistic personality disorder, now you have a more cheerful or energetic narcissist or a sober narcissist. This is a good thing, but it still leaves you managing the symptoms of narcissistic personality disorder. Over time, if you are in a relationship with someone who is experiencing narcissistic personality disorder plus some other diagnosis, you may notice that some issues may improve with treatment, but that some patterns, particularly the key symptoms of their narcissism, such as entitlement, lack of empathy, poor emotional regulation, and deficits in self-esteem, never improve. However, the guilt about a partner's other health issues, such as addiction or other mental illness, can also be associated with conflict about communicating with them or consideration of leaving the relationship.

The big-ticket symptoms we would like to see changed—the lack of empathy, the chronic entitlement, the grandiosity—tend to be most resistant to change, since they are linked so strongly to the core deficits of the disorder, such as an inability to regulate self-esteem. These are the symptoms that may be entertaining in small doses, but rarely pleasant for a partner who has to co-exist with the narcissistic personality day in and day out. Sometimes, you may observe a temporary shift in these patterns if the narcissist gets caught in a big-ticket lie, such as infidelity, but since these patterns are so linked into the core pathology of the person with the narcissistic personality (seeking admiration and validation), he will likely return to his patterns soon enough.

If They Are Not Going to Change, Then What?

When I set out to write this book, it was this section, the "Should I Stay" section, that actually got the project underway. It would be easier to offer only one option, or entitle the book *Your Partner's a Jerk, Now Leave*. But it is never that simple. In working with clients, and simply hearing about cases of people in narcissistic relationships, a tremendous struggle was the Catch-22 of not wanting (or feeling unable) to leave but feeling uncomfortable and hurt by their situations.

When I have worked with clients who were struggling with the landscape of a narcissistic relationship, they found it useful to share and discuss the patterns of the relationship. Upon discussing the patterns, they found that what felt like chaos was actually quite predictable, uncomfortable but predictable. We identified the narcissistic patterns that were distressing them and were actually able to predict the patterns. Many clients were grateful for the framework but also disappointed because this was indeed a pattern, and all the wishful thinking in the world would not change it. However, they also related the fact that for many reasons they knew they would not or could not leave. Preparing people for how to stay is a more nuanced issue. Many of the clients I have worked with, people I have interviewed, and people I have talked with who are in relationships with deeply narcissistic partners are not ready to leave. It is not my approach to tell people "you need to go"—my clinical responsibility is to work with clients where they are at, support them, help them connect the dots, provide them with education about the dynamics at play, and then work with them to develop tools that will help them live a healthier and more fulfilling life. In this chapter, I will give you those same tools.

Manage Your Expectations

Yuck. This is not an attractive way to have to think in a relation-ship. Healthy relationships are about growth, shared experiences, respect, and joy (and if you are lucky, some romance and sensuality as well). Healthy expectations in a healthy relationship are about excellence, new opportunities, and mutuality. If you are reading this book, it is likely that those healthy expectations either never existed or were abandoned long ago. You are now in a place of survival, getting through the days. If the bar was set any lower, you would have to tunnel to get under it. Your partner has been phoning it in for a long time, and you have been accepting the calls without asking for anything else. You likely learned to live on crumbs long ago, you have shaped and reshaped yourself to stay in this relationship, you gave in to a variety of conditions—including control, deceit, rage, neglect, insults, gaslighting—and are now ac-customed to living under this regime.

I remember talking with a couple, and in meeting with one of them one day, the husband very clearly laid out what he expected from his wife. He said "I expect always and forever to be her sin-gular priority. Everything, including our children, are to come second to me. I expect us to do everything out of our workplaces together. And I expect that she will never keep a secret from me. I in turn, would never keep a secret from her. I also believe that any time spent with friends should only happen when the two of us are together, because I do not want anyone else to take top billing." What I found refreshing about this (yes, refreshing) was that it was absolutely honest. This person made his rather extreme wants known. These were articulated even before this couple got married. He also said, "I will never compromise on this. Ever." Needless to say, things did not go well for them. But at some level, she believed that he would change his rather extreme tune over time. Tunes rarely change. People do let us know what they want, but too often we believe that if we stick around long enough they will change their answer. In the case of narcissistic personality, that does not typically happen.

The darker dynamics of narcissism imply that one person in the relationship gives just about everything, and the other (the narcissist) just takes, tossing out crumbs like a latter-day Marie Antoinette when it suits them. People in relationships with narcissists often frame their chronic capitulation as "compromise," but they will also feel frustrated by it because it is so one-sided and they still have certain expectations. Because they are told that "compromise" is part of a relationship, they feel guilty about being frustrated, and it becomes a vicious cycle. If the relationship is reciprocal, compromise is effortless. Give and take becomes an elegant dance, and it stops feeling like compromise because the gives are rewarded.

After months or years of the hills and valleys of a life with a narcissistic partner, you become aware that your needs are not being met, but you are not ready to pack it in. This kind of relationship is so taxing and so soul-killing, because it is so repetitive. When your expectations get repeatedly dashed, every day can feel like a childhood birthday party where no one shows up. While most people in these situations may believe that they have simply "adjusted" to the daily disappointment, you likely have not. It is almost too painful to face.

These can be small-ticket disappointments—your partner does not show up on time, does not come home for dinner, cancels your date night, or does not listen to you—or big ticket disappointments—your partner cancels your summer vacation, is late to your child's birthday party, or does not support you in a professional decision. They hurt, and they pile up like cordwood. Disappointment becomes your new normal, but that said, it never really does, because each time a new opportunity comes up to get it right, you believe he will get it right. You believe that, this time, it will be different.

Even though your expectations are regularly dashed, you may still have a regular routine in your lives together, such as morning routines, bedtime, work or family responsibilities, meals, general daily routines, and it is quite likely that these go off on schedule more days than not. The dashed expectations are merely part of this schedule. And you are so embedded in it, that sometimes you cannot see the toll they are taking. Just like the story of John and Rachel presented at the beginning of the book, she got so used to eating cold dinners that she started to believe that lasagna was meant to be eaten at room temperature.

But not all dashed expectations are "procedural." It is easy to understand disappointment that is embedded in behavior (for example, showing up late, not showing up at all, forgetting a birthday). The more challenging disappointments are the lack of empathy, the lack of connection, the lack of support. When a person enters a relationship, he or she is hoping for a shared sense of purpose, empathy, and respect. When that is missing day after day, and year after year, that is more profoundly impactful than a missed party or dinner date. It can leave you feeling completely alone. The only thing worse than being lonely is being lonely in a relationship.

So day after day, you keep waiting for your partner to respond to you in a way he likely never will. What if you could mindfully find a way to stop waiting for a bus that is never coming to this stop? What if you could get your needs met, not let yourself be swept away with the negativity, the indifference, and the disconnection? Much of achieving this has to do with managing your expectations. And that starts with how you share information in your relationship. A bit later in the chapter, I will give you some tools or "fixes" for how to share different kinds of information in your relationship so that you receive the support you need, protect yourself, and avoid or learn to turn away from some of the worst reactions in your partner.

The Territory and the Price of Admission

Much as we associate relationships with passion and novelty, familiarity is the glue that keeps them together. Let's then think of this as familiar territory. Many of us live in a place for a while, and if it is hilly, we get accustomed to it, and pedal harder. If it is hot, we just wear lighter clothing. Relationships are the same way. Anyone who has lived in a place for a long time will not expect the geography to change overnight. When you wake up on a February morning in Chicago, you do not expect it to be 80 degrees. When you live in Los Angeles, you do not expect the freeways to be wide open on a busy morning. When you live in Iowa, you do not expect 12,000-foot peaks outside your window. And when you live with a narcissist, you should not expect him to start behaving respectfully and empathically. Familiarity is not always easy. Familiarity can also be the familiar unpleasant feelings and patterns. But familiarity is still what you know, and even if it is abusive, it is strangely seductive and comforting.

Sadly, and yes, cynically, relationships do have a price of admission. You have started to recognize this price since day one but pushed it away because it did not feel good to think that way. By now, whether you want to acknowledge it or not, you are aware of the price of admission in your particular relationship. In a normal relationship, this may be small aggravations—he wants to watch football every Sunday, she doesn't like the cold, he doesn't like your cousins in Pittsburgh, she leaves her towels on the bathroom floor— and you work around them (or you don't). In fact, it may not even feel like a "price." If these things are deal breakers, you figure it out or you leave. The price with a pathological narcissist can be a bit higher, but in a way it is no different than the towels on the floor. However, because the narcissist's "asks" are more psychologically challenging, they are also less obvious than the towels on the floor.

Yes, communication is always the first stop on this train, but many times the "price of admission" with a narcissistic partner may push buttons that make you vulnerable: inappropriate relationships, problems with boundaries, criticism, cold indifference. In my work with clients who are trying to make decisions about how to move forward with a narcissistic partner, one of the greatest stumbling blocks is recognizing the so-called "prices of admission" and acknowledging that they are in fact real. People are so wedded to the idea that their partner can change that the concept of a fixed price of admission or of an unchanging territory are hard to accept (and also feel cynical). In addition, a narcissistic partner who is highly successful provides a comfortable life and at times of exuberant grandiosity can be loving and generous. This can be seductive, but there may be a price of admission there. That wealth and comfort may come at the price of inconsistency, unpredictability, and running hot and cold. So when you reflect on your comfortable life, it may be uncomfortable to reflect on what it is *really* costing you.

In my work, I have heard many scenarios of women being swept away by (usually relatively older) gentlemen who can offer wealth, access, comfort, and freedom from having to work. Probabilistically, these men do possess more traits of narcissism than the average bear. The women then become quite offended when their wealthy paramour starts engaging with other young lovely women. They never look too happy when they are told that it is simply the price of admission. Most women are socialized to believe that they will be the Cinderella who charms the prince from all others. You may charm the prince, but think harem rather than monogamy. There is a cynicism that accompanies this thinking, but there is also a reality—and while the price of admission may sometimes be clearly financial (I will keep you comfortable, but I am going to do my own thing), it may also be psychological (putting up with control, coldness, or distance) to keep the relationship going.

Where this is most frequently observed is in the area of "inappropriate" relationships—relationships that may not have devolved into full-blown affairs but are not likely to pass the "smell test" for appropriate conduct by a person in a committed relationship.

Remember, the narcissist needs cargo ships of narcissistic supply sailing into the harbor every day. No one person or situation can provide this, and because they are so frequently on the quest for novelty and new forms of validation, they will burn out on what you can bring pretty early and need more. In addition, because narcissists are so Machiavellian (remember that Dark Triad?), they also tend to hedge their bets and keep a few irons in the fire at all times. If the two of you have a fight, they maintain a B-team to turn to for validation, encouragement, and flirtatious texts, instead of being self-reflective or communicating about growing your relationship together or managing the rough patches. A common scenario is the narcissist who maintains fuzzy boundaries with former partners, flirtatious co-workers, and random folks he meets here and there. Often, by the letter of the law, nothing has ever ostensibly "happened" with these electronic boundary violations, but the tenor of the messages, the fact that the messages are coming in the middle of the night, and the secretive conduct of your partner are unsettling for you. The narcissist "needs" the flirty banter, inappropriate photographs, and other fluffing to get through the day.

So you do what most relationship books suggest (and is an essential first step) and you communicate. Ideally, you do so in a manner that is not emotional, erratic, and accusatory but instead is collaborative, and you take ownership of your feelings. You let your partner know that these late night communications and inappropriate messages leave you feeling uncomfortable. Your partner may even clean up his act for a while, but narcissistic supply trumps all and the greater likelihood is that your partner will change the password on his phone or the names of the senders on the incoming messages. Professionally, I have worked with numerous clients and witnessed gallons of tears in frustration about "what I found on his/her phone." They often admit that monitoring their partner's phone becomes an addiction, a mix of fear, disgust, and obsession about what they will find next. The relationship slowly devolves into monitoring and anxiety and brings out the worst in them. The narcissist is not going to change; he will maintain or at least encourage these improper relationships. So either adjust to his electronic antics or get out—there is no option number three. I challenge every relationship out there to pass the "phone test." Pretty simply, would you feel comfortable passing your smartphone to your partner with all of your passwords and full access? Would he be willing to do the same? If the answer is no, then take a long hard look at what both of you are doing.

Reflect on this with regard to parenting as well. If you have children, you already know this; there were times when you felt like a de facto single parent. In some ways, with a narcissistic partner it can be worse than being a single parent, because you have to do all of the heavy lifting, but then your partner will still weigh in and perhaps attempt to control it when it is convenient. If you have not yet had children, you may not get the rosy-cheeked family tableau you envisioned. That disappointment can be staggering, because a child implies a permanent commitment and a far higher sense of responsibility. If you have a child with a pathological narcissist, you may need to mentally start planning on being a single parent (at least when it comes to the hard stuff). He may show up for the fun days, but the day-to-day drudgery is likely to be all you.

So here we are back at the price of admission. Regardless of which behavior you are trying to change, a narcissist's behavior may improve slightly once you communicate, but you can set your clock on the fact that it will not stop. The price of admission is that your narcissistic partner is going to keep doing this, and if you stay, then this is the territory. This is not about judging his behavior but about monitoring your reaction. If it doesn't feel good to you, then think about how to manage your reaction, but do not expect his behavior to change. This is where managing expectations can become particularly challenging, because one thing you cannot do is manage feelings. Susan Sontag once said, "One can never ask anyone to change a feeling." She is absolutely correct—you feel the way you feel. Expect your partner will behave this way, expect you feel this way, and understand that this is the price of admission in this relationship. Bottom line: If you intend to stay, get used to the territory. Don't be surprised when it is cold in the winter; if you intend to stay, put on a coat.

The Three-Part Rule

As I mentioned earlier, part of managing your expectations relates to how you share information within your relationship. This is easy to remember. There are only three parts:

1. Good
2. Bad
3. Indifferent

The premise of all three becomes the same. Stop setting yourself up for disappointment. One of the most challenging elements of the narcissistic dynamic is that they are not tuned in to you. And at the rare times they are tuned in to you, they will often criticize you, minimize you, view your successes as a threat (remember, they are devoid of self-esteem), and/or mock, degrade, or humiliate you. Yet, you keep going back, telling them the "stuff" of your life, having it laughed at or ignored, feeling deflated, then doing it again the next day. Rinse, lather, repeat.

Let's break down the Three Part Rule and look at how you can better share news—the good, the bad, and the indifferent.

THE GOOD

Something good happens to you. You get an award at work. Someone compliments you on your dress. You receive a promotion. You have a good day.

➡ **Rule:** Don't share any of the good experiences in your life with your narcissistic partner. I know that seems like an extreme position. Treat this like an exercise. Reflect on the last five times you told your partner something wonderful that happened to

you—this could be as big as a promotion or as small as the kindness of a store clerk or finding a four-leaf clover while pulling
weeds. How were these pieces of good news received? List each
piece of news, then next to it, the response you received. As a really
useful exercise, try this in the next few days. Share some good
things with your partner and see what comes back at you.

Obviously, I do not know your answers, but I am willing to bet,
if indeed you have a narcissistic partner, at least 4/5 if not 5/5 were
unkind responses or you were downright ignored. They were anything from him not listening and saying "what did you say?" to
"it's about time" to "does the promotion mean more money or is it
just a bullshit title?" or "I'll bet you're going to be too big for your
britches soon," "I'm sure you will start screwing your boss next,"
"the only reason the clerk commented on your eyes is because he
was hoping for a tip," "why do you need so much validation from
other people?" or, simply never responding to the text you sent
him, sharing the good news. Sound familiar yet?

Interestingly, research on memory, recall, and cognitive bias
suggests that you will remember negative events and nasty words
more clearly and frequently than positive words or experiences.
Ensure that you do this exercise honestly. Dig deep. Try to recall
if there were instances when your partner was your cheerleader,
which is fantastic, because there may be patterns there. He may be
more willing to compliment you for example as a parent as that
may be less threatening than your role as a professional.

That raises the question, if your responses to this brief exercise
show that this is a pattern, then why do you do it? Why do you
keep sharing good news with your partner? By way of an example, imagine that you have a precious and fragile treasure like
a piece of crystal given to you by your great grandmother. Would
you hand that precious treasure to someone who you knew
would break it? For example, would you hand it to someone who
is intoxicated? A small child? Probably not. Why? Because you
knew there was a strong likelihood that such a person would

break it. They may not break it deliberately, but rather because they just do not know better, and even if you educated that drunk person or that three-year-old on how precious this object is, they still may break it, because they do not have the ability to do anything else.

Your good news or your aspiration is not exactly a crystal wine glass or museum treasure. In fact, I would argue that it is more precious; wine glasses and treasures are just things. It goes back to the idea of carelessness, and just like in a court of law, not knowing it was a bad thing to do or not knowing that it was experienced as bad or hurtful, is not a plausible defense. Adults know better.

So again, let's return to the question, why do you do it? Why do you keep telling your partner the good things that are happening in your life only to have them ignored, ridiculed, or criticized?

You do it because you think this time it will be different (that darned hope raising its head again). You are in the rosy glow of the good news or good experience, and you can't imagine someone else viewing it as anything but good. A darker interpretation could be that perhaps you don't think you deserve the good news, and so you take it to the one person you know will spoil it. It may also be a familiar dynamic for you, having your husband laugh or minimize your meaningful promotion at work could be similar to when your father or mother would mock you or put you down. These patterns tend to run deep.

Sadly, familiarity, even abusive familiarity, keeps people in the game. There is something perversely satisfying about someone behaving the same way every time. Even if they are being critical. You know the good news will typically be met with sarcasm, mockery, belittlement, or insults, and inevitably it is. Like the sun rising in the East, you can count on it.

It is not good for you. Chronic criticism will erode your self-esteem, inoculate you with self-doubt, and it can be a contributor to symptoms of anxiety and depression, including worry, helplessness, hopelessness, worthlessness, guilt, and a sense of emptiness and purposelessness.

There is another layer to this. We have been talking about sharing "good news" (something that has already happened to you), but there is something even more important to share that may be far more fragile. That is the sharing of your aspirations. It is amazing how cavalier we are with our dreams, particularly new dreams, ideas, or ventures. We share them recklessly with other people, wagging our tails and tongues like puppies, as we wait for the other person to get as excited as we are. Taking a new aspiration to a narcissistic partner is a recipe for psychological disaster. He or she may go after good news that has already happened (such as a promotion or a raise) in a different manner. Most good news is a reflection of some external entity validating you, so you already got a nod there, and while it hurts to have your partner minimize it or insult it, the good news is a fact. This is quite different than sharing a dream or a hope. Most narcissistic people are not good dream catchers. Their own issues get in the way of being authentic and enthusiastic cheerleaders. And this can be lethal.

Dreams are like children. For those of you who are parents or pet owners, this will ring true. We are typically careful to vet the qualifications and/or reputation of any person with whom we will leave our children or animals. We take great pains to choose people known to us and our kids or people with certain credentials. You may enjoy spending endless weekend hours with your drinking buddies or your distracted bohemian friend, but you may not entrust your kids to them, because it may not be in the kids' or pets' best interest. The same responsibility applies to dreams. It could be a critical mistake to entrust our hopes and aspirations to the wrong person, lest they mistreat or neglect them. But we are not nearly as careful with our dreams as we should be.

In a healthy relationship, your partner is a great "dream-catcher." However, when that unformed dream is laughed at, questioned, or belittled, it may not recover. Worse, you may scrap the whole idea. Learn from these mistakes, and don't even think about continuing to bring these aspirations to a narcissistic partner.

You don't want to leave this relationship, but you are getting slowly bled out from not having your good news and your aspirations received with what they deserve. They deserve congratulations, encouragement, joy, support, and interest. You may not, however, ever be able to get that from your narcissistic partner. So what do you do?

The Fix

She met him and fell in love with his creative vision. He was a senior and seasoned professional in a field in which she was just starting out but was getting early acclaim. Early on, he was a fan, giving her feedback, supporting her, and she always valued and praised him for his excellence in his work. As time went on, he became more and more critical of her creative work, undermining her, mocking her, and over time as she noticed he was becoming more disengaged, she would try to draw him in by sharing with him the wonderful things happening in her career. Over time, it became clear that anytime she would tell him good things, or ask for his opinion, he would be cold and critical. She felt disappointed and started doubting her performance, taking fewer chances, and selling herself short. Over time, she stopped sharing anything with him about her career, just to save herself the criticism and grief. He would sometimes be surprised when her work would be on public display. She found herself calmer and enjoying her career more than ever before. She would share her career developments in therapy, with friends, and with colleagues, and she realized that she once again felt inspired, in control, and serene in the face of the many demands, ups, and downs of her career. She recognized that he would never be able to celebrate her successes in any sort of cooperative manner, and so she found a way to celebrate her career and stop doubting herself. It just didn't involve him.

Remember, this is about managing your expectations. Step one: Make a list of people and places. This is a list of your "good-news people"—the cheerleaders, the supporters, the ones who believe in you on good days and bad. These may be friends, family, co-workers, or members of a club or religious community or school community. When the good news hits, tell them *first*. Sharing good news with your "good news people" can become a habit more quickly than you think. By taking the dreams and positive experiences to them instead of your partner, you are protecting yourself and growing yourself. Doing this will give you the opportunity to enjoy the news and value yourself enough to share it with a supportive mirroring person.

So what do you do with your partner and the good news or new aspiration? You have two potential paths here:

1. tell him/her nothing; or
2. tell him/her after you have carefully and joyfully shared it with others.

Option one is a bit riskier. Your partner may find out, and this can yield even more tension and stress in your relationship. Especially if the good news or new goal will have implications for the household, or is something that will be mentioned and noticed by others, and at some point he or she will need to know. With option two, because you took the good news to better "receivers" first, you may be more equipped to withstand the indifference, insults, or undermining your partner will bring upon hearing your good news. You may be able to stand your ground or not be as shattered by the usual reactions from your partner.

Ultimately, the fix is not to take your narcissistic partner the good stuff first. Relish it, enjoy it, share it with others who care, and take care of you first. Then you can share the news with him or her but not with the vulnerability of a small child who is about to face a rejecting parent, but rather as a strong adult, with head held high, who is already aware of your worth, your value, and will not let another's rejection sully your experience, your hopes, or your achievements.

THE BAD

Bad news happens, too. Lost jobs. Flat tires. Broken windows. Late bills. This news is obviously twice as challenging for a person in a relationship with a pathological narcissist. Unlike with the good news, not only is the bad news itself a challenge but also your partner will likely not be a source of comfort and may only bring more stress in the wake of this bad news. Just as with the good news, let's talk about strategies to minimize your damage.

➡ **Rule:** Just like with the good news, don't share it. And when you do, prepare it.

Many of the same themes from the "good" apply here as well. However, when you are sharing bad news or information, you are more vulnerable. There is a wide variety of issues that will qualify under bad news: layoffs at work, illness of a family member, argument with a friend, car problems, bad grades for your child. If you think a narcissist is cruel in how he or she receives good news, it can be even worse with bad news.

Types of Bad News: The first question that has to be addressed is the "type" of bad news. Sadly, because you may be in a narcissistic relationship, you do have to take the time to conduct this kind of "bad news assessment" (in a different relationship you would just freely share news—good, bad, or indifferent). The types of bad news can generally be classified into three bad news buckets:

1. Bad news that almost exclusively affects you and that represents an inconvenience to you (difficulties in the workplace, argument with a friend, traffic that you have to deal with on a commute)
2. Bad news that has implications for your family, household, or finances and by extension affects your partner (for example, loss of a job, a broken-down car,

broken dishwasher, child sent home for behavior issues in school, problems with a tax form)
3. Bad news that raises extremely personal vulnerabilities (illness in a family member, death of a loved one, illness or a health issue in you)

Each of these types of bad news may require very different approaches.

I. Bad news that almost exclusively affects you and that represents an inconvenience to you

A line often attributed to Chekhov goes something like this, "any idiot can face a crisis; it's this day-to-day living that wears you out." Traffic, money problems, broken appliances, flat tires, challenging co-workers, taxes. It's the stuff of life and most of us adjust to it more days than not, but sometimes these inconveniences can take a toll on us. Typically we vent, and in an ideal universe we share our challenges with our partners. Then they talk us through it and we take it on again.

However, if there is one thing a narcissistic person cannot tolerate, it is being inconvenienced. Even just hearing about your bad day is an inconvenience. This can be compounded if your bad day results in a literal inconvenience for your partner (bad traffic resulting in you arriving late, the broken appliance resulting in a lack of clean clothing). The word convenience often seems more applicable to devices or objects—a cell phone is a convenience, a dishwasher is a convenience. A person should not be classified as a convenience. When you are in a relationship with a narcissist, it can slowly dawn on you that things work well as long as you are convenient. Thus, at times you are not functional or useful or convenient, you may become nonexistent. When you are convenient to a narcissist (for example, you pick him up at the airport, call in a favor for her, keep the household running, have sex with him, look pretty), do not expect much more than a passing thank you. However, when you are inconvenient, and that could be anything from making a request of him, being unavailable due to a prior obligation, asking for his time, asking him to show up, or simply sharing something problematic that he cannot or does not want to deal with, the typical reaction is often irritability or just plain meanness.

So here you are, having experienced something challenging, and either wanting to talk about it or problem solve, and instead of addressing the stressful situation, you are actually adding another stressor to your list: your partner's irritability or indifference. It is not unusual under these conditions, when you share these kinds of day-to-day problems with him (problems that affect you far more than him) for him to barely listen, stare at a computer, TV, or cell phone, yawn, get frustrated, or simply leave the room.

This kind of daily negligence and disregard for your stressors is one of the issues that many people highlight as one of the most exhausting, because they feel as though they are in a relationship alone.

2. Bad news that has implications for your family, household, or finances, and by extension affects your partner

This is a much more challenging scenario, because before, the bad news was your problem—your commute, your PTA meeting, your kitchen appliance. Ergo, your partner could ignore it or just be a little grumpy about you wasting his or her time.

In this case, it's higher stakes, because now your partner's life will be interrupted. A lost job may mean less money in the household, a disruptive child means time spent in a teacher meeting, a glitch in a home repair may mean needing to get someone in to fix it and the cost of getting it fixed. You likely have had a long-term cycle in which you share this kind of "disruptive" bad news, your partner gets angry, and then over time, you become more and more reluctant to share such information because of fears and discomfort with your partner's reaction. But then you get painted into a corner, because the information ultimately has to be shared and will become more of a problem because you delayed sharing it.

Remember the initial premise: Narcissists hate being inconvenienced. They also hate anything that pierces the balloon of "everything's perfect." Thus, anything that besmirches the façade of your lives can often receive a disproportionately negative and strong reaction from a narcissistic person. In some ways, it can feel like your partner is turning something that is not at all personal (a broken appliance) into what feels like a vendetta by the world (and you) against him or her.

3. Bad news that raises extremely personal vulnerabilities

This is the most painful of the three scenarios, because it is here that someone wants and needs a connected and present partner. It is here that you want to hear that everything is going to be okay, that your partner is here for you, a hug, words of reassurance, hope.

Sadly, upon presenting personal or sad information to a narcissistic partner, many people will encounter emotional coldness or indifference. I recall one person telling me that in the days her mother was dying, her narcissistic husband kept hassling her to go to the hardware store. While this had occurred years ago, she is still mired in thinking about the coldness of her husband during some of the darkest days of her life. This is emblematic of the narcissists' superficial emotional world—they just can't go deep. So when faced with something deep and dire—a serious illness in your loved ones, a health crisis for you—they simply lack the emotional bandwidth and capability to be there. Their complete obsolescence at such times, and once again the sense that they are being "inconvenienced," can not only lead them to be unsupportive at such times but also just plain nasty. As you attempt to wrap your head around a dismal situation, such as the deterioration of a parent and the management of their healthcare, your partner may be grousing about how long you will be out of town and who is going to feed the cat. This can be devastating for you if you are already trying to face down what feels like an insurmountable crisis.

These patterns may also appear in situations of loss. During a period of mourning, empathy becomes essential. Grief is a time of extreme vulnerability, and when faced with cruelty, neglect, or indifference at such moments, it can feel like a slap in the face. Once again, your grief and mourning may represent an inconvenience. Narcissists lack the emotional vocabulary necessary to have these kinds of conversations. The last thing you want to do when you are grieving is to comfort and soothe them, because they do not want to face your sadness. Strong emotions make narcissists uncomfortable, and grief may be one of the strongest emotions we experience. Since the cycle in your relationship is to always have to make sure the narcissist is "taken care of" (to appease the beast), in your darkest hours you may have to appease and soothe *them*. Ironically, if they are experiencing the loss, they will often stop the clocks and turn into their own self-focused, self-referenced mourning period, expecting all lives to halt for them, and with the belief that their experience of grief is unique in all of human experience.

The lack of support in the face of a crisis represents one of the more devastating conditions that people in narcissistic relationships face. Many people hope that their relationship is in fact their insurance on a rainy day, the person who will be their rock during times of struggle. It is quite demoralizing to learn that decades were put into a relationship, and then when the rubber really met the road and a real crisis was upon you, your partner was not only nowhere to be found but also actually unavailable while your heart was breaking.

This can become extremely challenging when you are the one facing a health crisis of your own. This is a unique and specific situation, because illness in a partner can raise a wide array of reactions in the narcissist, ranging from anger and irritability that their narcissistic supply is otherwise preoccupied to resenting the attention your illness may bring to you to actually becoming anxious and in fact even helpful because they are concerned about losing your availability and presence. They may even rally for a few days or weeks. As a rule, narcissists do not make good adult diaper-changers; they are not built for it, and once again, there can be a real sense of feeling let down at precisely the time when you may not have the mental, emotional, and physical strength to manage your partner's disconnection.

The Fix

I. Bad news that almost exclusively affects you and that represents an inconvenience to you

Reflect on the most recent four or five daily stressors you have brought to your partner and on his or her reactions. It was most likely indifference or perhaps irritability. You may have also received little in the way of support, solution, or strategy for how to manage the problem together.

Expect nothing, and stop taking the day-to-day "stuff of life" to your partner. You are already frustrated by these stressors and sharing them with your partner only adds to the frustration, or even makes it worse. Your coping abilities are already tapped out, and now you are wiping them out. It can be frustrating or even isolating to not share these day-to-day stressors with your partner, because it leaves you feeling alone in your relationship. You are already in it alone and managing these stressors alone, and now we are taking an additional stressor off of your plate. By not sharing your daily stressors with your partner, you do not have to deal with his or her indifference, lack of empathy, and disconnection. That's one less stressor to deal with.

Just as with the good stuff, find empathic people with whom to share these daily stressors. Call a supportive friend on the way home. Talk with co-workers about work issues. Talk with other mothers about child-related issues. Talk with people who actually care and can offer support or even solutions. Share and hopefully solicit solutions via social media networks. Find other outlets, including exercise, meditation, and distraction. These may not fix the traffic, but they may leave you better able to cope with day-to-day stressors.

Ultimately, realize you are in much of this alone. Currently, you are waiting for your partner to be a partner. A healthy partner helps with finding solutions, hearing your concerns, letting you vent, and providing you with support. This typically does not happen with a narcissist, and as a result resentment is a frequent visitor in your life. Your partner is not going to react this way; it is not part of the narcissist's regular vocabulary. Your relationship is not a collaborative process, and with a narcissistic partner, it likely never will be. Many times, the exhaustion comes from waiting and waiting for your partner to finally get it right one day. It will *never* happen. There is an honesty, painful as it is, to just taking care of it yourself, and perhaps taking back some of your power.

2. Bad news that has implications for your family, household, or finances, and by extension affects your partner

Of all of the situations, this may be the hardest to deal with in terms of expectation management. If you are in this relationship, some of this will have to be shared, especially if it involves an issue that has ramifications, such as children, your residence, or long-term financial issues.

The "fix" here is preparation. Ingmar Bergman once said, "Only someone who is well prepared has the opportunity to improvise." So prepare, and part of this is to mindfully, calmly take the emotion and the expectation out of it. That way, you may also be better prepared to roll with the ups and downs of the conversation. You know very well that the bad news and the inconvenience will be poorly received. Many times people will use a long prelude to bad news in hopes that it will soften the blow. It won't.

Here is an example of a "bad" approach to giving this kind of news to a narcissist: "I know you had a tough day, and after a hard day it is hard to hear more difficult stuff. I hate to be the bringer of bad news, but don't worry, I will take care of it, but I wanted to let you know something about the car. It's not a big deal, and I have already dealt with the insurance company, and I hope you are okay because I know how busy you are."

After a prelude like that, your narcissist has his or her teeth on edge and it doesn't soften him; it hardens him. Your prelude makes sense. You have been here before and you know what is coming.

In some ways your attempts to "take care of him" and prepare him for the bad news is actually an attempt to prepare yourself for what is about to happen. You cannot control his reaction. You can only manage your uptake of his reaction.

You need to channel your inner Zen master and calmly cut to the chase:

> "I hit a pothole and damaged the front tire of the SUV. I had to get the car towed and will be getting the final estimate tomorrow, but they are expecting it will be approximately $2000. The deductible is $1000."

Then let the fireworks fly. You know they are coming, so steady yourself for the explosion. If you expect the tantrum, and *you know that there is no communication tool that will change them or redirect them,* calmly go to an internal mantra, let your partner go on his rant, listen to whatever solution he offers if any, and be prepared to find your own mode of transportation tomorrow. Basically, this strategy involves cutting to the chase and offering up answers right away. You have been "massaging" and managing your partner for so long, usually in fear of his reaction. That ship has sailed. Prelude or no prelude, there will be a reaction, so prepare and then improvise. You will survive his reaction. Think of it as pulling off a scab really quickly.

At this point, you have established that this person will not change (and in case you have not established this, I am reminding you again: He will not change). Thus, sobbing and crying and escalating this further represents a loss of your power and energy and will not result in a different or better outcome. You can already anticipate his reaction, and there is no evidence to assume it will be different. It is incumbent on you to problem solve the solutions ahead of time (yes, it will all fall on you). Your fear of his reaction is what has delayed you in the past and often allowed things to get worse, and your frustration at his unwillingness to help has devastated you in the past. With this strategy, you (a) stop the procrastination and delay; (b) stop the long preambles to "prepare" him for the inconvenient news (which often results in more hurtful reactions); (c) expect nothing so you are no longer disappointed; and (d) may feel more effective because you are not wasting time and effort waiting on someone else but rather addressing the problem at hand.

3. Bad news that raises extremely personal vulnerabilities

If you are going to stick this relationship out, you need to take care of you—especially under these circumstances. When you are facing profound experiences, such as parental illness, illness in a child or other loved one, or the actual loss of a loved one, you will feel vulnerable, weak, and tapped out. This is even more acute when it is your own health challenges. This is a time you need to find anyone in your network who will help you through; do not wait for your narcissist to ride in on his horse. He may be able to play White Knight for a day or two, but mourning, healing, and caregiving are long games, and to engage in these processes, you need resources and supports. At this time you can keep the matter-of-fact façade of your relationship, but turn to places for help where you know it will come. Do not try to draw water out of the dry well of narcissism.

View this as a long journey, and behaviors such as self-care (sleep, eating well, exercising, daily practices such as meditation) should be in your arsenal now. Self-care is like filling an account you will need to draw upon in the future. It is a reasonable assumption to believe that if you are in a relationship your partner will be there for you down the road. Sadly, with a narcissistic partner, plan on that account being chronically overdrawn and unavailable. As such, today is a great day for you to start taking care of you, so you can face down challenges big and small (even without the support of your partner). This chapter is intended to be a wake-up call that you need to take care of you. This also means that you need to cultivate your social support networks now. As noted throughout the book, the absence of depth and consistency from your partner means that you need it from other

sources. Be there for them as they will be there for you. These relationships will be important for you at all times of your life. When
a person is in a narcissistic relationship, other healthy relationships are essential and pay out dividends that can save your soul.
It is within these relationships that your empathy gets mirrored
back and reinforced. It is critical that you take care of yourself and
maintain connected relationships with those around you. Not as
a means of preparing for crises but to enrich your life, and yes, it
is likely that these relationships will be there for you (when your
partner is not).

THE INDIFFERENT

This is all the neutral minutiae: the weather, the new supermarket
that is being built in your town, the bird that just landed on the
windowsill. You better pay attention to it, because these are going
to be the only details you can talk about with your narcissistic
partner. The indifferent issues—and there are many of them in our
lives—are the filler. They are the neutral trifles that are happening
between the big events. Typically, these are the topics we may be
able to engage in with a stranger—they are universal themes and
observations about the world around us. Think about when you
have fallen into a conversation with a stranger at a bus stop or an
airport. You likely just talked about a delayed flight, the rain, or a
doughnut you were eating.

➡ **Rule:** Pay attention to everything that once felt like it was
not worth talking about (for example, the weather); this will be
your "go-to" when it comes to initiating a conversation with your
partner, because it is safe and will allow you to minimize criticism.
These seemingly "trivial" topics will allow a place of connection
for you and your partner, and even if he remains disconnected at
such times, the disconnection loses its power because the topic
does not matter.

When you stay, and are making it "work," then the indifferent parts of life become a life preserver of sorts. It is generally "un-valenced," meaning that it holds little personal relevance or emotion. While it can sting to be criticized or mocked or neglected about an accomplishment, or an aspiration, or an important event or a loss, you can't really take the weather personally. Few people want to live in silence if they are in a relationship, and the indifferent filler can keep the conversation moving, without giving the narcissist a hurtful target. He or she will likely find ways to insert some negativism here as well, perhaps mocking your opinion, calling you out for not being knowledgeable about a topic, or even labeling you as "dull." Smile serenely and carry on. Your narcissist does not realize the triumph—you just dodged a bullet and did not play out the usual old patterns. He may even be frustrated, since he can't get the same reactions out of you, and may have to find a new psychological punching bag.

The Fix

In some ways there is a secondary payout in accessing the "indifferent" aspects of your world as fodder for conversation, because it forces you to be mindful about your environment. You will actually have to pay attention to the little things around you so there is something to chat about. The focus then becomes mindfully avoiding the topics that leave you vulnerable, and also breathing and reflecting on whether you are ready to share about the fight you had with your sister, or just making the conversation about the impending snow-storm. Cultivating the filler can allow you to stop the one-sided be-rating you regularly face, as well as the chronic disappointment of being ignored or unheard. It can also help you to avoid uncomfort-able silence. Narcissists are never really listening anyhow, so whether or not they respond to your daily weather reports or other prosaic observations is now officially irrelevant. Now you are taking care of you and no longer falling into the usual traps.

Does the 3-Part Rule Work?

Yes, it does. Managing expectations can be undertaken at two levels. 1. No longer sharing significant or vulnerable information with your partner, and 2. Sharing it and being ready for the reaction and the disappointment. In both cases, you can and should employ other sounding boards—friends, family, colleagues, members of your community, therapy, pastoral advisors—to give you the chance to participate in the human experience of a shared life.

Over the years, I have had multiple clients who had narcissistic spouses, and I realized that no one had been listening to them for years. They had rich inner worlds, hopes, histories, and unique experiences that had gone unshared for years. Watching them share their stories and receive feedback was curative in and of itself. Therapy can often be a wonderful first step to healing from not being heard. I never held an agenda for them to leave, and our work prepared them to stay, but to no longer cultivate disappointment. They slowly found ways to nurture new friendships, become involved in their communities, and reach out to old acquaintances. As their needs got met—in therapy, with friends, and most critically in finding meaning and purpose in their lives that was no longer being mocked or minimized by their partner (because they were not putting it on the chopping block by sharing it)—they were now better able to withstand the one-sided rigors of their relationship and reported that, surprisingly, things were going better now that they were no longer waiting for a balanced relationship.

You actually do not need to tell anyone you are doing this—that you are managing expectations and responding in new ways—you can just do it. When this approach is discussed with others, it is labeled as cynical, and many people will ask if you do not share anything with your partner, then what is the point of the relationship? Shouldn't we be helping the narcissist listen to his partner, instead of his partner shutting down? I have no doubt that this approach will be labeled as cold, calculating, and cynical. This approach could be labeled as "passive aggressive" or playing "hard to get" (to which my question would be "what exactly are you trying to get?"). To reiterate, communication is the ideal goal, but you are reading this book because communication did not work, and likely never will. Do not undertake the 3 part rule because you think it will get your partner to change or pay attention, if you approach it like that—then it is in fact passive aggressive and also likely to yield the same old disappointment. When you embrace the 3 part rule, you must do so in a way that reflects that you are aware of your partner's limitations, are avoiding the same painful communication traps, are attempting to build a support network, and are no longer waiting for the rescue fantasy. Just as there is no magic pill that someone can take to lose 10 pounds, there is also no magic therapy technique that will make a narcissist empathic and available. A relationship characterized by censorship, lack of sharing, and distance is not for everyone and is not optimal. However, since the narcissistic partner will not change, and you also want to maintain the relationship, these techniques may facilitate saving yourself while remaining in a suboptimal situation. Cynical? Perhaps. Survival rarely looks like a fairy tale.

Will This Be Easy?

No. The narcissists in your life may actually get a bit squirrely if you don't give them some ammunition. Their paranoia may kick in and they may accuse you of holding back or assume something more sinister.

Finally, however, you always have the ultimate ace in the hole: *Let them talk about themselves.* Smile, nod, offer some understanding, toss them a little narcissistic supply and encouraging words. After all, you did decide to stay. Remember a basic ground rule: You always bring your best self into this. Do not get into the mud and criticize, berate, or even question them. Just smile, nod, encourage. They never really listened to you or cared what you had to say anyhow, so focusing on positive vocalizations like encouragement is good for your psychological health and may maintain a sense of peace in your relationship and a place of grace for you. Who knows, they may even learn a little by watching you. Because you have learned to no longer attempt to get your needs met by them, and are focusing instead on the positive elements of the relationship, they may actually mirror this behavior back from time to time (just do not let it lull you into complacency and start sliding back into old rhythms).

Because you are cultivating your ability to get needs met outside of your primary relationship in terms of support, connection, encouragement, and kindness, you are not as depleted as before. You can actually listen to what your narcissistic partner has to say, and perhaps even find it interesting, or even want to support it. For years, you imagined reciprocity: You tell me yours, I will tell you mine, and we will share it and grow together. That is highly unlikely. The years of frustration about chasing that hope left you depleted.

I would be remiss if I did not mention some of the "risks" of building a social network and finally addressing your needs directly. After years of being ignored, neglected, criticized, or silenced, you begin reaching out to others and building a network, and you start giving yourself permission to be heard. A key dynamic that keeps narcissistic relationships in place is denial— denial by both you and your narcissistic partner. The narcissist has little insight or empathy, so there is a general denial of his treatment of his partner, and the other person in the relationship often needs to remain in denial in order to wake up every day and stay in a relationship with someone who is not present. Once you start developing other social connections, the denial starts getting scraped away. Other people will start noticing you, often for the first time in years. They may listen, and empathize, and care, and support your dreams, and safeguard your fears. It can be ripe ground for falling in love with someone, largely because for the first time in a long time, someone is finally seeing you. It does not mean you are a bad person, or an amoral person, but it can be disarming. Be mindful, establish boundaries with which you are comfortable, and reflect on what these kinds of shifts may mean. It may be a wakeup call or a slap in the face. It can also be terrifying. A key recommendation is to solicit the guidance and support of a trained mental health provider to help you navigate this territory. It's not necessarily a bad thing to experience these feelings, how you act on them is a personal decision. No matter what, these awakenings are important pieces of information to consider as you navigate this new way of being within your relationship. People in narcissistic relationships slowly start to negate themselves a day at a time; they gradually devalue themselves. When you finally start coming out of this space, the world will notice.

The supported and wiser version of you may be better able to withstand the day-to-day challenges and the many patterns we have discussed, including self-doubt, frustration, confusion, and anger. Most important, you are not waiting for something that will never happen, you are getting your needs met, and you are not going to permit your hopes, dreams, and accomplishments to be criticized or undermined. In essence, you have learned to "consume" your partner in a new and realistic way.

The "I Love You" Paradox

Clarifying the three most confusing and misunderstood words in the English language may help you stay (or go, or just stay sane). The meaning of these words often relates to the issuer. We all say them—to parents, children, friends, siblings, lovers, dogs, and cats.

In a romantic relationship, the words "I love you" can carry assumptions: If you love me then you will support me, keep me safe, listen to me, respect me, honor me, have sex with me, laugh with me, take care of me when I am old, kiss me, stand by me.

Lots of assumptions for three little words. So reflect right now on what "I love you" means to you. When you say those words to someone, what does it mean? It may mean the things listed above, and it may not. One of the greatest challenges I encounter when working with couples, even regardless of whether one of the partners is narcissistic, is misunderstandings over the words "I love you" and second-guessing someone who says those words. A rule of thumb is that you are not allowed to question someone who says "I love you" to you. As far as that person is concerned, he said the words and he means them. The difficulty is that his definition of "I love you" and your definition are likely completely different.

Couples can fall down the rabbit hole of arguing about the "I love you" crisis. "If you act like this, then you don't really mean it." The real challenge is not the words, or whether the other person means them, but rather being clear on your definition, your expectation, and ultimately how you want to be treated. Think about how you feel in this relationship, the quality of your communication and collaboration, and your partner's behavior. If these things do not sit well with you, then all the "I love you's" in the world may not have meaning. However, when your partner says it, he means it. Do not waste your time with the wrong argument. Reflecting on "I love you" may be one of the most useful ways to reflect on how you really feel in this relationship. "I love you" can be a careless, tossed-off phrase—stop giving it so much meaning and pay attention to the other person's actions and regard. Saying "I love you" is easy; being present and engaged in a relationship is a different matter. Avoid this argument by saying it if you mean it, and not assuming it means the same thing to your partner.

The Revelation

There are several fantasies that have kept you in this relationship. Debunking these fantasies does not mean you have to leave, but remain aware of the key classic fantasies that have held you hostage.

- ► My partner will change.
- ► One day s/he will see how wonderful I am, and what we have together.
- ► One day s/he will have that moment and s/he will see the light and apologize for everything.

None of these are likely to happen. Your partner may in fact be a nice person for days and months at a time, but the first time a big-ticket stressor rears its head, you will be back to business as usual. Each time something more interesting than you turns up—at work, a person, an opportunity—he will ignore you again. The disappointment each time this takes place can be paralyzing. With each good day you have, hopes soar, and the higher they soar, the more pieces there are to pick up once things crash again. A typical trajectory here is enjoying a nice vacation during which he relaxes, you relax, and then you get a little brave and start trying to talk about meaningful subjects again and realize that he isn't listening. Or an event occurs in which he feels somehow let down, and it all comes crashing down again. If anything, you almost need to embrace the good days as "holidays" of a sort, and since every day can't be a holiday, enjoy it and gird yourself for the usual on more days than not.

In an earlier chapter, I presented the idea of being "enough." Always remember, you are *more* than enough, always have been, always will be. The narcissist also never feels like he is enough, so he is always seeking attention and affirmation from the outside. If he is never enough, then no one else is either, but he is not aware of this dynamic. It would be an entirely different experience if he sat with you and said, "I am very empty, and I will never feel like I am enough, so I know that I will always treat you like you are not enough, even though you are." If your partner had that level of insight, then he would not be narcissistic.

This leads to the biggest hope of all—that he will someday "get it." You will get the big apology, the Hollywood moment, the act of contrition, the hope of redemption. It's not going to happen. That myth is what has led you to destroy yourself for years. The belief that someday he will see how wonderful you are, and he will apologize and thank you for standing by his side.

Redemption is built into religious texts, mythology, fairy tales (our Beast, the Frog Prince), and films. It is one of the primary messages of all world religions: Through love comes redemption. It is a dangerous sell, because it can be true and miraculous, but in the case of narcissism, redemption will almost never occur. More and more love will not bring the change you hope for. I have never seen real redemption with a pathological narcissist or a person with narcissistic personality disorder. Never. But it's a big world, and I am sure such stories exist. Ronningstam's work, which suggests the possibility of a corrective emotional experience and corrective relationship, is quite possible but it requires considerable luck and timing. The odds are not in your favor.

By definition a personality disorder is almost impossible to change, and the nature of narcissism is such that insight is highly unlikely, unless it is self-serving. So do not project stories of redemption you observe in others onto your pathologically narcissistic partner. Your hope has wasted a lot of your emotional energy. Perhaps the redemption in this story needs to come back to you. To take care of you. To draw people closer to you that support and love you. You may not get the swan song from your partner, but you can start taking care of yourself right now.

Letting go of these myths and hopes is not easy, but it is essential if you want to keep this relationship going. The myths and hopes exhaust you, leaving you waiting for something that may never appear. In the process, you keep trying harder and harder, get fewer and fewer needs met, and start losing yourself. You may have believed until now that the hope is what kept it going; in fact, removing the hope may be how you can survive in this relationship.

Removing the hope will help you find your way to taking care of you (instead of trying to get your partner or someone else to notice you). It will lead you to cease expending resources on making the impossible happen but instead ensure that you receive the support you need, the encouragement you need, and the sounding boards you need. Managing expectations is about as romantic as getting socks on Valentine's Day, but understanding these rules allows you to stay and salvage what you can, while still maintaining as authentic a life as possible while you are in this relationship.

CHAPTER 8

SHOULD I GO?

One day everything will be well, that is our hope. Everything's fine today, that is our illusion.

—VOLTAIRE

You have decided to leave a relationship that is no longer working. This should be a good thing. But yet, this can be as confusing and challenging as staying in this messy web. You are in a relationship with a narcissist, you are slogging through the Dark Triad, your trust has been betrayed, you haven't been noticed or heard for months/years/decades, you have been ignored, and life has been empty. You have craved connection from the one source that could not bring it. You may have lots of cheerleaders at this point, showing you the finish line and supporting you every step of the way.

This relationship has likely become an invisible prison, with your self-doubt as the bars of your own cell. There are many forces operating at once: a strange sort of protectiveness about your broken relationship (it may be broken, but it is yours), feelings about the investment you have made in terms of time and resources put into the relationship, and a fear of the unknown (the devil you know may feel better than the angel you don't). The bottom line is that despite the bad treatment and the toxic conditions, you may also still be deeply in love with this person.

The question then becomes "what are you afraid of leaving?" Perhaps the hardest thing of all is to leave the illusion. Illusions are often more seductive than reality, and for years you have been nothing short of an advertising executive, branding your relationship for the world so masterfully that you even started believing in it. You had to, and that is why you stayed.

But remember, part of what you are leaving is an illusion, a mirage—something that actually is not there. And it is not real.

And yet, it hurts.

The relationship with the pathological narcissist is often very activating, because you kept it alive by writing a vibrant narrative around it. Your story may, in fact, have been more real than the relationship itself. In some ways, it is harder to leave an illusion than a reality. In addition, the hardest part of all is leaving the hope. You likely remained in this relationship for such a long time because of the power of hope. The hope has been your scaffold for so long that ending the relationship is just as much about stepping away from the scaffold that has supported you as it is about stepping away from your partner.

As you now realize, this relationship was running on hope more than it was running on reality. The future orientation of doing the right thing, of "trying to be perfect," of trying to be "enough," of strategizing and figuring out how to keep your partner's interest, and the hope that your partner would finally notice you kept it going. Perhaps at this point, with the recognition that this narcissistic pattern is never going to change, the hope has finally been shelved. This recognition is not an easy place to land. While this is a form of resignation, and finally, quiet acceptance, it is not easy.

What Does It Mean to End It?

Ending a relationship is stressful, challenging, and psychologically difficult. Whether it has been going on for months or years, breaking up is hard to do. It is also likely that you have been musing about this for a long time and slowly arrived at this place. As you think about ending the relationship, you will have to consider all of the following. First up are the very real and practical factors:

- Children
- Money
- Other family
- Cultural factors
- Religious beliefs

Next are the psychological factors—the barriers and variables that may be less visible:

- Fear
- Shame
- Anger
- Regret
- Nostalgia
- Being in love

Depending on your situation, many of these factors have all likely contributed to keeping you in for longer than you wanted or than was healthy. Obviously, the prevailing wisdom in our culture, especially for married couples, is to work it out. For most relationships, it is fiscally, familially, and culturally more expedient. Divorce is in fact hard on children and on the people in the marriage. There are still numerous cultural and religious prohibitions against divorce. The more of these factors you confront, and the longer the relationship, the more challenging it will be to address these practical factors. There is, however, no prize for endurance, and to endure this kind of relationship is not a healthy life.

Commitment Versus Investment

Some psychologists have applied logical, quantitative tools to understand commitment in relationships from a straightforward investment model. Understanding this model may help you understand why you stuck it out and why it is so hard to leave. Caryl Rusbult, who was a professor of Social and Organizational Psychology at the Vrije Universiteit in Amsterdam, laid out an investment model that focuses on the concept of commitment and breaks down the elements that commit a person (or not) to a relationship. The theory posits that there are three factors to be considered to understand commitment and the likelihood of making a change: satisfaction (what you get from the relationship), alternative quality (the outcomes you expect from the next best option or alternative), and investments (what you would lose if you left, and these could be practical things like possessions and children, and more intangible things like your shared histories and experiences). These three things work together and allow us to look at the mental "calculations" we make in our relationships. In simple terms, we consider issues, including what we are getting out of our relationship, whether there is someone else out there who might be better for us who is available and a good option, as well as what we might lose if we left. We do that algebra of the heart and if the numbers favor staying, we stay. If the numbers favor leaving, we leave.

This theory actually works quite well in relationships in which both parties are invested in the relationship for similar reasons. It does not work as well when one of the parties is a narcissist. People who are highly committed in their relationships care deeply about the well-being of their partners and they subjugate their own needs and even transform them to do what is best for the relationship and for their partner. Commitment brings lots of dividends, and the alternative has to be pretty damned good to pull most people out of their investment and to endure the loss of time and history. When your partner is narcissistic, satisfaction tends to run low, but you keep holding out for the day when your partner will be in the game. While some people bristle at the idea of a relationship being viewed through the lens of an "investment" model, it is an honest way to assess it.

Narcissists are masterful at compartmentalizing. This is basically putting everything in their lives into neat and tidy boxes and often not realizing that life is messy and things are not always so neat and tidy. As a result, they can compartmentalize work, relationships, and family and not reflect on the interdependence of all of these factors. It is also why narcissists are so easily able to engage in infidelity. They rather simplistically view their extramarital relationship or cheating behavior as being in a different "box" than their marriage and these relationships serve very different needs. Their lack of empathy means that they view their affair and their marriage as separate spaces and do not reflect on how the affair may devastate their spouse or partner. Their grandiosity means that they think they have it all figured out and are able to juggle a wife and girlfriend (and maybe even a few other dalliances on the side). Interestingly, many narcissists very much value their role as parent and spouse and would actually be devastated at losing those roles. Once again, the compartmentalization means that they view their marriage in a more distant and intellectualized manner ("I am a family man" or "I am a matriarch") and do not want to give up this identity (not realizing that being a husband and father is more than just a title). The affair addresses a specific need, and they have no intention of giving up either the marriage or the mistress if they can help it (word to all of those out there who are the mistress or partner in an extramarital relationship with a narcissist, unless he gets caught, do not plan on him making you his main act, no matter how many times he reassures you).

Compartmentalization means that narcissists often view the investment of a relationship differently than other people. Actually, a narcissist having an affair often makes a lovely husband—his needs are getting met, and he may come home quite cheerful and ready to jump into the spouse and father compartment with cheerful good humor. There is nothing more cheerful than a satisfied narcissist, and it can be devastating to realize that the pleasant months or years of your marriage were a by-product of your partner's deception.

Relationships *are* investments, and we do deposit tangible and intangible resources into them. We are more likely to keep doing that if we are getting a return, but interestingly, people in relationships with narcissists defy this investment model and stay in year after year, despite getting little satisfaction. The investment model, however, argues that it is not only the satisfaction that matters but also the investment that you make. If you put money into a bank account and the bank kept taking it and emptying out your account, odds are that you would find another bank. But the investments in a relationship are quite different—time, history, hope, family—and these are harder to quantify or walk away from, even if they are being squandered by your partner.

Over the years, the obvious return on your investment has not been very high, so it may be that the "perception" or the "hope" is what kept you in it. In addition, it is also quite possible that the activation of old familiar scripts (that confusing familiarity that we erroneously label "chemistry") adds a layer to this that the investment model cannot account for. The investment model is intuitive and simple and appealing, but it does not really work when you reflect on a relationship in which there is more illusion than reality.

Prepare for Narcissistic Rage

You will not be permitted to go quietly into the dark night.

First, let's revisit the concepts of narcissistic rage and inconvenience. Narcissists do not want to be inconvenienced, they tend to be paranoid, they do *not* like to be played, and they do not tolerate anything that feels like abandonment particularly well. In addition, a breakup, especially one that will remove their children from the home or requires a splitting up of assets that may negatively impact their lifestyle and that may leave them looking "bad" to the world, is *highly* inconvenient.

If you are the one who initiates the end of the relationship, your partner's strong emotions may overpower you. Expect rage, sorrow, withdrawal, more rage, retaliation, pettiness, and—especially in the case of a divorce—lots of litigation (divorce attorneys probably make half of their take on the backs of narcissistic divorces because they are so messy). The strong emotions may also discourage or frighten you. Again, to reiterate an earlier point, if this is a situation that is devolving into violence and danger, you will need to mobilize legal and public safety entities to address the situation. (See the Appendix at the end of the book for more information.)

Typically, narcissists' emotions are more about empty threats, cold anger, cruel stunts, calls from attorneys, rage and more rage, and just general bad behavior, and it can become exhausting. I have had a front row seat at some challenging divorces, and it became a white-knuckle ride for the receiver of all of this narcissistic rage. More than once, I would witness the deflation, exhaustion, demoralization, and sometimes suicidal thoughts of the people who were enduring this mess. The narcissist is masterful at being able to reload and launch into endless angry invectives, even after everyone else is completely broken down.

Narcissistic Ego and Injury

Why can't narcissists just *go gentle into that good night?* Much of it is ego. None of us like to be left, abandonment never feels good, and even the most transcendent among us will have a moment of grief and discomfort when someone decides to pack it in and bid farewell. But in the case of a person who is pathologically narcissistic, it goes deep. Being left is an awakening of their vulnerabilities, and their inability to regulate emotion becomes their undoing. Whereas many of us may go quietly to lick our wounds, eat some ice cream, drink some vodka, and cry it out, the narcissist feels inconsolable. However, this inconsolability manifests in a very unsympathetic way. Narcissists' propensity to rage and their emptiness make it nearly impossible to regulate the strong emotions that accompany a perceived abandonment, and as a result they have a terrible tantrum.

This brings us to the concept of narcissistic injury. A narcissistic injury is a threat to the grandiose (and fragile) sense of self of the narcissist. Your leaving, or your threat of leaving, is the reminder that he is fragile. Remember, the narcissist's dilemma is that under the powerful and charismatic bluster he shows to the world, he is actually extremely vulnerable and dependent. Your decision to leave reinforces that vulnerability and the narcissistic injury is deeply felt. The reaction to narcissistic injury is typically narcissistic rage. Because their reaction feels so disproportionate, it can be frightening, but because the injury that they have experienced is so piercing and such a threat to their grandiose and entitled self, it's a deep and primitive pain.

The fear of this rage reaction is what keeps many people in the relationship. For a very long time. Repeatedly, people attempting to end relationships with narcissists have said to me, "if I knew it was going to be this bad, I never would have started this process," but when it was all done, they were extremely grateful that they did. Some level of preparation for the rigors and harrows of what is about to unfold is good (at a minimum to make arrangements at work, for children, and for your own mental health). However, it can also be terrifying and you may be tempted to avoid such a difficult period. Many people think, "I put up with it for 10 years, maybe I can do it longer."

Sadly, this can also be a frightening time. Not just in situations that are violent and require restraining orders and the justice system. The threatening e-mails, text messages, and calls, the threats of legal action, the sense of being followed and of having your name besmirched to family members, friends, and anyone else who will listen are extremely upsetting. Many people who endure a narcissistic breakup will say that they had to start anew—and learned who their real friends were. After the smear campaign, it was only those who knew them best who were still standing, and after it all settled down, many also said that it was nice to start fresh and weed out all the suckers from their prior life.

Some people reading this may think *my situation isn't that big a deal, we didn't live together, we were not married, or we did not have children together.* A narcissistic breakup is difficult whether it is after months or years. Obviously, the more entrenched and "invested" you are, the more practically and psychologically challenging it may be. However, the reaction is likely to be over-whelming no matter what your situation, simply because you are dealing with a narcissist.

How to Prepare to Leave

If you are reading this book or have been in a narcissistic relationship, then odds are that you have been struggling with this relationship for some time. You may already be dissatisfied, frustrated, depressed, ashamed, or experiencing self-doubt. So this is not an easy time to make a challenging transition, as your reserves are already depleted. The bottom line is that leaving is not going to be easy. You will need to prepare both in practical and psychological ways.

PRACTICAL PREPARATION

Providing guidance on practical preparation for ending a relationship with a narcissist can vary widely, depending on your circumstances and how long you were together. Obviously, these preparations will have to be far more elaborate if you are ending a lengthy marriage or if there are children involved versus ending a shorter term dating relationship. However, in both cases, prepare to be challenged.

Here are some practical steps to consider. Not all may be relevant to your situation, but some may be useful:

- ▶ Document everything.
- ▶ Keep friends and family in the loop.
- ▶ Get therapy or counseling.
- ▶ Obtain legal assistance.
- ▶ Make structural changes (changing locks, ensuring bills—especially cell phone bills—are put in your name and credit cards are locked, safeguarding finances).
- ▶ Be mindful of your social-media exposure.
- ▶ Prepare to move out quickly.

Document everything.

These are unpleasant steps. In the case of a divorce, you will need legal assistance and a divorce attorney who should be briefed on the psychology of the case. However, documentation matters. Because pathological narcissists are such skilled liars and deflectors, you will be doubted and literally lied to about everything. If you are starting to pull the plug, begin putting things in writing. Keep a log and journal of relevant facts that you may need for litigation or simply for sanity. Save e-mails and text messages. You may need this documentation, even if it is not for legal purposes. For example, if your partner starts turning on the charm again, and you start feeling like you are getting sucked back into the vortex, this documentation can also be a wake-up call, a sort of psychological slap in the face to keep you from going back in.

Keep friends and family in the loop.

Up until recently, you may have also held back from sharing the more gruesome details of your relationship with other people. As noted earlier in the book, this may have been out of shame, to protect your partner, or because you may be a private person. It's time to start sharing. It does not have to be lurid or defamatory, but share with others what you have experienced personally. There are both procedural and personal reasons for this. Procedurally, if people become aware of the landscape of your relationship, they may also be able to provide you with the type of support you need at this time (for example, a safe place to stay without questions). It can also be normalizing to talk about your experience (and it is quite likely that they have been noticing it for years, even if you did not share it with them). They may also be an essential resource if you start getting pulled back in. They become that Greek chorus that can remind you of what it was (and still is).

However, your friends and family may also be in the narcissist's line of fire. When the narcissist starts blazing his rage, everyone in proximity will be hit. Your narcissistic partner may blame your friends and family for encouraging you, for filling your head with "ideas," for speaking badly about him, and he may also spew his venom onto them. This can be hard to experience, as you may likely feel responsible for the stress your friends and family are experiencing. Remember, that you are not spewing this hatred, your partner (soon to be ex-partner) is. And your friends and family will recognize it. By being directly in the firing line of your partner, it may also result in more support for you as they directly experience what you have been enduring for a while now. Your narcissistic partner has been and likely still is quite charming, so it may take a little while for those close to you to let go of their conception of your partner as a good guy. As he gets frustrated, he will show his true colors. However, if he has charmed those around you, it can be quite alienating for a while, as people may question you and may even advocate for him. Stand your ground; you know the back story. You do not need to defend your decision—you did not come here lightly.

If you have children, or this is the dissolution of a long-term marriage, you are definitely going to need the support of your friends and family—it may be practical (for example, childcare, a place to stay) and it will definitely be psychological. But be judicious. Not everyone will be a cheerleader. Sometimes relationship breakups can bring out the worst in people, and your own family members may be struggling with their own narratives about shame, divorce, or just "looking bad" to the world. This is definitely not the time to have to appease other people as you weather this storm, so choose your supporters wisely.

Get psychotherapy.

Psychotherapy is *essential* to grow and heal. Be sure you work with a therapist who knows the landscape of narcissism. Be wary of anyone who may try to push you back down the path of "communication" (you have likely already been down that road) or who holds to a charming belief that your narcissist will change. There are plenty of well-intentioned folks in the mental-health field who carry the banner of "everyone can change"—a positive and rather sweet supposition, and not true in this case. Remember, you are paying the therapist, and if it does not feel good, you can find another. But in the hands of a skilled and wise therapist, you will have the opportunity to share your fears and your experiences and have an objective sounding board.

Therapy may also be an important support for your children. Divorce is challenging for children, regardless of the circumstances, and providing them with an objective space in which to share their feelings and fears can be essential. In the case of dissolving a relationship with a narcissistic partner, therapy becomes required. Narcissistic parents are not above using their children as pawns, manipulating them with money or information, or sharing highly inappropriate details with them. Your role is to protect your children, and working with a therapist skilled in managing divorce transitions with children (ideally one with expertise in narcissistic personality) can help with this process. Do not get into the mud with your partner and try to outplay him. Maintain appropriate boundaries and conduct where your children are concerned, and work closely with mental health professionals to safeguard your children's transition.

Obtain legal assistance.

While many divorces can be handled via mediation, divorces with narcissists often require attorneys. The narcissist's tendency to pull out the rage and translate it into expensive and unjust litigation may necessitate legal assistance. Laws regarding divorce, child custody fiscal responsibility, and division of assets vary from state to state, and you are advised to seek out appropriate legal counsel from an attorney in your jurisdiction. Ensure that you have your own advocate and facilitate this process by ensuring you have as much documentation as possible.

Make structural changes.

These are hard to think about, but often essential, and they can include changing locks, separating finances, shutting down accounts, and informing employers if needed. Work with your legal counsel to ensure that you can make these changes, and ensure you do so in a timely manner so that your finances are not at risk. Establish a bank account with funds only you can access. But again, be sure you consult with an attorney so that you are not accused of acting in a way that could be construed as financial misconduct. You want to be sure that you do not find yourself on the wrong end of a partner's financial revenge scheme—and that may involve removing your name from any joint accounts ASAP. Again, ensure that you consult with your attorney and financial advisors about these issues.

In addition, if you had a shared phone account, make sure you establish your own mobile account immediately. Finally, certain shared smartphone services may permit your partner access to apps that allow your location to be made known. Ensure that you remove any geo-tracking features from social media and other networking and mobile apps if you have any concerns about your partner using your location as a means of ongoing harassment.

Sadly, you may have to take even more extreme steps, such as getting a new phone number. In the space of a breakup, their rage will often leave them with more destructive energy than you, so any tools, tricks, and techniques you can employ to minimize contact will help in the process of letting go.

Be mindful of your social media exposure.

Believe it or not, at this stage, social media can start becoming a toxic landscape for you. Again, if you have minor children, and this is a divorce situation, any photo of you on social media, even just holding a glass of wine at an elegant event, can become co-opted and turned into ammunition against you. Be very careful to not use social media as a platform to lambast or criticize your spouse, as such invectives may come back to bite you legally. As tempting as it may be to let the world know that you are caught in your own personal hell (or that you are surviving just fine), avoid doing so at all costs. Your social media may be probed minutely, so any and all posts can become weapons. Your best course of action may be to shut down for a while.

On the other side is your partner's conduct on social media. We have already established that narcissists do not go deep in any relationships. We also know that social media is the narcissist's mother ship—a playground of admiration-seeking and validation. Finally, we know that the post-breakup world for them is usually about rage and revenge. The rage often gets harnessed into revenge. Even if you are completely done and mentally checked out of the relationship, photos of your partner's new girlfriend, purchase or trip, angry posts about you, or angry posts about relationships may be unpleasant and stressful to read or to look at. Migrating out of the social-media space as you navigate your way out of the relationship can be an easy way to make life easier and protect yourself. Research suggests that time spent on social media in the post-breakup phase can significantly hamper the process of mourning and moving forward. However, your partner's bad judgment may be useful for you to document. Even if you do not feel able to do this, you may want to ask a trusted friend who still has access to your partner's social media feeds to document these posts, because they may become an important part of your records as you attempt to resolve the legal aspects of this situation.

Prepare to move out quickly.

You do need to be prepared to get out quickly if needed. While you may be able to manage strong emotions, your partner is not. When his rage kicks in, do not be surprised if you come home to find the locks have been changed or your belongings sitting on the front lawn or strewn about the home. If damage is done to your possessions, as noted above, document or photograph anything you may need in formal proceedings (or just as a reminder). But be prepared that your narcissistic partner's rage may mean a need for a hasty retreat. Stow some essentials in your car, office, or a family member or friend's house. Have credit cards or cash. While it can be upsetting and distressing to deal with this, if you are prepared, then you won't have to scramble in the midst of the chaos.

PSYCHOLOGICAL PREPARATION

Here are the harder steps—the "psychological" preparations you must make in order to begin this transition, as well as the attitudes and behaviors that will help you transition out. Just as in the "should I stay" section, these are all about managing expectations.

Be prepared for the following:

- ▶ Ignore the blame and accusations.
- ▶ Remember that your partner will never change.
- ▶ Don't fall for the honeymoon period.
- ▶ Embrace your emotions—and take care of yourself.

Ignore the blame and accusations.

Narcissists not only lie but also project. Because they engage in projection (taking what they are feeling and projecting it onto someone else), and because they do not take responsibility for anything or anyone, they blame. As you go through the process of undoing your relationship, be prepared for endless blame and accusations. It may even feel absurd at times—a well-reasoned concern about communication issues within your relationship over the years will deteriorate into your partner accusing you of a random shortcoming that occurred five years ago. Narcissists tend to accumulate grievances and pull them out at will any time they attempt to "defend" themselves. This process is exhausting, and enduring such accusations can challenge your patience. Responding in kind and hurling back similar accusations is not a good idea because you cannot win at this game. By now you have established that your narcissistic partner is a better and dirtier fighter than you. You know his accusations are irrelevant. Meet his behavior with dignified silence, because you learned long ago that your partner never listened anyway.

Remember that your partner will never change.

The mantra of "they will never change" has particular importance now. When you initially start the process to end the relationship, while rage is all but guaranteed, it is also quite possible that he will try to draw you back in. If you recall the early days of your courtship, in many cases, you remember your partner's charm, confidence, and flirtatiousness. Narcissists do not like to lose and may not want to end this relationship—or at least not have you leave them first. Do not get romantic and think it is because this is a grand love story and he does not want to lose *you*. After enduring insults and rage in the wake of your breakup, do not be surprised if he tries to win you back. And after months or years of an uncomfortable or even miserable relationship, it can feel good to go back to the beginning and be courted again. It is even likely that you will believe him (you did once before!), and that this time your story will be different and he will change. It won't last. If he wins you back with good behavior, it will only be a matter of time before his narcissistic traits surface again. After years of wishing for this change of heart from him, it will feel good for a moment, but it will be devastating when the inevitable return to bad habits happens.

Don't fall for the honeymoon period.

Repeatedly, in the interviews for this book, and among the people with whom I have consulted, most people remembered the sweeping and seductive early days of their relationships. To return to this "new and improved" version of your partner, especially after years of desolation, can be tempting. This can be even more compelling if you have children and a life together—the belief that the passion that caught you in the first place "is back" and things will work themselves out. You have been here before, perhaps not as far out the door as you are this time, but there were undoubtedly times in your relationship that were catastrophic and then your partner put on the good behavior for a few weeks or months. Hope can be dangerous in a narcissistic relationship.

This book is not about judging you for your decision or trying to convince you to leave if you are not ready. If your partner's about-face is convincing, and you decide to stay (first, please re-read the "Should I Stay?" chapter), then do so, but armed with the knowledge that he will not change, so at least you are prepared for the landscape. Behaviors may shift temporarily, but the core issues will remain. The challenge of getting sucked back in is that each ensuing time you try to get back out, it is that much more difficult.

Embrace your emotions—and take care of yourself.

You have been "appeasing the beast" for so long that you may not be aware of the mental and practical resources you have consistently expended to keep the relationship alive. Reflect back on what the past years may have been for you: walking on eggshells, living in disappointment, not being heard, having your trust betrayed, and trying out new strategies every day to get your partner to listen, to notice, or to care. As your partner slowly transitions out of your life, pay attention to how you feel. The theme highlighted by nearly everyone I spoke to was relief.

The feeling was that for the first time in many years, they exhaled. They were no longer waiting for something that was never going to happen. They were no longer being careful with every word, every action. When it initially dawned on them how tightly wound they had been for so long, many of them also expressed sadness. Sadness about time wasted, energy wasted, and a life spent in quiet despair. Similar to the stages of mourning, another common reaction is anger. Anger about what they tolerated. Anger about the bad treatment. Anger that their partner may have gone on to his next partner and a new life, seemingly without consequences. Anger that they tried their best, and it was never noticed. Anger that somehow their partner will get it right with their next partner, and wondering what was wrong with them.

The feelings will also shift and change every day. The initial relief felt wonderful for many people, but others were surprised by the sadness and anxiety. These negative emotions left many people wondering if they had made a mistake. Change and transition are difficult, especially in relationships. Think back to the relationship itself; you had good days and you had bad days, and coming out of a breakup is no different. But as with all such issues, there is no reason to carry this alone, and consulting with a therapist to talk some of this through can be useful. Taking care of yourself at this time is also essential, though it may seem like a cliché. Simple tools, such as sleep, exercise, healthy food, and healthy people, are nothing short of a prescription for managing difficult emotions and transitions.

These feelings of relief, anger, sadness, and fear are normal. They are a natural part of letting go. Grief and mourning are even more complex processes when the grieving is about something you feel conflicted about doing. There is more likely to be regret, frustration, anger, and even hopelessness. One of my favorite writers and poets, Rilke, says the following about feelings: "Let everything happen to you. Beauty and terror. Just keep going. No feeling is final." This process of letting go is not going to be easy, and it will often be uncomfortable. But allow the feelings to emerge, and before you know it, these feelings will have passed, and you will be stronger.

The Quest for Justice

The swan, who had been caught by mistake instead of the goose, began to sing as a prelude to its own demise. His voice was recognized and the song saved his life. (Aesop)

A swan song is fabled to be the beautiful song that the swan sings as it dies, a beautiful goodbye. If it had words, it may be the swan apologizing for all of the other people it hurt or devalued.

Don't wait for it.

This is the piece that undoes most people. Somewhere along the line, we were told that life is fair and life is just.

It's not.

Least of all in matters of the heart.

A message that so many people want to hear after enduring the soul-sapping territory of a narcissistic relationship is an apology, an act of contrition, a recognition of all that you did for him, of all that you endured. An attempt to set it right. Waiting for this apology, for the "justice," is often what prevents you from letting go. As though receiving that swan song will be what you need to move forward. You will have to learn to move forward without the swan song, without the great confession, without the empathy. It never existed before, why would it magically appear now?

A complaint I hear repeatedly is that "it's not right that they got away with this." According to whom? And exactly what did they "get away with?" Lots of people co-opt the concept of karma and believe that someday the bad guy gets his day. That the balance sheet has to even out at the end of all of this. That is not how karma or life works. Letting go of this belief is just as important a part of mourning as honoring your feelings. Your narcissistic partner does not OWE you anything.

A painful lesson was learned and getting out is not going to be easy. Your landscape has changed, forever. When this is over, it is quite likely that you may be less trusting, more suspicious, but also wiser. Survival always changes us. Perhaps the main justice is that you got your life back.

Maybe It's Me?

Many times people in relationships with narcissists blame themselves—and they keep trying harder and nothing works, which feels even worse. It is actually easier to blame yourself for a situation than it is to blame someone else. Taking responsibility can sometimes allow you to maintain a sense of control over a situation and attempt to "fix" yourself rather than having to take on something or someone else. Obviously every relationship is a two-way street and both parties take some responsibility. But wouldn't it be interesting if you could have an opportunity to witness what life would be like if your narcissist disappeared for a while (or forever)?

A story about some monkeys may give some insight into this . . .

Robert Sapolsky, professor of biology and neurology at Stanford University, is one of the foremost researchers on stress in the world. A twist of fate in his research yielded what I found to be one of the most profound findings he has reported to date. He had been conducting longitudinal research on baboons in Kenya for more than 20 years. One year, the dominant "alpha" males in one particular troop had eaten meat from the dumpster of a nearby park that was tainted with bovine tuberculosis and subsequently died. These dominant alphas were the "mean guys" in the tribe.

They organized their lives around terrorizing the females and the lower-ranking males, and because the dominant males were bigger and wanted to fight all the time, they won. These dominant males brought conflict and violence into all of their interactions.

The females and the lower-status males just had to adjust to the presence of these nasty dominant males. This was stressful for the females who were often injured by the dominant males and for the lower-status males who were chronically bullied. Sound like anyone we know? I don't think baboons can be diagnosed with narcissism, but the alpha model may be as close as we can get.

After the dominant alphas died, the first guess would be that the remaining and surviving males would take their place in the hierarchy and become the new alphas, maintaining the social order of bullying, violence, and hierarchy (up until then the non-alpha males in the troop just worked cooperatively with the females and had to endure the abuse and nastiness of the alphas).

They didn't. The remaining males continued to be cooperative with the females. There was more affection and increases in mutual grooming.

Once the alphas were gone, the remaining members of the new cooperative baboon tribe behaved more cooperatively, less violently, and they were actually healthier. Their hormone levels were consistent with lower levels of stress. And for now they are living happily ever after. Researchers in the field interpreted the findings of this study through the lenses of diplomacy, social ethos, and cultural behavior. The clinical psychologist in me sees it a little differently.

Sapolsky's study of baboons in Kenya has much to do with our musings on narcissism. In the wild when you remove mean, violent, abusive baboons then everyone is ultimately better off. Most baboon troops are not so lucky, and in fact when Sapolsky compared this "alpha-free" troop with others that still had the dominant males in place, the "alpha-free" troop evidenced some better outcomes. Interestingly, Sapolsky opines that it would just take a few "jerky" adolescent males entering this particular troop again to throw off the amiable balance. That is consistent with people;

sometimes it takes just one hardcore narcissistic personality to throw off an entire system, whether that is a family, a workplace, or any other group.

Imagine if you could remove every narcissistic, self-serving, abusive, entitled (dominant-alpha) person from your tribe . . . every last one. How would your life look? According to this research, it appears that it may be more stress-free. You would probably enjoy your day-to-day life more, work more collaboratively with others, and deal with less abuse. Far more significantly, your health would likely improve.

Perhaps the answer is to distance ourselves from the human equivalent of the "dominant baboon" and hopefully not bring them into the tribe in the first place. The bottom line is that the time spent with narcissists, and especially narcissistic partners, makes us less healthy. Our cortisol and other neurohormone levels are likely to be higher, and this contributes to a whole cascade of physical and mental-health issues. Work by researchers such as Janice Kiecolt-Glaser and her colleagues clearly illustrates that relationship conflict is not good for us, and relationships with narcissists do tend to be colored by more conflict.

Odds are that, once the narcissist is removed from your life, your life will be healthier, riddled with less conflict and stress, and more collaborative. Sometimes it's not you.

What if *They* Leave *You*?

At first breath, it may seem like a relief to have them lower the boom and exit. To get rid of them on their terms and avoid some of the poison and the anger. Ironically, it may not be as easy as you think. After your time served, and years spent trying to make it work, it can be quite galling to have your partner pick up and leave. Many times, the narcissist does decide to head out for greener pastures— typically a new partner—and even though getting rid of him is ultimately healthier and better for you, it still stings. The sting of being rejected. The sting of not feeling good enough. The sting that no matter how hard you tried, it was never enough. While that has nothing to do with you, it is a difficult pill to swallow when they decide to pack it in and leave.

Remember that the narcissist is unable to engage in deep empathic and intimate relationships. Leaving for them is often easy, because they never invested the same depth and breadth of resources into the relationship. For you, even though it has been a world of disappointment for years, the life you built together does feel real. To have someone walk out *will* hurt and you *will* mourn. For as challenging as this relationship is, if you are in love with someone, and it ends, it hurts.

You may have a cheering section telling you that you dodged the proverbial bullet, and you may even be able to accept this intellectually. But when someone leaves, it is an adjustment, and in some ways even harder because of how confusing the relationship has been. Because you are so accustomed to making everything right in the relationship, you may even be tempted to blindly fight for it (because you have been doing it for years). Slow down, and reflect on what the terrain has been like with this person. Be mindful of whether you are fighting for this out of fear, nostalgia, spite, pride, or an old familiar pattern. This is an opportunity to create a new path, new relationships, and stop living in a relationship vacuum. Before you fight for it, be clear on exactly what it is you are fighting for. Keep in mind too that you may not be narcissistic, but you do still have an ego. It is tempting to fight back on the end of the relationship, especially if your partner initiates it, out of pride. Pride and love do not make good roommates. At this point let your ego be a place of strength, not pride.

Avoiding Another Narcissist in the Future

Hard as it is to believe, you are likely to do this again. The deck is stacked against you, and the likelihood that you will choose someone like this again is pretty high. Remember the idea of familiarity and chemistry, and activating old scripts of disappointment.

In these pages you have the tools to pay attention to the signals, a roadmap and checklists of narcissism, the certitude that the patterns will never change, and your unique vulnerability to the narcissist. It is appealing to think that once you survived it you will never repeat it. It is critical that you remain mindful of the signs and signals—and the awareness that often the narcissist is the most seductive character in the room, the one with the most resources, the most charm. Before you grab at the low hanging and rather tempting fruit, pay attention. After this experience, you may learn to look at the less charismatic but far kinder people who may be less "obvious." If we valued kindness as much as we valued swagger in our society, we would save many people lots of heartache. Be aware of your vulnerabilities and start looking for the qualities that make for a better long-term partner—compassion, kindness, respect, and empathy—rather than the flash in the pan qualities of charisma and ego. That so-called "magic" tastes better when it grows over time.

Healing

It will get better. For no other reason but the passage of time. Ending a relationship with a narcissistic partner can often leave lingering echoes of frustration, anger, and regret. But contrary to the prevailing wisdom of poetry and love songs, all broken hearts do heal. They may come out a little sore on the other end, but not only will the hurt dissipate but also you will be wiser.

Eleanor Payson, a marriage and family therapist who has expertise in working with people recovering from narcissistic relationships, argues that there are three phases of healing when you are leaving or in a relationship with a narcissistic person: awareness, emotional healing, and empowerment. The awareness may very well encompass the fact that the current state of affairs will never change, and in light of this awareness, you are making some decisions—difficult decisions, but at least they are decisions that will modify the status quo. The therapist of one woman whom I interviewed for the book said to her "you will stay in this until it becomes too painful to stay." The awareness carries with it possibility, possibility that things in your life can become better. This is consistent with qualitative research by nursing professor Kathryn Laughon conducted with women who have been the victims of intimate partner violence. When it came to the point of making major changes in their lives and their relationships, they basically said, "You're not ready 'til you're ready." Precisely the same stance applies in relationships with narcissists. No one else can tell you this. Only you know.

The emotional healing requires a combination of ingredients: time, self-care, support, and therapy. This is a path that will be different for everyone, and it may take longer for some than others. There is no hard and fast number here; you may find yourself struggling a year later, and that is okay. Do not put yourself on a timeline. There are other things you can do to expedite and ease this process. As noted above, therapy with a skilled therapist can give you a consistent sounding board. Reaching out to friends can give you support, laughter, and a sympathetic ear.

Self-care should always be built into a healthy lifestyle, but it is often something that erodes when you are in a relationship with a narcissist. John Helliwell, an economics professor at the University of British Columbia, and Robert Putnam, a professor at the Kennedy School of Government at Harvard University, examined large samples from throughout the U.S. and Canada and found that our relationships—not just marriage but also family, neighborhood, religious and community ties—are associated with physical health and a sense of well-being. Your relationship has been a bit of an illusion and likely not contributing to this essential social capital, and you may not have the other strong ties (that often deteriorate while you are in a relationship with a narcissist). Maintaining your social ties and relationships is critical to your health.

The vacuum of the relationship offers little incentive to value yourself, and the lack of mutuality means that your partner is doing little to take care of you. This is a skill that can be learned. Some of the elements include maintenance of healthy routines like getting enough sleep, eating well, exercise, and engaging in activities that bring you meaning and purpose. For years, attempts to care for yourself or engage in meaningful pursuits were often thwarted, undermined, or criticized by your partner, or you were so busy trying to please him that you neglected taking care of yourself. Years of shipping narcissistic supply into the harbor has likely left you tapped out. At the risk of sounding clichéd, the healing is only going to unfold if you love yourself, and the first step consists of taking care of yourself.

Empowerment is a tough mountain to climb after years of giving your power away. The void of the relationship with the narcissist and the attendant self-doubt and erosion of self-esteem can wrest the word empowerment out of your vocabulary. Awareness may be the first step in the establishment of empowerment: learning the language of self-advocacy, giving yourself permission to be respected, never allowing someone else to insert doubt into you. Interestingly, a fair number of people who have come out the other side of these narcissistic relationships have been drawn to being trained as therapists, life coaches, or have done lots of reading and education on the process they just survived. Empowerment is also about meeting your own needs—and that may be the hardest lesson of all. It was likely your inability to do that in the first place that allowed this relationship to develop, but a big part of healing is being able to offer yourself the empathy that your partner never gave or will ever give. Ever.

A Few Last Mantras

Now that it is over, remember . . .

- ▶ S/he will never change.
- ▶ I no longer have to live in disappointment.
- ▶ I can speak my mind and be heard.

- ▸ I no longer have to second-guess myself.
- ▸ I no longer have to doubt myself.
- ▸ I am now free to live authentically and not keep cutting off parts of myself to make this work.
- ▸ I got my life back.

CHAPTER 9

THE NEXT CHAPTER

I have always believed, and I still believe, that whatever good or bad fortune may come our way we can always give it meaning and transform it into something of value.

—HERMAN HESSE

Y ou may still be in it, you may be out of it, but you likely feel like you are transformed. All human relationships transform us, some more than others. The risk of the narcissistic relationship is that it transforms you so profoundly and painfully that you feel that you are no longer you. Slowly over time you have cut off bits and pieces of yourself, so you feel as if you have lost your true self. A key part of the walk forward is to not allow this relationship to define you or break you. I do not believe you will have lost your true self forever, but I do agree that it will take a while to get it back. You are not a victim, even though you may feel like one. Do not allow living in a world of entitlement, indifference, mistrust, discouragement, and control rob you of your own gifts, and of your own humanity and empathy.

The irony that writing a book on narcissism exhausted me and left me depleted is not lost on me. I write for a living, it is what I do, and yet this book was different. In some ways, being so immersed in this topic for such a long time was like being with a narcissist, and perhaps offers some insight into how it starts feeling like a psychological flu. The symptoms of this flu include ongoing malaise from the emptiness, the superficiality, and the inauthenticity of this disorder. In speaking with people about the topic on airplanes, in coffee shops, in my office, and at parties, I was struck by the resonance of the topic but also by the misunderstandings about narcissism. It is my hope that this book has expanded your understanding of the broad strokes and the subtleties of what is clearly a modern epidemic. A disorder that is being kept in place and multiplying under perfect cultural conditions. Our culture is presently a petri dish for narcissism. Relationships are going to be the greatest casualty of this proliferation.

I wrote this book because I directly observed the damage these relationships can create. They injure the soul. Much like a physical injury or an old sports injury: On most days, years after the injury, you may not feel anything, but then step the wrong way, and the pain courses through you. That is what happens after these relationships. Your soul can remain slightly bruised for a long time. Wear the bruise as a badge of honor, a life fully lived, and lessons learned. Let the bit of pain remind you to be mindful and pay attention to the red flags.

Most people with whom I spoke said that their lives were never the same again after a relationship with a narcissist. It was years before the self-doubt began to fade and they felt whole again. They had spent years walking on eggshells and feeling unheard. Self-doubt continued to characterize their lives, whether in new relationships, at work, in friendships, or even in daily decision-making. Those habits were hard to break, and while every single person, without exception, indicated that they felt relieved when it was over, that relief would often be accompanied by a cascade of other emotions, including regret, anger, sadness, and fear that they would never be the same again.

Life Lessons from Others Who Have Survived

With the people whom I interviewed, and with my own clients, I asked the same question: What advice would you give to someone in this situation? Their answers are a primer of survival as well as life lessons on how to avoid these situations and better manage them if they happen again. Keep in mind that not all of these people have left these relationships.

- Do what is best for you; if you are not happy in a relationship, end it.
- Don't contort yourself to please someone else.
- You have to stand up for yourself and understand what you want.
- Put yourself in the picture.
- You can care about others while you care about yourself.
- The only way to get perspective is to walk away.
- You live on hope and that gets you through, and it is also dangerous.
- Don't take the first person that comes along, sometimes we do that because we are afraid that no one else will come along.
- Don't sell yourself short.
- Leave.
- Never believe that you are not good enough.
- Tell people about your situation and they will help you.
- Ask the people around you their opinion of your partner and listen to the answer.
- Pay attention to the red flags.
- It will never be enough.
- No matter how "perfect" you are, the first time you make a mistake, that is what they will focus on, as though all of the good things you do never happened.
- Don't let someone else control your life.
- People like that don't change.

Taken together, these responses, most of which come from people who were in these relationships for 20 years or longer, focus on distancing themselves, recognition of the futility of the situation, and the need to value yourself. These insights often took more than a decade to percolate. In many ways, these are lessons that should be learned at the front end—how to avoid confusing compromise with negating yourself. "Relationship-speak" in our culture is so rife with discussion about compromise (which is in fact a very important part of normal relationships) that by labeling the surrender that often has to occur in a relationship with a narcissist as "compromise" it can keep your submissive and fruitless behaviors and expectations alive. Their lessons and this book are meant to illuminate when to fold your hand and walk away, or stay with a new set of expectations and rules.

Pay Attention to RED FLAGS

The theme of red flags pervaded all of the interviews I conducted, and when these were gathered up and specifically questioned, the most consistent theme is that, without exception, the red flags were made apparent within the first three months of the relationship. Not one person said that on the day of their wedding they were entirely comfortable with their choice. Nearly all of my clients and interview participants indicated that those red flags were signs of what would become consistent themes in the relationship. Here are some examples:

* *Anger issues—he would get angry about the smallest things. He was also unkind to my pets, my friends, and my family.*
* *Everyone told me not to marry him or at least to wait a little longer.*
* *I found that I was saying 'I'm sorry' a lot. I was constantly rationalizing his anger and blaming myself.*
* *He lied a lot and all the time about everything, to the point where I started believing him.*

❖ *He was not very communicative, and he also did not listen.*

❖ *He would never help me with the small things and would take for granted that I would be there.*

❖ *He disregarded my feelings from the beginning.*

❖ *He needed complete attention and adoration from other women.*

❖ *He would frequently accuse me of lying, cheating, and be-having badly—with no basis in fact. I found out later, he was doing everything he had accused me of.*

❖ *Whenever she did not like how things were going, she would break up with me, and then take me back quickly.*

❖ *He was always posting on social media about his life, but it was as if it was a separate space from me, and he wanted the world to still recognize him as single so he could "play" at another kind of life.*

❖ *He was very inconsistent. He would be angry and then loving.*

❖ *He was very secretive about his e-mail, his phone, his text messages, and his social media. Over time, and I am not a suspicious person, I came to find out that he maintained an entire life of inappropriate messages with other women, from our first date to the day our marriage ended. I let it pass in the beginning; I wish I had known it would be a pattern.*

❖ *He was selfish about his time and his money.*

❖ *He was very vain and very focused on his appearance.*

The themes, and these are typically the themes that can unfold early, are anger, blame, lack of empathy, admiration seeking, and lying. Interestingly, most of these relationships began a long time ago, well before the advent of social media. In newer relationships, social media and devices are shaping the landscape of modern relationships. Smartphones and social media are grenades in the hands of narcissists. They permit 24/7 maintenance of admiration-seeking, boundary violations, suspicion, and secrecy.

It is quite simple to look at the stories of other people and believe that we would not fall into the same traps. It is likely that if you look at your own story, many of your red flags are similar to those listed above. These red flags do not occur in isolation, they occur in a context, a context of becoming acquainted with a new person, new experiences, the fun, joy, and perhaps relief of being in a relationship. In a new relationship there will be moments of tenderness, attentiveness, sensuality, and simply being in love with being in love. It becomes a figure-ground issue. When we are focused on the nice shiny new relationship, we can ignore the ground (context or background) of carelessness on which this new relationship is unfolding. Over time, the red flags may proliferate more than the positive behavior, and so it is easy to look back at them with 20/20 hindsight.

The Power of Narrative

Equally telling are the responses to the red flags. The answers were human. We are not robots, designed to identify a so-called "red flag" and mechanically respond to it. We bring our own histories, narratives, expectations, and hopes to each of the actions we experience in our environment. Here are some examples:

❖ *It was time to get married, and my family was pressuring me to settle down.*

❖ *His jealousy and control made me think that he really cared for me, and I think I felt special because even though all of those other women would send him messages, he chose me.*

❖ *When he would get angry and share his fears, I thought he was showing his vulnerability.*

❖ *I romanticized the red flags.*

❖ *I was in love and didn't want to see things that would ruin that.*

❖ *I felt like I had to protect him.*

❖ *I liked being the "white knight" and rescuing her.*

✤ *I wanted to get married. I wanted a family.*
✤ *I believed he would change.*

More than anything, these responses suggest the power of narrative. When these red flags appeared early on, the narrative was "shaped" in a way that was at times romantic, passionate, and even practical. The old saying of "love is blind" applies here, and before these patterns set in, hope is often what allows people to look the other way when the red flags arise. Over time, the narratives become a bit more realistic, hope begins to fade, and it becomes brutally clear that these patterns of mistrust, anger, and deceit are here to stay. Then there is no fairy tale that can be written around these warning signs any longer.

Trying to Appease the Beast

While the red flags would be ignored for many years, people I have spoken with have shared the myriad ways they would try to make it "work." It is backbreaking and heartbreaking work to make a relationship with a narcissist succeed. Until people came to the realization that their partner would never change, and that nothing they did would make a difference in their conduct, they exhausted, depleted, and destroyed themselves to make it work, to prove themselves, to win over their partners. By and large the responses here show that people believed that if they made life easier for their narcissist or improved themselves, then their relationship would work. For periods of time they were correct, but is it really a relationship if your sole function is to please and make someone else's life easier? Sadly, once upon a time, especially for women, that was the prevailing ethos of marriage. In some cultures, it remains that way. In fact, if you read magazine articles or even current books out there on "how to snag a husband," there is still the prevailing advice to put on your 1950's apron and greet him with a smile. Here are some examples:

❖ *I dyed my hair blond and stayed skinny.*

❖ *I earned all of the money and kept the kids out of the way.*

❖ *I did all of the cleaning and almost all of the cooking.*

❖ *I bought her anything she wanted and never asked her to work. I borrowed money to maintain her in the lifestyle she wanted.*

❖ *I took care of the house, took care of the kids, tried to give him the perfect situation because then I thought everything would be fine. And when he would cheat, I would try harder to make everything just right.*

❖ *I tried to be the "cool chick" and would never ask any questions, even when I knew he was lying and cheating, was never there for me, and never listened to me.*

❖ *I would walk on eggshells and do everything I could to control everything, so he would never have to experience any discomfort.*

❖ *I knew he had a tortured youth, so my job was to take that pain away.*

❖ *For a while I tried talking, then I tried yelling, and then I became silent.*

❖ *I took him on expensive vacations, and spared no expense, even though I would have to work extra hours to make it happen.*

❖ *I made enough money so that he would only have to work two to three days per month.*

❖ *I would make sure I called him every hour so he knew what I was doing.*

The frustration and fallout of the relationships would come in the wake of the exhaustion from attempting to "appease the beast." Most people interviewed acknowledged that if their appeasement strategies worked then that would have been somewhat more satisfying. But even after making sure life was a well-oiled machine, shielding the narcissist from any discomfort or sadness, it was never *enough*. That realization is often what broke the spirits of the people in the relationship. And that may have been a good thing. Ultimately, a human relationship should not be built on what you can *do* for someone, but simply on a mutual partnership. A narcissistic relationship can often devolve into superficial attributes, such as jobs, schools, titles, resources, addresses, photo-shopped images, status posts, quiet children, well-appointed homes, and possessions. That is only a small sliver of what life and human relationships are about.

Why Did You Stay?

This is in fact a book entitled *Should I Stay or Should I Go*? Thus, the reasons for staying are just as interesting and important as the reasons for leaving. Both paths carry their own narratives. The reasons for staying represent narratives about coping with the red flags and the bad behavior. The reasons for staying are also quite complex and while many times people focus on the "external" reasons for staying, there are often deeper personal reasons as well. So I asked many people the simple question, "Why did you stay?" Below are some of the most common answers:

- *Religion, children, money*
- *Fear*
- *Guilt*
- *I believed he was a sensitive artist.*
- *I loved him.*
- *I built a story around the idea that he needed my love to create.*
- *I believed the excuses, forgot the bad times, and remembered the good ones.*
- *It was financially easier, and easier on the kids.*
- *I believed he would change.*

Reasons for staying are often universals—and even people who are not in relationships with narcissists stay for these reasons. These reasons may have particular poignancy in a narcissistic relationship in which you are being treated badly, but people stay because they stay, and the classic reasons are guilt, kids, money, fear, love, and culture. Those reasons are equally compelling here, and even when bad behavior would occur, people were and are able to get back in the saddle and focus on the good times. That would also be supported by an emotion such as fear. Fear about being alone, fear of disappointing others, fear of failure, fear of the unknown. Fear would often result in people becoming more and more skilled at training their lens back at the good times, or on the narrative or the nostalgia or the framed photographs that helped them endure the emptiness and keep fighting another day. These are all valid and powerful reasons to stay, and most people will stay, until it no longer can be endured.

Interestingly, it is often at this point that clients may drop out of therapy. In therapy, where they are sharing the painful details of their relationships, even they recognize that the dots are adding up in a way that suggests that "only a fool would stay." The discomfort about that recognition combined with their fear makes it easier to drop out of therapy, which serves as a reminder of their current circumstances. At this point, clients will also slowly start cutting themselves off from the rest of their friends and sometimes even family, because they do not want to reflect on their relationship. It is easier to remain blind and in denial.

Why Did You Leave?

So when things ended, I asked my patients and those I interviewed, "why did they end it and leave the relationship?" It was not always the sweeping fantasy of someone heroically walking out the front door and saying "I am mad as hell and I am not taking this anymore!" Among those who experienced the end of these narcissistic relationships, it took many forms:

✢ *I left to protect the children from his anger and influence.*

✢ *I finally talked openly with family who provided me with financial assistance to hire attorneys and get the resources to get out.*

✢ *He came home and told me he met someone else, left me, and married her.*

✢ *He kept up the relationship with the other woman he was dating at the same time he was dating me and chose her.*

✢ *My son gave me a note that told me that his father had been having an affair for years. The other things he did to me were far worse, but somehow this was the thing that made me pack it in and leave.*

✢ *I went into intensive psychotherapy and the therapist helped me articulate it and make the phone call in which I asked him for a divorce. I did it on the phone; I knew I would not be able to do it in person.*

✢ *He went back to his wife.*

These were rarely graceful exits. Sometimes the narcissistic partner left (always for presumably greener pastures), and at others a breach of trust led someone to leave the narcissist. In some cases it was the support or concern about other people, such as children, that finally galvanized a person enough to get out. While the entire network of people around you may be secretly gleeful that you finally are out of the situation, it still hurts. Because many of these situations did not occur gracefully (being left for other people) the hurt was often augmented. Leaving a nasty narcissistic partner may ultimately be the best thing that happens to you but there is a reason people stay in these relationships, and even if these reasons are not always psychologically healthy, they are what you know. Leaving the familiar is always challenging.

Write Your Own Happy Ending

The final chapter becomes where many of these people end up and the words that most commonly arose were *redemption, happiness, free,* and *euphoria.* But at the same time, there was acknowledgement that these echoes do not dissipate quickly: *it takes a long time before you get their voice out of your head; once the euphoria passed, I became depressed; I kept asking "why did this happen to me?"; hurt and devastated, I keep making the same mistakes.*

This entire journey of narcissism is a reminder that happy endings do not just happen; they need to be written. Orson Wells says it even more brilliantly when he says, *"Every story has a happy ending, it just depends on where you end it."* This next anecdote captures all of this elegantly with a top note of triumph. The pathological narcissist will never change, and while it hurts, you will recover. Perhaps, sometimes, while you cannot wait for karma and justice, the universe gives you a little gift to believe that the scales do balance out.

I put up with his selfishness, his cheating, and his bad behavior for 17 years. I took care of the house, kids, everything to give him the perfect place and life. I believed that if I did that, everything would be fine. I would feel let down when he would behave badly; it made my self-esteem low. I would wonder, what is wrong with me that he would treat me like this? What am I doing wrong? He came home and said he was moving out, he met someone, and then he got married. It was a very hurtful time and it put me to my lowest. At this time of being at my lowest I started working a lot more, tried to be there for my kids. I felt like I was going to die, and I went into a deep depression. It took me years to get out of that fog. We knew the same people and lived in the same community, so I would still have to see him around and now I had to see his new wife. It was really hard to withstand that. Frankly, I hated him. I think what bothered me was that after 17 years, I wondered if was he going to change and be a different person. I was relieved to see that he did not change for her;

he stayed exactly the same, now he was her problem. Needless to say, it didn't work out for them either.

Infectious Narcissism

Narcissism is a funny pathology because it can also be somewhat infectious. That is not to say that spending time with a narcissist will make you narcissistic, but spending time with a narcissist can result in a certain level of social withdrawal and a loss of emotional vocabulary. If you speak a language, but then do not use your language for years because you do not have the opportunity to speak it, your language skills will become rusty. It is the same experience with emotional language as well. In a relationship with a narcissistic partner, over time, that emotional vocabulary may not be used, and you may find yourself less able to express and articulate your feelings. In addition, after years of not having your experiences mirrored and having to jump into survival mode (which can be quite selfish, as survival requires that), you may find this "style" pervading your other relationships as well. Years living with a narcissistic partner in which you did not experience empathy often means that you may have unplugged from your own empathy and may be vulnerable to treating other people the way your partner treats you. It is your new normal.

An interesting observation is that people who have had narcissistic partners for years can start to become quite clipped in their other relationships, in essence mirroring their lives with their partners. Be mindful of this, because this style could easily alienate the supports you need and limit the full range of emotional experiences you share with other people. The recovery process of healing from a narcissistic relationship, whether you stay or go, includes reflecting on the micro-changes you had to make to survive this relationship and how to bring yourself back to a full, rich, and engaging emotional world.

Is It Me or Is It Them?

If this has happened to you more than once or it has been happening for a long time, you may have spent a fair amount of time wondering "is it me?" Narcissistic relationships often work because your narcissistic partner takes no blame, and you take all of it—it all equals out. Obviously, when going through a relationship like this, it is important to be self-reflective and think about patterns in which you have engaged. However, when it comes right down to it, if you are being treated badly, or a relationship does not feel healthy, and if you have communicated and attempted to address it in a meaningful manner, it does not matter. Narcissistic partners are masterful at leaving someone feeling like they are doing something wrong. Relationships are complicated, and yes, while it would be nice to heap 100 percent of the blame on your narcissistic partner, it is a two-way street, so take the time to think about how you behave in this relationship. If this is a pattern, this self-reflection becomes even more important. What attracts you to a partner? Whose narrative are you living out? How do you respond to conflict and criticism? How do you communicate? By sussing out some of this, you can learn from this experience and build a healthier relational space for yourself.

How Do I Avoid this Dark Alley Again?

You are now in possession of everything you need to know to identify a pathological narcissist. But that knowledge is not enough to stop you (despite knowing all of this, I have chosen narcissistic partners, too). Knowledge is *not* enough. When you are in a relationship with a narcissist, you gradually learn to start ignoring and denying your feelings. Just because your narcissistic relationship ends doesn't mean that this pattern ends. When you blunt your emotions, you run the risk of repeating this pattern. Let the feelings flow so you do not forget them. Many people just jump from lily pad to lily pad of different kinds of narcissistic partners. Few things feel as good as falling in love, and narcissists put on a better show than anyone else. Remain wary, as it is easy to go back in and enact these patterns with a new partner.

In addition, do the psychological heavy lifting of reflecting on your self-concept. Many of us devalue ourselves, and these are often ancient scripts. There is nothing like a narcissistic partner to validate those scripts. But your partner did not write those scripts; those scripts existed long before him and will remain long after he is gone, unless you start tackling them head on.

You want to avoid doing this again?

Make sure you value yourself.

Fear of being alone often drives a person back into a relationship quickly. In that rush, or even basking in the glow of a new partner who actually pays attention to you, it is easy to ignore the red flags. You did it once, which increases the odds that you will do it again. When you meet new romantic love interests, pay attention to how they listen, how they share, and review the list in the beginning of the book. If you find yourself making extensive excuses for them, remain aware of that pattern. Remember that we talk about that magical glow of "familiarity"; be mindful and alert that you are not choosing the rejecting or unavailable partner with whom you have to start jumping through hoops again. The terrain of the familiar is seductive. The only way to ensure you do not get drawn back into that poppy field again is to pay attention, check in with yourself, and communicate clearly and early.

You should be a more discerning partner now. When you reflect on the fallout of your past relationship, you may now recognize the traits that really matter to you in a partner. The younger version of you may have chosen on the basis of status, wealth, attractiveness, sociability, and who you thought your mother would like. You may have chosen from a place of devaluing yourself, believing no one else would come along. After enduring this experience, you may now identify other qualities—kindness, mindfulness, commitment, trust, respect—that make for good relationship raw material. You may have also shifted as a person, and more specific characteristics, such as spirituality, sense of purpose, or shared interests, may matter more. You may be more than willing to look past more superficial characteristics, such as appearance, career, or age in favor of deeper level characteristics from which a committed and healthy relationship can be built. In this way, perhaps the narcissistic relationship may lead you to a partnership that is mature and will allow you and your new partner to grow in a deeper way. If you can contextualize this arduous narcissistic relationship and find some meaning in it, you will then be better able to endure, cope, and grow in the wake of it.

The other risk is letting the pendulum swing too far to the other direction. This experience can leave you shattered. You may be tentative, hesitant, or cut bait too early when you meet someone new. As with any injury, including a broken heart or a broken spirit, take it slow and remain open. Live in the present and avoid forcing a narrative. After months or years of denying yourself in your narcissistic relationship, enjoy life. Develop yourself, your interests, your passions, your hopes. Cultivate you. Love would be a nice add-on, and the stronger you become, the better your instincts. You will be better prepared to choose a partner who is a collaborator, a support, and an equal. Take off your shoes. You are no longer walking on broken glass.

What About the Other People in My Life?

Odds are that if you have one narcissist in your life that you have others. These may be family members, friends, co-workers, or neighbors, and you may be reading this book and realizing that these patterns are also manifested in other people in your life besides your partner. When you leave the door open for one narcissist to enter, others tend to follow. Because you have become accustomed to these patterns and rhythms, you are also likely to tolerate them.

While this book focuses on the particular space of your intimate, committed partner, the patterns, suggestions, traits, and recommendations issued herewith can and should be considered for use with other pathological narcissists in your life. There are unique elements to romantic relationships that may lead us to make "unhealthier" choices on the basis of our histories, but we may also have the same propensity to hold on to narcissistic friends, be challenged by narcissistic co-workers, and cower in the face of narcissistic family members. The same rules apply: managing expectations, preparing for rage, understanding how they make you feel, and the fallout that can come from letting these people go or holding on to them. And, finally, knowing that they will never change.

A final question about narcissism relates to children. It would require another book to definitively address issues of narcissism in children. By definition, children are narcissistic and focused on self, their brains and psyches are developing, and we as parents, caregivers, and teachers have to teach them and demonstrate empathy, mutuality, respect, and emotional regulation. We do that by being present, listening to them, monitoring our own behaviors, and regulating our emotions. Technology, multi-tasking, consumerism, and the winner-take-all ethos are making it harder for us to do our job. But we must. Now that you are fully aware of the havoc wreaked by narcissism, and the emptiness of life that accompanies it, remain mindful of shepherding any children in your purview away from this path. By doing this, we can develop children who ideally do not become narcissists, as well as children who have a strongly developed sense of self, who do not fall prey to the narcissists who will be an inevitable part of their landscape.

So What Happens to Narcissists?

It is curious and morbidly fascinating to watch a narcissist grow old. Narcissists bank on youth, status, and access to opportunity, wealth, and life—things that often fade with time. The luckiest of narcissists remain financially successful and retain their high status right until the end of their lives. This will often keep them armed with a steady stream of houseguests, admirers, sycophants, and young partners. The narcissistic supply can sail into the harbor until they finally call it a life. It often remains an empty life to an outside observer, but they are content, and if you are not sucked into it, it is really not your problem.

However, for those who do not experience this kind of homerun, it is not pretty. Narcissists get greedy, get played, their rage gets the best of them, or their grandiosity and entitlement does them in, and they can find themselves later in life with very little and muttering about what could have been. I have observed many older narcissists who are put out to pasture, relying on the largesse of more successful friends, or settling into suboptimal living situations of roommates and loneliness (in most cases, their families turned their backs long ago). The narcissist's stock in trade has always been external attributes—appearance, success, possibility, possessions—and when all of that goes, a lifetime *not* spent cultivating their internal worlds can leave them unable to regulate the existential crises of old age, with few long-term friendships or relationships built up over the years. Superficial friends don't drive you to the doctor.

They tend to become hollow men (and women) and will hold court and tell the same stories about their glory days, the places they lived, the things they owned, the people they knew, the lives they lived. Narcissists often end their stories lonely and broken. We live in an ageist society, and retirement can be quite lovely for those who cultivated a full life and relationships—a time to reap the fruits of a life well lived. With the status, bells, and whistles gone, the denouement of the narcissist tends to be the saddest part of the story. Family may reappear toward the end, to claim inheritances and other superficial bits and pieces, or solely out of guilt since that was often the only currency in these relationships.

Not all stories have happy endings—they simply have endings. And that's okay.

Keeping Your Humanity

It is challenging. If you have not had protracted contact with a narcissist in your personal life, family life, or career, then you may not have a handle on what this is like, and you may still believe in second chances and redemption (and you are most likely not reading this book). If you want to give someone 100 chances, then do so. With a narcissist, you already know how it will turn out. If you are going to give your partner these second chances, just make sure your expectations are in line with reality. For example, if you take back a narcissist who was unfaithful, set a clock on when it will happen again. Adjust your expectations to the infidelity that is inevitably coming back. Perhaps you enjoy your family life and other qualities of your relationship enough to tolerate that behavior. Being with a narcissist means having difficult conversations with yourself.

If indeed you are dealing with more of a "pure" narcissist, and less of the more malevolent Dark Triad, then you have likely directly observed that narcissists can actually appear vulnerable at times, and even downright sad (the psychopaths don't tend to go there). This can definitely pull for sympathy, and connection and kindness, which are completely appropriate reactions to someone else's pain. Narcissism, like all human psychologies, is not black and white; it sits on a continuum and human experiences like vulnerability, sadness, and hurt can build up the connective tissue between the two of you and leave you feeling confused when he returns to being cold or neglectful or controlling.

Narcissists are human beings, they in fact do have feelings, and they do get hurt—they just lack an adequate emotional vocabulary to share any of this. As such, their periods of distress and hurt can feel disconnected, or they may channel inappropriate emotions, such as rage or criticism, at those times. Their personalities are not wired for intimacy and closeness. But they *are* human beings. Understanding them may actually make you a better friend to them or, if you stay, a better partner. Being compassionate does not mean throwing yourself under the bus. Their lack of empathy does not mean you have to be cold towards them. All human beings are deserving of love, warmth, and compassion—do not destroy yourself in the process of giving it. Give it, and in the case of the narcissist, do not expect much back. It is not likely to be a relationship of depth or closeness, but it can be shaped into something civil, and perhaps even a collaborative friendship. With love, it is the process of giving that restores us. The world gives it back in myriad ways; do not solely look to your partner for it. That myopia of only looking for love from your partner can lead you to miss the abundance of love, connection, and beauty around you. Understanding does not mean "making excuses." It means accurately anticipating behaviors and outcomes.

Ultimately, it is important that you check in with yourself to ensure that you are being realistic and not waiting for the "fairy tale ending." Your landscape has altered, but not necessarily for the worse. It is out of the ashes that kingdoms can rise. It really comes down to your willingness to shift your focus out of the past and into the present and the future. There is often a post-traumatic phase after getting out of such a relationship, playing an endless loop in your head "how did this happen?" "what do I do now?" "it's not fair," and "I am never going to find happiness." You may continue to second-guess yourself, walk on eggshells, and think about all of the energy you put into being perfect, endless arguments, and living in denial. It is possible you still have to do some of that if you are raising children together, but on a regular basis you do not need to do that any longer. All of that wasted energy can now go to your own growth, health, and living a real life.

On compassion, the Dalai Lama says "only the development of compassion and understanding for others can bring us the tranquility and happiness we all seek." After an experience with a narcissistic partner, it is far too easy to lose that compassion. You are empathic and compassionate, and those are gifts, this relationship does not have the power to rob you of that and in turn rob you of your inner happiness. This is but one episode in the complex tapestry that is your life. Remain aware that you do not abandon your humanity, kindness, and gratitude in the face of this. Take a long look at the good people around you and feel grateful for them. Take a long look at the people who have challenged or even hurt you, dig deep, and find that compassion. This relationship has inflicted enough damage in your life; do not allow it to keep stealing your sense of well-being by stealing your compassion. If other people have given you reason to trust them, then trust them. And hard as it may be, compassion toward your narcissistic partner may be the most curative part of this journey. Compassion is often embedded in forgiveness but not blind forgiveness, and take heed from the wise words of Desmond Tutu who said, "Forgiving is not forgetting; it's actually remembering—remembering and not using your right to hit back. It's a second chance for a new beginning. And the remembering part is particularly important. Especially if you don't want to repeat what happened."

Towards the end of the Lord of the Rings trilogy, there is a particularly beautiful line. Tolkien writes, "Your time may come. Do not be too sad. . . . You cannot be always torn in two. You will have to be one and whole, for many years. You have so much to enjoy and to be and to do."

Remember, always remember. Keep your heart open, your mind wise, and your soul mindful. Learn from your experiences, but do not let them define you. Your narcissistic relationship likely had both beauty and challenge, and it is a part of the glorious story that is your life. Whether you remain or part ways . . . wish them and yourself well. And in your fashion, you love them and they love you.

APPENDIX

DOMESTIC VIOLENCE RESOURCES:

If you are in a violent situation and believe you are in danger call 911.

The National Domestic Violence Hotline is 1-800-799-7233 (1-800-799-SAFE) (TTY 1-800-787-3224).

The National Resource Center on Domestic Violence (www.nrcdv.org)

Local communities will have specific programs, information and shelters available. These resources will connect you to local assistance and services.

Other resources include:

American Psychological Association (www.apa.org)

Centers for Disease Control (www.cdc.gov)

BIBLIOGRAPHY

FRONT MATTER

Marcel Proust (1913-1927). *In Search of Lost Time/Remembrance of Things Past.*
Sigmund Freud (1930). *Civilization and Its Discontents.*

CHAPTER I

Eugene O'Neill (1939). *More Stately Mansions.*
F. Scott Fitzgerald (1925). *The Great Gatsby.*
Anais Nin (1959). *The Four Chambered Heart,* The Swallow Press, Chicago
William James (1899). *William James: The Essential Writings* (1971), (ed. Bruce Wilshire, SUNY Press).

CHAPTER 2

Antonio Machado. (translated 1983). *Times Alone.*
Andrew M. Colman (2015). *A Dictionary of Psychology,* Oxford University Press.
Alan Rappoport (2005). *Co-Narcissism: How we accommodate to narcissistic patients.*
Christopher Bagley (2013). Kanye West: The Transformer, *W Magazine.*
Mark Seal (2009). Madoff's World, *Vanity Fair.*
American Psychiatric Association (2013). *Diagnostic and Statistical Manual of Medical Disorders—5 (DSM-5),* American Psychiatric Association Press.
Delroy L. Paulhus and Kevin M. Williams (2002). The Dark Triad of personality: Narcissism, Machiavellianism, and psychopathy, *Journal of Research in Personality,* Volume 36 (6).
Heinz Kohut (1971). *The Analysis of the Self: A Systematic Approach to the Psychoanalytic Treatment of Narcissistic Personality Disorders,* University of Chicago Press.

Otto Kernberg (1975). *Borderline Conditions and Pathological Narcissism,* New York, NY: Aronson Press.

Alexander Lowen (2004). *Narcissism: Denial of the True Self,* Touchstone.

Frederick S. Stinson (2008). Prevalence, Correlates, Disability, and Comorbidity of DSM-IV Narcissistic Personality Disorder: Results from the Wave 2 National Epidemiologic Survey on Alcohol and Related Conditions, *The Journal of Clinical Psychiatry,* 69.

Jean M. Twenge and W. Keith Campbell (2009). *The Narcissism Epidemic: Living in the Age of Entitlement,* Free Press/Simon & Schuster.

American Society of Plastic Surgeons (2013). *2013 Plastic Surgery Statistics Report.*

Mad Men (2007-2015). A & E Networks.

CHAPTER 3

Fyodor Dostoevsky (1880). *The Brothers Karamazov.*

Theodore Millon (1996). *Disorders of Personality: DSM-IV-TR and Beyond.* New York: John Wiley and Sons.

Elsa Ronningstam (2005). *Identifying and Understanding the Narcissistic Personality,* Oxford University Press.

CHAPTER 4

Herman Hesse (1910). *Gertrud.*

Carrie Haslam and Tamara Montrose (2015). Should have known better: The impact of mating experience and the desire for marriage upon attraction to the narcissistic personality, *Personality and Individual Differences,* Volume 82.

Joe Navarro and Toni Scyarra Poynter (2014). *Dangerous Personalities: An FBI Profiler Shows How to Identify and Protect Yourself from Harmful People,* Rodale Books.

Pamela Regan (2008). *The Mating Game: A Primer on Love, Sex, and Marriage,* Sage Publications.

Jane Austen (1811). *Sense and Sensibility.*

Helen Fisher, Arthur Aron and Lucy Brown (2005). Romantic Love: An fMRI Study of a Neural Mechanism for Mate Choice, *The Journal of Comparative Neurology,* Volume 493.

Paul K. Piff, Daniel M. Stancato, Stéphane Côté, Rodolfo Mendoza-Denton and Dacher Keltner (2012). Higher social class predicts increased unethical behavior, *Proceedings of the National Academy of Sciences,* Volume 109 (11).

CHAPTER 5

Gustave Flaubert (1852). Trans. by William G. Allen. Correspondence, letter, July 6, 1852, to Louise Colet.

William James (1899). *Talks to Teachers on Psychology and to Students on Some of Life's Ideals.*

Martin Seligman (1972). Learned Helplessness, *Annual Review of Medicine,* Volume 23.

CHAPTER 6

Paulo Coelho (1994). *By The River Piedra I Sat Down And Wept,* Harper Collins.

CHAPTER 7

Viktor Frankl (1946). *Man's Search for Meaning.*

Joel Paris (2013). *Psychotherapy in an Age of Narcissism: Modernity, Science, and Society,* Palgrave MacMillan.

Ingmar Bergman (cited in Lise-Lone Marker and Frederick Marker, *Ingmar Bergman: Four Decades in the Theater* (1982)). Cambridge University Press.

Elsa Ronningstam (1996). Pathological Narcissism and Narcissistic Personality Disorder in Axis I Disorders, *Harvard Review of Psychiatry,* 3 (6).

CHAPTER 8

Voltaire (1756). *Poeme sur le desastre de Lisbonne.*

Caryl E. Rusbult (1980). Commitment and satisfaction in romantic associations: A test of the investment model, *Journal of Experimental Social Psychology,* Volume 16 (2).

Rainer Maria Rilke (1929). *Letters To A Young Poet.*

Robert Sapolsky and Lisa Share (2004). A Pacific Culture among Wild Baboons: Its Emergence and Transmission, *PLOS Biology* 2 (4).

Eleanor Payson (2002). *The Wizard of Oz and Other Narcissists: Coping with the One-Way Relationship in Work, Love, and Family,* Julian Day Publications.

Kathryn Laughon (2007). Abused African American Women's Processes of Staying Healthy, *Western Journal of Nursing Research,* Volume 29.

Janice K. Kiecolt-Glaser and Tamara L. Newton (2001). Marriage and Health: His and Hers, *Psychological Bulletin,* Volume 127 (4).

Janice K. Kiecolt-Glaser, Ronald Glaser, John T. Cacioppo and William B. Malarkey (1998). Marital stress: Immunologic, neuroendocrine, and autonomic correlates. *Annals of the New York Academy of Sciences*.

John Helliwell and Robert Putnam (2004). The social context of well-being, *Philosophical Transactions of the Royal Society B: Biological Sciences*, 359 (1449).

CHAPTER 9

Herman Hesse (1922). *Siddhartha*.

J.R.R. Tolkien (1955). *The Return of the King*.

ACKNOWLEDGMENTS

This was not an easy book for me to write. It was three years in the making, and the culmination of years of clinical work, interviews, education, and research. The subject material was challenging, and while narcissistic personality disorder is an intriguing intellectual exercise, it ceases to serve merely as an exercise when it is real stories, real people, real hurt. It took a merry band of thieves to gather around me, encourage me to stay the course, and make this possible.

To Anthony Ziccardi, Katie Dornan, and everyone at Post Hill Press, thanks for picking a scrappy fighter out of the crowd and giving her a voice. Stephanie Krikorian, whether on the beach in Easthampton, my dining table in Benedict Canyon, or in myriad e-mails and phone calls, you never let me give up and pushed me to a half-court shot. You helped shift my identity as a writer through your belief in me. Lara Asher, your advocacy of me as a writer has been redemptive, and your editorial brilliance was a game-changer. Thank you for being a dear friend and lady of letters who would not allow me to stop writing. Jill Davenport, thanks for the jacket photograph of me, and for 37 years of glorious friendship. You have the incisive ability to photograph me from the inside out and keep me honest.

To Robert Mack, for resolutely reminding me to tell the story of ego without any ego. To Margaret Spencer, for reminding me that Tom and Daisy were careless. Dr. Pamela Harmell, in our work together, I articulated half of this book. You have been a through-line for me for more than 20 years and remind me that therapy is equal parts science and magic.

To my steadfast friends Kara Sullivan, Christine Anderson, Lisa Readman, Mona Baird, Debbie Thompson, Emily Shagley, Tonia Mendinghall, Shery Zarnegin, Vanessa Williams, Kathiann Mead, Toni Lewis, Tasnim Shamji, Beth Corets, Cheryl Johnson, Jenifer Maze, Kieran Sullivan, Bryan Donovan-Rossy, Miguel Rossy-Donovan, Perry Halkitis, Jennifer Wisdom, Shari Miles-Cohen, Keyona King-Tsikata, Scyatta Wallace, J.Travis Walters, Hector Myers, Steve Brady, Eric Borsum, Eric Miller, Hitomi Uchishiba, Elizabeth Linn, Fary Cachelin, Shellye Jones, and in memory of my beloved Monique Sherman. To Ellen Rakieten, I got the line about Chicago and the winter in there! Thank you all for being my cheerleaders and sounding boards.

To the men and women who provided hours of interviews and shared with me the resilient survival stories of their narcissistic relationships. I remain deeply grateful that you were willing to share your stories in precise and sometimes painful detail. I hope that these words knit your narratives into something that may help guide others. Aurelio Burgos, Nya Lowden, Ana Morales, Miranda Hernandez, thank you for your administrative assistance with this book. To all of my students at California State University, Los Angeles, you endure my lectures on narcissism every quarter, and I learn more from your questions than you know.

Morgan Wilson, this is our second book together! Your patience and provision of love, safety, hundreds of miles driven, and connection to my children allowed me to focus in the midst of the chaos.

Bill Pruitt, thank you for reminding me to not lose sight of the stars and the moon and the eclipses and the eucalyptus; it would have been easy to do. Life is, ultimately, a labyrinth.

Pamela Regan, your encyclopedic knowledge of anything related to human mating and relationships, your friendship, your intellect, and your generosity of spirit in sharing your big brain gave this book a stronger voice. To Kaveri Subrahmanyam, Gloria

Romero, and Diane Lewis, despite our occupational travails your friendship and brilliance during a very challenging period in my career kept me laughing and strong. Myriad colleagues, mentors, and other scholars and clinicians in the field have been terrific sounding boards. I have also had occasion to attend numerous seminars and training on personality disorders and narcissism, and I remain grateful for the excellent work clinicians and scholars are doing in this area and for the support of California State University, Los Angeles and the National Institutes of Health for my teaching, research, and scholarship.

Charlie Hinkin, you remain father and ex-husband extraordinaire, and your support was a game changer as I went into the homestretch. Padma, Joe, and especially my beautiful Tanner Salisbury, you continue to be my reminder of strength, love, and clarity. Sai and Rao Durvasula, I know you didn't think this psychology thing would work out for me, but I think it's going okay. At the end, all of us learned the most important lesson of all about unconditional love. Here's to many more years of enjoying that together.

Maya and Shanti, you remain magnificent muses. A mother could not be more proud and I love you. Thanks for letting me be "integer mom." You fill my heart and my life with music and joy. Thanks for pulling me out of my head and back into life. (And please don't date or marry a narcissist).

ABOUT THE AUTHOR

Dr. Ramani Durvasula is a licensed clinical psychologist in private practice in Santa Monica, CA and Professor of Psychology at California State University, Los Angeles, where she was named Outstanding Professor in 2012. Her research on personality disorders and health has been funded by the National Institutes of Health for 10 years. She is the author of *You Are WHY You Eat: Change Your Food Attitude, Change Your Life,* as well as the author of numerous peer-reviewed journal articles, book chapters, and conference papers. Dr. Durvasula was the co-host of Oxygen's series *My Shopping Addiction* and has also been featured on series on Bravo, the Lifetime Movie Network, National Geographic, the History Channel, Discovery Science, and Investigation Discovery. She has been a featured commentator on nearly every major television network, as well as radio, print, and Internet media. *Muses and Visionaries* magazine features her opinions and guidance in their regular column "On the Couch with Dr. Ramani." Personality disorders are a central focus of Dr. Durvasula's research and clinical practice, and she works with men and women on managing these issues as partners, employees, parents and friends. Dr. Durvasula brings a unique expertise as a professor, clinician, researcher, author, media commentator, and mother. She resides in Beverly Hills, CA with her two daughters.